Cases on Uncovering Corporate Governance Challenges in Asian Markets

Rashedul Hasan
Coventry University, UK

A volume in the Advances in Logistics, Operations, and Management Science (ALOMS) Book Series

IGI Global
PUBLISHER of TIMELY KNOWLEDGE

Published in the United States of America by
IGI Global
Business Science Reference (an imprint of IGI Global)
701 E. Chocolate Avenue
Hershey PA, USA 17033
Tel: 717-533-8845
Fax: 717-533-8661
E-mail: cust@igi-global.com
Web site: http://www.igi-global.com

Library of Congress Cataloging-in-Publication Data

Names: Hasan, Rashedul, 1987- editor.
Title: Cases on uncovering corporate governance challenges in Asian markets / edited by Rashedul Hasan.
Description: Hershey, PA : Business Science Reference, an imprint of IGI Global, [2024] | Includes bibliographical references and index. | Summary: "This publication aims to promote good governance practices among Asian firms, prevent corporate failures evident in advanced economies, and promote more ethical business practices in Asia"-- Provided by publisher.
Identifiers: LCCN 2023044070 (print) | LCCN 2023044071 (ebook) | ISBN 9781668498675 (hardcover) | ISBN 9781668498682 (paperback) | ISBN 9781668498699 (ebook)
Subjects: LCSH: Corporate governance--Asia. | Business ethics--Asia. | Corporations--Corrupt practices--Asia--Prevention.
Classification: LCC HD2741 .C344 2024 (print) | LCC HD2741 (ebook) | DDC 658.40095--dc23/eng/20231128
LC record available at https://lccn.loc.gov/2023044070
LC ebook record available at https://lccn.loc.gov/2023044071

This book is published in the IGI Global book series Advances in Logistics, Operations, and Management Science (ALOMS) (ISSN: 2327-350X; eISSN: 2327-3518)

British Cataloguing in Publication Data
A Cataloguing in Publication record for this book is available from the British Library.

Advances in Logistics, Operations, and Management Science (ALOMS) Book Series

John Wang
Montclair State University, USA

ISSN:2327-350X
EISSN:2327-3518

MISSION

Operations research and management science continue to influence business processes, administration, and management information systems, particularly in covering the application methods for decision-making processes. New case studies and applications on management science, operations management, social sciences, and other behavioral sciences have been incorporated into business and organizations real-world objectives.

The **Advances in Logistics, Operations, and Management Science** (ALOMS) Book Series provides a collection of reference publications on the current trends, applications, theories, and practices in the management science field. Providing relevant and current research, this series and its individual publications would be useful for academics, researchers, scholars, and practitioners interested in improving decision making models and business functions.

COVERAGE

- Networks
- Information Management
- Services management
- Finance
- Marketing engineering
- Risk Management
- Production Management
- Decision analysis and decision support
- Political Science
- Computing and information technologies

IGI Global is currently accepting manuscripts for publication within this series. To submit a proposal for a volume in this series, please contact our Acquisition Editors at Acquisitions@igi-global.com or visit: http://www.igi-global.com/publish/.

The Advances in Logistics, Operations, and Management Science (ALOMS) Book Series (ISSN 2327-350X) is published by IGI Global, 701 E. Chocolate Avenue, Hershey, PA 17033-1240, USA, www.igi-global.com. This series is composed of titles available for purchase individually; each title is edited to be contextually exclusive from any other title within the series. For pricing and ordering information please visit http://www.igi-global.com/book-series/advances-logistics-operations-management-science/37170. Postmaster: Send all address changes to above address.

Titles in this Series

For a list of additional titles in this series, please visit: http://www.igi-global.com/book-series/

Innovation Capabilities and Entrepreneurial Opportunities of Smart Working
Beatrice Orlando (Department of Economics and Management, University of Ferrara, Ferrara, Italy)
Business Science Reference • © 2024 • 300pp • H/C (ISBN: 9781799887973) • US $240.00

Integrating Intelligence and Sustainability in Supply Chains
Badr Bentalha (National School of Business and Management, Sidi Mohammed Ben Abdellah University, Morocco) Aziz Hmioui (National School of Business and Management, Sidi Mohammed Ben Abdellah University, Morocco) and Lhoussaine Alla (National Schools of Applied Sciences, Sidi Mohammed Ben Abdellah University, Morocco)
Business Science Reference • © 2023 • 330pp • H/C (ISBN: 9798369302255) • US $275.00

Global Perspectives on Soft Power Management in Business
Kannapat Kankaew (Burapha University International College, Thailand)
Business Science Reference • © 2023 • 360pp • H/C (ISBN: 9798369302507) • US $275.00

AI and Emotional Intelligence for Modern Business Management
Bhawana Bhardwaj (Central University of Himachal Pradesh, India) Dipanker Sharma (Central University of Himachal Pradesh, India) and Mohinder Chand Dhiman (Central University of Himachal Pradesh, India)
Business Science Reference • © 2023 • 370pp • H/C (ISBN: 9798369304181) • US $250.00

Strategies and Applications of Islamic Entrepreneurship
Ahmad Rafiki (Universitas Medan Area, Indonesia) Alfatih Gessan Pananjung (Bahrain Institute of Banking and Finance, Bahrain) and Muhammad Dharma Tuah Putra Nasution (Universitas Pembangunan Panca Budi, Indonesia)
Business Science Reference • © 2023 • 313pp • H/C (ISBN: 9781668475195) • US $250.00

Entrepreneurship Ecosystems and Their Opportunities and Challenges
Mohammed El Amine Abdelli (University of Brest, France) Shajara Ul-Durar (University of Sunderland, UK) and Hala Wasef Hattab (British University in Egypt, Egypt)
Business Science Reference • © 2023 • 337pp • H/C (ISBN: 9781668471401) • US $250.00

IGI Global
PUBLISHER of TIMELY KNOWLEDGE

701 East Chocolate Avenue, Hershey, PA 17033, USA
Tel: 717-533-8845 x100 • Fax: 717-533-8661
E-Mail: cust@igi-global.com • www.igi-global.com

Table of Contents

Detailed Table of Contents

Corporate governance practices in the Asian market have come under intense scrutiny in recent years after a series of high-profile corporate scandals exposed weaknesses in the legal framework, enforcement, and monitoring. These scandals have highlighted the need for more transparency, accountability, and responsible business practices. In response, many Asian countries have instituted institutional and regulatory reforms to improve corporate governance practices and strengthen shareholder rights. While challenges remain, the evolution of corporate governance in Asia represents an important step toward establishing more responsible and sustainable business practices in the region.

India has recently witnessed several allegations of corporate governance lapses and failure. The alarming situation prompted the government and the regulators to take serious note to make the companies accountable for the allegations and to bring in regulations to contain the policy leaks. The governing body and the board of directors must abide by ethical standards, demonstrating an unwavering commitment to discipline, transparency, fairness, and accountability for their actions. This work uses a case study approach to examine various recent corporate governance failures in India. The examination is made in the following dimensions: accountability, transparency, equitability, responsibility, ethical conduct, board independence, risk management, corporate social responsibility, stakeholder engagement, and regulatory compliance. The study scrutinized various classic and recent corporate governance lapses in established corporate entities and startups and in Indian banks. The measures implemented by regulatory bodies, including the RBI, SEBI, and the MCA, were analyzed.

The glass ceiling is a metaphorical concept which represents the invisible barriers and biases that limit the advancement and upward mobility of individuals, particularly women and other underrepresented groups, in their careers. It alludes to the cultural and institutional barriers that keep capable individuals from rising to the top of leadership roles or realising their full potential inside the organisations. Taking cognizance of this matter, various nations around the globe have legislated and recommended gender-based quotas in corporate leadership which inevitably intends to ensure the appointment of women in leadership positions of renowned companies. Accordingly, this chapter intends to explore the factors which contributes to glass-ceiling phenomenon through the empirical survey and compare the affirmative actions implemented by of Asian nations to address the concerns related to glass ceiling. The chapter will also analyse the efficacy of the approaches adopted by China and India in ensuring gender diversity in the boardroom and executive designations.

The Luckin Coffee case presents an opportunity for an important analysis of corporate governance challenges of Chinese businesses and regulators because of the 2020 scandal and the fact that it carries on business in China and is a publicly traded company in the US. In the past, company failures have led to local and sometimes global queries about the processes through which companies' objectives are set and pursued. The regulatory changes ensuing from corporate scandals can be far-reaching, controversial, and leading to global regulatory contagion. In the Luckin scandal, its real and potential implications involved two of the world's dominant economies. The concerns from the Luckin scandal are the issues on which this chapter is focused. The chapter explores the concepts and regulatory solutions that are relevant to the Luckin scandal. The dynamics of the Chinese market and the consequences of the scandal are explored in the chapter. Ultimately, the need for caution in the discourse on regulatory response to scandals such as the Luckin case is articulated in the chapter.

Ayondo Ltd. (Ayondo) (now known as RSQ Technology Ventures GmbH) was the first financial technology (fintech) company to be listed on the Catalist Board of the Singapore Exchange (SGX) on 23 March, 2018. However, the company was suspended from trading on 1 February, 2019, less than a year after listing. This case highlights corporate governance issues related to Ayondo, and also, fintech companies in general, in the context of Singapore. Examples of issues discussed are the roles of (a) board of directors; (b) sponsor in listing; (c) auditors; (d) regulatory bodies; (e) investors. These issues have ramifications for stakeholders. This case also includes lessons gleaned from the corporate governance issues and some actionable recommendations. This case study covers only the corporate governance issues of Ayondo in the period leading up to its listing and shortly thereafter. It does not include other ongoing issues subsequent to the listing.

The effectiveness of board characteristics on the financial organization's performance has been examined in several studies. Studies that looked into the characteristics of the boards of state-owned enterprises (SOEs) are scarce. Therefore, this chapter aims to scrutinize how nominee directors and Indian SOEs' perform. The findings consider that nominee directors raise the performance of the SOEs utilizing a variety of performance parameters and control variables. The research backs up agency theory. The conclusions have specific ramifications that the government and decision makers must address.

This chapter is intended to understand how environmental, social, and governance issues are integrated in the annual report of Bangladeshi banking companies from 2020 to 2022. This understanding, in turn, can help investors determine how to integrate ESG analysis into their own investment processes. This study considered the top 30 banks operating in Bangladesh for three years (2020 to 2022). Discourse analysis was used to identify the textual narratives disclosed in this study. Finding of this study showed that many banking organizations are presenting their ESG disclosure in a separate section of annual report and other organizations report such information in the form of sustainability report or corporate social responsibility section. Despite all the regulatory interventions, the level of ESG reporting especially governance is not up to mark in Bangladesh. The main factor for integrating ESG is to face risks and opportunities that can impact the long-term performance and sustainable finance.

This chapter addresses how corporate governance supports shareholder-director conflicts and company success. Islamic financial institution (IFI) governance and performance have not been studied, yet corporate governance has affected previous financial crises. This examines IFI board size, ownership, CEO duality, and pay committee independent directors. Also studied is how Islamic corporate governance influences executive director pay. Thus, IFIs require an IWBCGF to handle current and future corporate governance issues. Qualitative corporate governance metrics research and qualitative Islamic principle evaluation helped exploratory studies attain these goals. The research shows that corporate governance strongly impacts IFI executive pay. These results show that executive directors require an Islamic-based comprehensive governance framework to navigate corporate governance issues. The study makes literary contributions. It tackles the lack of religious research on Islam and IFI corporate governance. It highlights IFIs' corporate governance and CEO remuneration.

2010 to 2022. The empirical findings gleaned from this study unequivocally affirm a statistically significant relationship between the existence of audit committee and the formulation of dividend policies within these financial institutions. Notably, audit committees have been revealed to exert a robust and statistically significant influence on dividend policy within these financial institutions. The implications of these findings extend beyond the confines of academia; they hold substantial relevance for regulatory bodies, financial institutions themselves, and their shareholders in the Malaysian context.

Preface

Welcome to *Cases on Uncovering Corporate Governance Challenges in Asian Markets*, a comprehensive and illuminating exploration into the intricate landscape of corporate governance within the dynamic Asian business sphere. As editor of this insightful compilation, I am delighted to present an assemblage of in-depth cases and analyses that shed light on the vital role of corporate governance in achieving organizational objectives while safeguarding the interests of stakeholders.

Corporate governance forms the very foundation of effective company direction and control, ensuring a harmonious interplay of stakeholder interests and the realization of organizational goals. In the Asian context, this construct has garnered increasing attention due to its undeniable relevance in fostering economic growth, sustainability, and ethical business practices. Yet, the region has faced its share of corporate scandals that have underscored the imperative of strengthening governance mechanisms.

This book serves as a beacon, guiding readers through the intricate labyrinth of corporate governance challenges in Asia. From dissecting notable corporate scandals to elucidating the root causes and consequences, each case offers valuable lessons for businesses, regulatory bodies, investors, and policymakers. My aim is to emphasize the criticality of proactive governance practices, advocating for enhanced board supervision, transparency, accountability, and ethical conduct within companies.

The objectives in compiling this publication are to meticulously analyze the major challenges afflicting corporate governance practices in Asia and to provide actionable policy recommendations for their improvement. By doing so, I aspire to facilitate the adoption of good governance practices in Asian firms, deter corporate failures, and encourage the infusion of ethical standards into business operations across the region.

The book is organized the book into focused sections, each addressing a critical aspect of corporate governance. From cultural influences on technological advancements, family-owned enterprises to environmental considerations, and emerging trends to future prospects, we strive to present a well-rounded view of corporate governance dynamics in Asian markets. This book seeks to serve as an invaluable resource for academics, researchers, practitioners, policymakers, students, investors, and corporate governance consultants.

CHAPTER OVERVIEW

Chapter 1 presents an in-depth exploration of corporate governance practices in the Asian market, focusing on recent high-profile corporate scandals that have exposed weaknesses in the legal framework, enforcement, and monitoring. The chapter discusses the imperative for increased transparency, accountability, and responsible business practices and explores the ongoing evolution of corporate governance in Asia. Reforms and regulatory changes aimed at strengthening shareholder rights are highlighted, acknowledging the steps taken toward establishing more responsible and sustainable business practices in the region.

Chapter 2 delves into recent corporate governance failures in India, emphasizing accountability, transparency, ethics, board independence, and regulatory compliance. Using a case study approach, the chapter examines governance lapses in both established corporate entities and startups, as well as in Indian banks. The measures implemented by regulatory bodies, including the RBI, SEBI, and the MCA, are analyzed, shedding light on the efforts to address governance challenges and promote responsible business conduct in the country.

Chapter 3 focuses on the persistent issue of the glass ceiling, exploring the factors contributing to this phenomenon that hampers the progress of women and underrepresented groups in reaching leadership positions within organizations. The chapter examines the implementation of gender-based quotas in corporate leadership in various Asian nations, particularly in China and India, to address the gender diversity gap in boardrooms and executive designations. The efficacy of these approaches is critically analyzed.

Chapter 4 centers on the Luckin coffee case, providing a thorough analysis of the corporate governance challenges faced by Chinese businesses and regulators in the aftermath of the 2020 scandal. The chapter explores the implications of the scandal on the Chinese market, regulatory responses, and the need for caution in shaping regulatory solutions. It delves into concepts and regulatory mechanisms relevant to the Luckin scandal and highlights the broader consequences for global economies.

Chapter 5 sheds light on corporate governance issues within fintech companies, using Ayondo Ltd. as a case study in the context of Singapore. The chapter discusses the roles of boards, sponsors, auditors, regulatory bodies, and investors, analyzing the implications of corporate governance challenges for stakeholders. Key lessons and actionable recommendations derived from the Ayondo case provide valuable insights for both practitioners and policymakers.

Chapter 6 delves into the effectiveness of board characteristics on the performance of Indian State-Owned Enterprises (SOEs), particularly focusing on nominee directors. Through empirical research, the chapter underscores the positive impact of nominee directors on SOE performance, backed by agency theory. The implications of these findings for government and decision-makers are discussed, emphasizing the need for strategic governance improvements.

Chapter 7 examines how environmental, social, and governance (ESG) issues are integrated into the annual reports of Bangladeshi banking companies from 2020 to 2022. The study offers insights into the presentation of ESG disclosures and the level of reporting in annual and sustainability reports. Despite regulatory interventions, the study reveals challenges in ESG reporting in Bangladesh, emphasizing the need for enhanced integration to manage long-term performance and sustainable finance.

Chapter 8 explores the relationship between corporate governance, executive pay, and performance in Islamic Financial Institutions (IFIs). The chapter analyzes IFI board characteristics, ownership, CEO duality, and the role of independent directors in pay committees. It emphasizes the necessity of an Islamic-based comprehensive governance framework to address corporate governance challenges and executive pay within IFIs, making significant literary contributions.

Chapter 9 investigates the 1MDB controversy, analyzing the system of financial misreporting that allowed for the misuse of funds and examining the cultural, sociological, and political contexts that exacerbated the problem. The chapter elucidates the effects of the scandal on the Malaysian economy, stakeholders' reactions, and the lessons it offers for corporate governance. Corrective measures and the importance of strong corporate governance are emphasized.

Chapter 10 discusses the limitations of the traditional Cheque Truncation System (CTS) and proposes an efficient and secure blockchain-based system for cheque clearing. The comprehensive framework presented encompasses paper check clearing, digital check issuing and clearing, check fraud detection, and check transaction security procedures. The chapter highlights the potential of blockchain technology to expedite the clearing process and enhance security and integrity within the system.

Chapter 11 examines the role of audit committees in influencing dividend policies within Malaysian financial firms. Using empirical data spanning over a decade, the chapter explores the relationship between audit committees and dividend policy formulation. The findings affirm a significant and positive influence of audit committees on dividend policies, underscoring the implications for regulatory bodies, financial institutions, and shareholders in Malaysia.

I envision diverse applications of this book, ranging from academic research and policy formulation to strategic decision-making by practitioners and investors. I am optimistic that this compilation will instigate meaningful discussions, inspire further research, and contribute to the evolution of corporate governance practices, ultimately fostering a vibrant and sustainable business environment in Asia.

I extend my heartfelt gratitude to the authors who have contributed their expertise and insights to this endeavor. Their dedication and commitment have been instrumental in creating a book that I believe will make a significant contribution to the discourse surrounding corporate governance in Asian markets.

Rashedul Hasan
Coventry University, UK

Chapter 1
The Evolution of Corporate Governance in Asian Markets

Aysa Siddika
https://orcid.org/0000-0001-7407-5150
Multimedia University, Malaysia

Abdullah Sarwar
https://orcid.org/0000-0001-6475-7393
Multimedia University, Malaysia

EXECUTIVE SUMMARY

Corporate governance practices in the Asian market have come under intense scrutiny in recent years after a series of high-profile corporate scandals exposed weaknesses in the legal framework, enforcement, and monitoring. These scandals have highlighted the need for more transparency, accountability, and responsible business practices. In response, many Asian countries have instituted institutional and regulatory reforms to improve corporate governance practices and strengthen shareholder rights. While challenges remain, the evolution of corporate governance in Asia represents an important step toward establishing more responsible and sustainable business practices in the region.

INTRODUCTION

Corporate governance (CG) is a structured set of systems envisioned for efficient monitoring and control of an organisation's strategy and process for better accountability and transparency (Aluchna & Idowu, 2017). It comprehends the fundamentals for responsible business operations through accountability, transparency and legitimacy in achieving broader economic goals (Monks, 2002). It balances

DOI: 10.4018/978-1-6684-9867-5.ch001

economic and social goals, promoting efficient resource use and accountability for stewardship, aiming to align the interests of individuals, corporations, and society. It encourages responsible resource use and accountability for resource stewardship (Iskander & Chamlou, 2000).

CG frameworks are expected to promote transparent and fair markets in accordance with regulatory requirements (Anon, 2015). In order to meet CG concerns, the framework typically combines elements of legislation, self-regulation, and voluntary commitments. A firm's CG entails the connections between its management, board of directors, shareholders, and other stakeholders. It defines the company's objectives, determines how they will be achieved, and monitors their progress (Anon, 2015). A single model cannot define good corporate governance. However, it is characterised by certain elements in common aimed at ensuring effective corporate governance frameworks. They ensure that shareholders' rights are protected, information is distributed fairly, transparency is maintained, and board members are held accountable.

Good corporate governance is vital to building up equity capital in the long run. It establishes market confidence, business integrity among potential investors and economic performance. Companies and countries must adhere to globally recognised corporate governance standards to fully exploit the global capital market and attract long-term investments. As a company seeks to build confidence with domestic and international investors, proper supervision and execution remain essential (Anon, 2015). Hence, an effective CG system will enable corporations to easily access the capital market and reduce capital expenditures. Good CG is also important for ensuring that management is disciplined. In order to identify those who may perform better than the existing management, the performance of the current management is evaluated and benchmarked (Roche, 2005).

This chapter examines the cultural and historical evolution of Corporate Governance in Asian markets, with a focus on Japan, South Korea, and China. In this chapter, you will be provided with the following information:

- The theoretical framework of CG
- Historical evolution of CG in Asian markets
- CG practices in some selected Asian markets
- Challenges and opportunities for CG in Asian markets.

The Theoretical Framework of CG

Theoretical frameworks for corporate governance have evolved over time to reflect changes in the business environment and new perspectives on the role of corporations in society. The most important theoretical perspectives include agency, stewardship theory, stakeholder, and institutional theories.

One of the most important theoretical stances, agency theory, emphasizes the function of CG mechanisms in bringing together the interests of shareholders and managers and sees the corporation as a nexus of contracts. Another important theoretical viewpoint is stakeholder theory, which assumes that companies are not only responsible to their shareholders but also to a broader range of stakeholders. It entails employees, customers, suppliers, and the environment. Stakeholder theory emphasises the importance of social and environmental sustainability and argues that organizations should be held responsible for their effects on society.

Agency Theory

Corporate governance research has primarily been based on agency theory, which concentrates on the separation of ownership and management, leading to principal-agent problems. With agents serving as managers, principals as owners, and boards of directors serving as the monitoring mechanism, this theory seeks to reduce issues brought on by the principal-agent relationship (Jensen & Meckling, 1976). Agency theory is supported by shareholders' and managers' distinct and consistent interests as well as by peoples' inherent self-interest and lack of willingness to put others' needs ahead of their own. The firm is a legal identity, bringing conflicting objectives into equilibrium within contractual relationships with employees, suppliers, customers, and creditors, with the intention of all parties acting in their own performance. A monitoring mechanism can prevent managers from taking actions that might not maximize shareholder wealth when ownership and management are separate (Jensen & Meckling, 1976). Hence the asymmetry in information leads to uncertainty in the principal-agent relationship. Influencing agents to act in the principal's best interests leads to agency costs, such as monitoring expenses and disciplining agents to prevent abuse, which is where the agency problem comes from. These costs include monitoring expenditures to limit aberrant activities, bonding expenditures to guarantee actions will not harm the principal, and residual loss to reduce welfare. Accounting plays a critical role in lowering agency costs in organizations through written contracts connected to accounting systems. The agency problem varies based on the ownership structures of different countries. In countries with dispersed ownership, investors may use exit options signalled through the reduction in share prices. Conversely, those with concentrated ownership and powerful shareholders often exert control over managers and exploit minority shareholders for their own personal gain (Spanos, 2005).

Stewardship Theory

Rooted in psychology and sociology, according to stewardship theory, top management acts as stewards and incorporates their objectives into the company. (Davis et al. 1997). It emphasizes the satisfaction and motivation of stewards when organizational success is achieved, as they work for shareholders and maximize their utility functions. This perspective differs from agency theory, which emphasizes individualism. Two theories on management, agency and stewardship, have different approaches to achieving success. Agency theory views individuals as economic entities (Agyris, 1973), while stewardship theory values trust and autonomy (Davis et al. 1997). The latter encourages responsibility and independence to maximize returns to shareholders, which can reduce monitoring costs (Davis et al. 1997).

In order to maintain their reputation as key decision-makers within the organization, executives and directors maintain their careers to be seen as effective stewards of the company (Fama, 1980) and frequently put a priority on maximizing financial performance and shareholder profits (Daily et al., 2003). This theory contends that managers' concern for their professional development and reputation motivates them to act in the best interests of shareholders, which reduces agency costs (Donaldson & Davis, 1991). The psychological aspect depicts that managers tend to perform better when they are satisfied with their job. Managers are better equipped to make wise decisions, according to Fama and Jensen (1983), if they have access to specific insider information about their organization. When managers are empowered to make independent decisions, it can boost job satisfaction and lead to better financial performance (Clarke, 2004). This emphasis on financial performance may also impact how employees perceive their own performance in relation to the organization's overall success.

Stakeholder Theory

According to Wheeler et al. (2002), a synthesis of organizational and sociological disciplines led to the development of stakeholder theory. Stakeholder theory, which was introduced to management in 1970 and gradually developed by Freeman (1984), included corporate responsibility to a broad range of stakeholders. In fact, rather than being a formal, unifying theory, stakeholder theory encompasses philosophy, ethics, political theory, economics, law, and organizational science. Stakeholder theory defines a stakeholder as any group or person who has the potential to influence or who is impacted by the accomplishment of an organization's goals (Abdullah & Valentine, 2009). According to Donaldson & Preston (1995), stakeholders encompass a diverse group of individuals and organizations, including investors, customers, employees, suppliers, trade associations, political groups, and governments.

According to Clarkson (1995), a firm can be viewed as a system with stakeholders that aims to generate wealth for its stakeholders. Stakeholder theorists believe that managers have a responsibility to serve a network of relationships that includes suppliers, employees, and business partners. In contrast to agency theory, which focuses on the owner-manager-employee relationship, stakeholder theory emphasizes the importance of this network group (Freeman, 1999). Sundaram & Inkpen (2004) argue that stakeholder theory aims to address the stakeholders who deserve and require management's attention. According to Donaldson & Preston (1995), Stakeholder theory gives importance to the interests of all stakeholders and acknowledges their inherent value, without giving preference to any particular group's interests over others. It emphasizes the importance of these relationships. Additionally, the company's decision-making procedures are influenced by these relationships (Freeman, 1984).

Resource Dependency Theory

In 1978, Jeffrey Pfeffer and Gerald Salancik, two experts in organizational theories, developed the Resource Dependence Theory (RDT). This theory emphasizes the impact of external resource dependencies on organizational structure, behaviour, and decision-making. It examines how entities and organizations interact with their environment, particularly in terms of acquiring and managing resources. The theory argues that organizations rely on external resources to survive and expand, such as capital, knowledge, technology, skills, and connections.

RDT emphasizes the importance of controlling and accessing resources in order to maintain power and make strategic decisions within an organization (Hillman et al., 2009). Organizations can enhance their competitive advantage and survival chances by managing external dependencies. Additionally, organizations must adjust their resource acquisition strategies in order to maintain stability and effectiveness as a result of environmental uncertainty. An RDT can provide valuable insight into the dynamics and interactions that influence organizational structure, behaviour, and decision-making levels in complex business environments (Hillman et al., 2009).

Furthermore, there are several other theories of CG, such as institutional theory, transaction cost theory, political theory, etc. Meyer & Rowan (1977) and DiMaggio & Powell (1983) are the authors of the Institutional Theory, which is a sociological and organizational framework that investigates how outside structures, norms, and values influence organizational behaviour. According to institutional theory, firms are influenced by the social and cultural context in which they operate, and their behaviour is shaped by the norms and values of their stakeholders (Mallin, 2017).

According to Cyert and March's (1963) transaction cost theory, a company is an association of people with various objectives and viewpoints. The fundamental premise is that firms have gotten so big that they can effectively take the place of the market in determining how resources are allocated. In this theory, transactions serve as the analytical unit (Abdullah & Valentine, 2009). Political theory suggests that shareholder voting support is more important than purchasing voting power, and political influence in corporate governance can direct decision-making. Government involvement in corporate decision-making and cultural challenges can influence governance developments. The political model of corporate governance can significantly impact profits and privileges, involving politics in the governance structure (Pound, 1988).

Historical Evolution of CG in Asia

Recent decades have seen significant changes in CG in Asia. Transparency and accountability were traditionally not emphasized in many Asian countries. Several corporate scandals and financial crises during the late 1990s and 2000s increased interest in CG. Several countries in this region have restructured their laws and regulations to address corporate transparency, accountability, and shareholder rights (Chen & Hsu, 2017). A number of initiatives have been undertaken, including appointing independent directors, strengthening audit committees, and implementing laws related to information disclosure and codes of conduct. Investors and international organizations have become gradually more committed to global CG standards (Chen & Hsu, 2017). CG in Asia has evolved towards more sustainable and responsible business practices despite the challenges The next section outlines the three stages of CG's historical development in Asia, namely:

- Pre-1990s Phase: Family-owned businesses and state-owned enterprises
- 1990-2000s Phase: Economic crisis and corporate governance reforms
- Post-2000s Phase: The emergence of independent directors and shareholder activism.

Pre-1990s Phase: Family-Owned Business and State-Owned Enterprise

Family-Owned Business. Prior to the 1990s, family-oriented business structures dominated the corporate landscape in many Asian economies (Nam & Nam, 2004; Claessens et al., 1999). A single family or a small group of families held the majority of the ownership, control, and decision-making authority in these structures (Roche, 2005; Claessens et al., 1999). Family-owned conglomerates were crucial in determining the direction of regional economic growth. These family-oriented businesses' defining traits can be categorized as follows.

Founder-Centred Leadership. A substantial amount of influence and control was exerted by the founder on the company's operations, strategy, and decision-making. It was evident that the founder's goals, principles, and management style were reflected throughout the company (Claessens et al. 1999). Hyundai Group in South Korea was founded by Chung Ju-Yung, Sony Corporation in Japan was founded by Akio Morita and Masaru Ibuka, AmorePacific Corporation in South Korea was founded by Suh Sung-whan, Tata Group in India by Jamsetji Tata, Li & Fung Group in Hong Kong by Fung Pak-liu, and Astra International in Indonesia were just a few examples of founder-centered leadership in Asia during the pre-90s. Overseeing various business divisions and making crucial strategic decisions, these founders were instrumental in determining the direction that their company would take.

Vertical Integration. There were a lot of vertically integrated family-owned conglomerates that covered various production and distribution stages. Due to this integration, the supply chain could be managed more effectively, and reliance on outside vendors was diminished. In the Philippines, Ayala Corporation was involved in various sectors such as banking, telecommunications, manufacturing, and real estate (Koike, 1993). Manila Water, a water distribution firm, demonstrated vertical integration from supply to distribution through their ownership. Mitsubishi Group, the largest conglomerate in Japan, engaged in vertical integration by owning coal mines, shipyards, and trading firms, which gave them control over important inputs and transportation for their various businesses. Samsung Group, a South Korean company, was involved in manufacturing its own parts for its consumer electronics products, including displays and semiconductors (Globerman et al., 2011).

Diversification. Family-owned businesses often engaged in diverse sectors, including manufacturing, trading, real estate, finance, telecommunications, automotive, heavy industry, and electronics (Gutierrez & Rodriguez, 2013). The Ayala Group, Gokongwei Group of the Philippines, and the Mitsubishi Group in Japan are prime examples of this strategy, with operations in finance, automotive, heavy industry, and electronics, thus mitigating risks and tapping into different markets (Gutierrez & Rodriguez, 2013).

Cross-Holdings and Business Relationships. Family-owned businesses often establish cross-shareholdings and business relationships with companies in the same group, creating a complex web of interlocking ownership that reinforces cohesion. A well-known example of this is the Samsung Group in South Korea, which maintained cross-shareholdings among its various subsidiaries to solidify the group's control.

Long-Term Orientation. Family-owned businesses often prioritize stability and continuity with a focus on preserving and enhancing the family's legacy over generations. The Tata Group, which was founded in the 19th century in India, is a prime example of a company that has focused on long-term growth and making a positive impact on society. Through its philanthropic efforts and commitment to sustainable practices, the Tata Group has demonstrated its dedication to leaving a lasting legacy. Similarly, Ayala Corporation in the Philippines, which has been around since 1834, has shown a commitment to sustainable development in the country by investing in real estate, telecommunications, and utilities. Other companies like CK Hutchison Holdings Limited in Hong Kong, Samsung Group in South Korea, and Jardine Matheson Holdings Limited in Hong Kong have also demonstrated a long-term focus on business growth.

Limited Minority Shareholder Protection. It was challenging for minority shareholders in Asian family-owned conglomerates to influence corporate decisions or oppose the actions of the controlling family because they frequently had few rights and protections. This was caused by a pyramidal ownership structure, in which the founding family held a sizable percentage of the voting stock with a small percentage of shares and had a greater influence to limit the power of the minority shareholders (Claessens et al. 1999). Examples include keiretsu in Japan (such as Mitsubishi, Toyota, and Sumitomo), chaebols in South Korea (such as Samsung, Hyundai, and LG), and various conglomerates in Southeast Asian nations (such as the Salim Group in Indonesia and the Ayala Corporation in the Philippines).

The control of family members over board seats and leadership roles led to conflicts of interest and gave rise to serious agency problems among the agent and managers (Roche, 2005) as well as the controlling family and minority shareholders (Nam & Nam, 2004). It reduced accountability to outside shareholders in many family-owned Asian businesses. Over time, calls for reforms and changes in CG practices arose due to the shortcomings of the family-dominated business model.

State-Owned Enterprises. Prior to the 1990s, industries and sectors that are considered crucial are owned and controlled by the government in the form of State-owned enterprises (SOEs). State-owned enterprises operated in strategic sectors like energy (China National Petroleum Corporation), transportation (Indian Railways), telecommunications (Telecom Authority of Singapore), and heavy industries, playing a central role in infrastructure development (Japan Highway Public Corporation, Japan) and social and economic development. Although they aim to promote economic development, employment, and equitable resource distribution, they often operate in monopolistic or oligopolistic environments with limited competition, subject to direct government control over their operations and pricing policies (Telecom Authority of Singapore, Pakistan International Airlines, Myanma Oil and Gas Enterprise, Philippine National Oil Company). While family conglomerates contribute to economic growth and innovation, state-owned enterprises play crucial roles in infrastructure development and nation-building.

1990-2000s Phase: Economic Crisis and Corporate Governance Reforms

During this phase, in contrast to Indonesia and Thailand, where corporations are primarily controlled by families, corporations in Japan are typically widely held. Furthermore, Indonesia, Korea, Japan, Malaysia, Indonesia, and Thailand all had significant state control (Claessens et al. 1999). In 1997-1998, the Asian Financial Crisis led to severe economic and financial turmoil in several Asian economies causing currency devaluations, stock market crashes, widespread corporate bankruptcies and economic recessions (Johnson et al. 2000; Radelet et al. 1998). Examples include South Korea's Daewoo Group collapse, Thailand's Tom Yum Goong crisis, Indonesia's crony capitalism, Malaysia's capital controls, and the Philippines' economic contraction and banking crisis (Hunter et al., 2012). The crisis also highlighted the importance of sound corporate governance practices.

Significant corporate governance reforms were implemented as a result of these crises, which exposed flaws in transparency, risk management, and accountability (Chang, 2007). The reforms aimed to address weaknesses, enhance transparency and accountability, and attract foreign investment. South Korea introduced the Corporate Governance Code in 1999, emphasizing transparency, shareholder rights, and board independence (Chang, 2006b). Accordingly, Japan initiated the "Big Bang" Financial Reforms in the 1990s (Patrikis, 1998) to encourage foreign investment and escalate the tradition of cross-shareholdings. Thailand established the Thai Institute of Directors (IOD) to promote corporate governance practices (Limpaphayom, & Connelly, 2004) through guidelines, and assessments for improved governance. Indonesia introduced measures to strengthen capital markets and corporate governance, while Malaysia launched the Corporate Governance Blueprint (Alnasser, 2012). Singapore issued a Code of Corporate Governance in 2001 to enhance investor protection and strengthen governance that emphasized board accountability, audit practices, and transparency in reporting (Conyon, 2006). The Philippines adopted a code emphasizing accountability, transparency, and equitable treatment of shareholders (Echanis, 2006). A stricter set of criteria for independent directors and audit committees were introduced by Hong Kong's Securities and Futures Commission in order to improve corporate governance practices (Michael & Goo, 2015).

Post-2000s Phase: The Emergence of Independent Directors and Shareholder Activism

Asian economies have recognized the value of corporate governance reforms for attracting foreign investment, preserving financial stability, and promoting sustainable growth (Walker & Fox, 2002). After 2000, there was a significant change in corporate governance in Asia, which was characterized by the emergence of independent directors and the growing importance of shareholder activism. Governments have paid more attention to transparency, accountability, and investor protection. The historical progression of corporate governance in Asia during this time can be summarized as follows:

Adoption of Independent Directors. In order to ensure objectivity and decision-making, independent directors (ID) are members of a company's board without significant financial or personal ties. They offer an outside perspective free of conflicts of interest. No material relationships, objectivity, board committee expertise, transparency, diversity of expertise, and accountability are important traits of independent directors. These directors contribute to a well-rounded and informed decision-making process, ensuring that a company's actions align with stakeholders' best interests while minimizing conflicts of interest.

In order to improve board oversight and decision-making, Japan introduced a Corporate Governance Code in 2015 that placed a strong emphasis on the appointment of independent directors. Companies were encouraged to form independent audit committees and have a minimum number of IDs. According to the Indian Companies Act of 2013, at least one-third of the board members of public companies in certain sectors must be IDs.

Shareholder Activism Gains Momentum. Shareholder activism is the active engagement of shareholders in influencing corporate decisions to improve transparency, governance practices, and shareholder value. This trend has gained momentum in Asia due to changing landscapes, key catalysts, targeted engagement strategies, and regulatory changes. Examples include Sony Corporation, Samsung Group, and Olympus Corporation. Regulatory changes and institutional support have contributed to shareholder activism, with governments and regulatory bodies facilitating engagement and institutional investors embracing activism for better governance. Challenges include cultural context, balancing short-term shareholder demands with long-term strategic vision, and the emergence of activist investors. Despite resistance in some Asian cultures, the movement has led to better governance, improved performance, and enhanced shareholder rights.

Key Reforms. The post-2000 period observed significant reforms in corporate governance across Asia. Following are some examples of significant reforms that various Asian countries executed to elevate corporate governance standards, increase transparency, and safeguard investor interests in the during post-2000 (.

South Korea: to encourage institutional investors to actively communicate with companies about governance issues, South Korea adopted a Stewardship Code in 2016.

China: to increase board independence, enhance financial reporting, and safeguard minority shareholders, China implemented a number of governance reforms.

Taiwan: to improve board effectiveness, shareholder rights, and disclosure requirements, Taiwan amended its Corporate Governance Rules.

Singapore: to advise businesses on governance procedures and promote transparency, Singapore introduced a Code of Corporate Governance.

Malaysia: to improve governance standards and practices and bring them into line with international best practices, Malaysia published a Corporate Governance Blueprint.

India: to incorporate independent directors and enhanced disclosure, The Companies Act of 2013 in India made significant changes to corporate governance.

Corporate Governance Mechanisms and Practices in Selected Asian Markets

CG mechanisms in Asia have evolved in response to many factors, including the global financial crisis, business scandals, and increased investor scrutiny. Asian countries are implementing regulatory and institutional reforms to improve corporate governance and strengthen shareholder rights. Another key corporate governance mechanism in Asia is audit committee strengthening (Chen & Hsu, 2017). The Audit Committee is responsible for overseeing finances with legal and regulatory requirements. In recent years, audit committees have become commonplace in many Asian countries as part of a broader effort to improve corporate transparency and accountability. These standards and requirements promote transparency and accountability, enabling companies to provide investors with accurate and timely information. Overall, CG mechanisms in Asian markets reflect a growing awareness of transparency, accountability and shareholder rights (Gillan & Kim, 2016). This is about long-term value creation and sustainable business practices.

The prominent role played by family and other major shareholders in corporate decision-making is one of the distinguishing characteristics of CG in Asia. It is rare for management to be separated from ownership control, and in two-thirds of firms that are not widely held, management is related to the family of the controlling shareholder (Claessens et al., 1999). Asian countries actively shape CG practices and monitor corporate behaviour. This may include regulatory oversight, direct ownership of state-owned enterprises, and using state-owned banks and other financial institutions to influence corporate decision-making.

Japan

Reviewing Japanese corporate governance reform highlights its transition from the main bank system to large-scale boards with internal directors. These features complement economic systems, such as lifetime employment and long-term contracts with suppliers, known as "keiretsu." These elements have traditionally served as an alternative to outside directors, regardless of their monitoring capacity function and effectiveness (Suzuki, 2019). Keiretsu is a Japanese term referring to a business network that includes different companies, including manufacturers, supply chain partners, distributors, and occasionally financiers. The Keiretsu originated in the Meiji era when the Meiji government sought to accelerate Japan's industrialization by creating family-controlled Zaibatsu. These enterprises emerged due to market failures, allowing capital markets to allocate resources efficiently and facilitate risk assessment. Each Zaibatsu was owned by a family with diversified interests, driving the pre-World War II Japanese industry and economy (Daidj, 2016). Keiretsu are characterized by two inter-corporate linkages: horizontal and vertical. Horizontal keiretsu dominate Japan's industrial landscape, while vertical keiretsu are organized around major firms and their buyers and suppliers, like Toyota and Honda (McGuire & Dow, 2009).

The structure and function of the two kinds of keiretsu are very different from one another. Vertical keiretsu has been recognized as a significant factor in the expansion of the Japanese economy, in addition to horizontal keiretsu, which has a long history in the Japanese economy ((McGuire & Dow, 2009). The Japanese economy is dominated by six major horizontal keiretsu, three of which are pre-war zaibatsu descendants and three post-war ones. Membership is diversified, but recent mergers have reduced it to four. Sumitomo and Mitsui merged in 2000, while Sanwa became part of the Bank of Tokyo Mitsubishi group in 2001. These developments are a result of significant regulatory and economic changes in Japan over the past decade (McGuire & Dow, 2009). Keiretsu firms have complex ties, primarily focusing on lending and equity ties, and personnel ties. The ownership structure is dominated by group holdings, with reciprocal holdings prevalent. These ties create a dispersed yet robust ownership network (Johnston & McAlevey, 1998). Japanese firms traditionally rely heavily on bank financing, but the bank-centred nature of horizontal keiretsu makes such ties especially important. Lending ties are reinforced by equity holdings and board memberships, and personnel exchanges and memberships on the "presidents' council" further reinforce these ties (Hwang & Kim, 1998; Morck & Nakamura, 1999). This combination of debt, equity, and personnel ties results in a highly intertwined network of stable financial stakeholders (McGuire & Dow, 2009).

The Japanese recession of the 1990s significantly impacted the governance of Keiretsu firms, reshaping their corporate structures, business practices, and relationships (Nakamura, 2006). The economic downturn exposed the risks associated with cross-shareholdings, leading to concerns about transparency and accountability (McGuire & Dow, 2009). Nissan Motor Co. had cross-shareholdings with other keiretsu firms, causing Nissan to reconsider its governance and ownership structure.

The crisis also highlighted the need for more objective and independent oversight within keiretsu firms, leading some companies to appoint independent directors to their boards, an example includes Toyota Motor Corp.

The recession also led to a focus on efficiency and profitability, with some underperforming businesses restructured or divested to improve financial performance. During the recession, Mitsubishi Corporation underwent restructuring and sold non-core assets in order to boost its financial performance. A greater shareholder focus was also observed, as the Japanese government and international investors called for improved corporate governance. Keiretsu firms began to pay more attention to shareholder rights and transparency, reducing their reliance on cross-shareholdings (Tricker, 2019). In order to address these issues, Mizuho Financial Group implemented changes to increase transparency, improve risk management, and appoint independent directors. Keiretsu firms came under pressure from regulators and market participants to update their governance procedures and conform to international standards. As a result, this led to changes in board composition, increased board independence, and a greater focus on transparency, disclosure, and risk management within the Sumitomo Mitsui Financial Group (Nakamura, 2006).

A hostile takeover attempt by Livedoor Corporation in 2005 exposed the issues at stake between shareholders and the current management, the acceptance of general shareholder rights by Japanese courts, the justifications for anti-takeover actions, and the legal restrictions on poison pills (Milhaupt & Pistor, 2008). This incident occurred around the time that the Japanese parliament was debating changes to the company law, which were later incorporated into the new company law in May 2006. The case demonstrated the necessity of safeguarding current shareholders from ineffective management while enabling value-adding takeovers to succeed (Nakamura, 2006). Company laws were revised to allow US-style corporate governance when the traditional method of corporate governance was called into question. It emphasizes shareholders, board restructuring, and performance incentives. Some companies experimented with hybrid governance, but some predict the moves towards the US or UK commonwealth model as Japan responds to globalization (Tricker, 2019).

Over the past decades, the cross-shareholding system between companies significantly dissolved, leading to a rise in foreign institutional investors' shareholding ratio. This led to a decline in the traditional mutual monitoring model among group companies, and increased institutional investor shareholding, significantly impacting the Japanese corporate governance system (Suzuki, 2019). Hence, the rise of foreign institutional investors in the 2000s led to the introduction of a global corporate governance system in Japan. California Public Employees' Retirement System (CalPERS), a large investor in Japanese companies, significantly influenced the reform of Japanese corporate governance practices. The Asian Corporate Governance Association recommended a transparent process for independent external supervision of management, and companies committed to appointing at least three independent external directors (Suzuki, 2019). Japan has since moved towards a market-oriented system, increasing the number of outside directors and disclosing more information to shareholders. Foreign shareholders' voices have become crucial in determining corporate governance reform in the highly globalized Japanese stock market (Suzuki, 2019).

South Korea

Large conglomerate groups known as Chaebol, which originated from small family-run businesses, have dominated South Korea's CG system. South Korean business has a dominant family ownership structure, with less than 2% of shareholders holding over 80% of company shares in 1996 (OECD, 1999). Due to this conventional structure, the corporation is controlled by its owners, who are frequently families. However, insider CG systems, like those in South Korea, frequently experience problems like abuses of power and a lack of transparency. With Confucian ethics encouraging a family-like environment, cultural influences on South Korean business have fueled the growth of hierarchical business structures (Solomon, 2012). The chaebol has developed strong, dominant leadership as a result, which has contributed to the nation's failure to address the Asian crisis in 1997. Abuses of power, lack of transparency, accountability and other CG weaknesses have contributed to the country's failure to address these issues (Balino and Ubide, 1999).

In economies, such as South Korea where insiders hold greater influence within a legal framework derived from Germany and Scandinavia, minority shareholders can find themselves inadequately protected (Solomon, 2012). With institutional investors holding only about 35% of companies, this exacerbates the issue (Solomon, 2012). To tackle this problem, the South Korean government has taken steps to enhance investor protection and broaden corporate ownership through the implementation of changes to the Commercial Code. This is a commonly employed approach to corporate governance reform in countries with codified legal structures, where voluntary codes of practice and policy documents are deemed sufficient. Over the past few years, the chaebol has lowered its debt-equity ratios by owning more equity. Additionally, the increase in shareholder democracy in South Korea has played a role in implementing changes in CG, particularly in terms of treating minority shareholders more fairly (Solomon, 2012).

The People's Solidarity for Participatory Democracy (PSPD) is a civic organization that promotes increased accountability and transparency. They have urged businesses like Hyundai to reimburse customers for losses brought on by unauthorized transfers of securities to trust funds. The legal changes that removed restrictions on institutional investors' voting rights and lowered voting percentage limits in 1998 have improved minority shareholders' rights in South Korea. The lack of interest in corporate governance among South Korean shareholders, though, may have stemmed from a lack of awareness of their rights and obligations. Additionally, by reforming annual general meetings (AGMs), Korean shareholders' rights have been enhanced. AGMs are frequently held on the same day in stock markets controlled by insiders, which has an impact on shareholder democracy. Companies have come under pressure from the PSPD to hold AGMs that encourage greater shareholder participation and attendance. The research reveals encouraging signs that Korean institutional investors were growing more interested in corporate governance in South Korea and that they felt they had a bigger role to play in terms of responsibility and the exercise of their rights (Solomon et al., 2002).

The International Monetary Fund and the International Bank for Reconstruction and Development, which provided bailout funds after the 1997 crisis, assisted the government in driving the reform (Min & Bowman, 2015). The Asian crisis and South Korea's CG reforms have led to improved governance of chaebol, even among the worst performers. Research shows that even chaebols were once considered the worst performers have significantly improved their governance since the crisis. However, many chaebols have disappeared due to globalization, partly due to their inability to compete globally (Solomon, 2012). The government decided to adopt an outside director system in an effort to more closely resemble the Anglo-American framework. The corporate reforms addressed issues like enhancing the legal responsibility of controlling shareholders, shareholder activism, the audit committee's independence, allowing a holding company system, and trustworthy and transparent accounting and management information. One of the most crucial aspects of the reform is the implementation of the outside director system (Min, 2013).

Three main aspects of Korea's government-initiated regulatory reforms are: changing the makeup of the board of directors (BOD), mandating the appointment of outside directors for publicly traded companies, and encouraging the use of an outside director system. Companies listed on the Korea Exchange were required by the Listing Act of February 1998 to have at least 25% outside directors on the Board of Directors. The Securities and Exchange Act was amended in 2001 and 2003 in response to the Code of Best Practice for Corporate Governance, which called for large listed corporations with assets over 2 trillion won to set up an Appointment Committee and an Audit Committee under the Board of Directors, both of which would be predominately made up of outside directors (Min & Bowman, 2015).

China

China's production of goods and services is primarily conducted by State-owned enterprises (SOEs), which evolved from holding property ownership and managerial rights to a contracting model resembling a U.S. corporation (Schipani & Liu, 2002). SOE governance models include traditional (1950s-1984), transitional (1984-1993), and modern corporate (1993-present). SOEs were government-affiliated businesses instead of true businesses that produced goods or provided services. However, modern corporate governance standards were necessary for SOE corporatization as the majority of SOEs were uncompetitive and static (Schipani & Liu, 2002).

From 1984 to 1993, the State-creditor's rights model—also known as the contracting model—was the dominant method of governance for State-owned Enterprises (SOEs). It aimed to turn SOEs into legal entities while retaining State property ownership, separate State ownership from SOE management rights, and hold SOEs accountable for their own profits and losses in the market. To accomplish these reform goals, the State-Owned Industrial Enterprises Law of China was adopted in 1988. The SOEs Law introduced three features: the factory director assumes overall management responsibility, creates a management committee, ensures and monitors guiding principles and policies, and permits enterprises to practice democratic management through employees' congresses. The contracting system implemented between 1987 and 1993, regulated SOEs' interactions with the government and factory managers. It set a fixed minimum profit, allowing SOEs to keep additional profits but still obligated to pay the fixed amount. This system reduced government interference and granted SOEs more autonomy. However, the contracting system and its interim model failed in SOE reform. Determining a minimum profit for SOEs, ensuring they could pay fixed sums when losses occurred, preventing personal exploitation of assets, and reserving insufficient profits for development were difficult tasks for the State. Therefore, SOE reform in 1993 aimed to create a modern enterprise system compatible with the market economy, influenced by the Western corporation model (Schipani & Liu, 2002).

To facilitate a market-based economy and create more effective labour, capital, and product markets, the nation adopted a gradual strategy. Significant market reforms began with the establishment of the Shanghai and Shenzhen Stock Exchanges in 1990 and 1991, which sparked additional reforms centred on internal governance mechanisms (Jiang & Kim, 2015). The main objective was to provide managers with financial incentives in addition to direct state control. However, due to a lack of effective external governance mechanisms, such as strong shareholder protection and competitive product and labour markets, the efficacy of policy prescriptions included in codes of "good" corporate governance remains in doubt (Mutlu et al.; 2018). China introduced CG reforms in 2001 that ensure publicly traded companies have outside directors on their boards. By bringing diversity, objectivity, and a focus on shareholders' interests, these directors were expected to enhance the performance of the company. However, due to its relationship-based culture, China has generated controversy regarding the efficacy of outside directors.

Various CG regulations are enforced by government bodies, including annual shareholder meetings, a voting system, director terms, director responsibilities, prohibitions, independent directors, and supervisory boards. Listed companies must hold annual meetings, implement shareholder resolutions, make significant operational and investment decisions, and evaluate top managers. Independent directors must not be related to the manager or top 10 shareholders. Supervisory boards consist of at least three supervisors, including representatives of shareholders, and must be employees of the firm. Supervisors are elected for three-year terms and have the primary responsibility of supervising and evaluating directors and senior managers. They can attend board meetings as nonvoting participants and propose the removal of directors or senior managers who fail in their duties or violate regulations. These regulations aim to promote transparency and accountability in Chinese-listed firms (Jiang & Kim, 2015). Regulations requiring disclosure of information expanded roles, an improved labour market, and reporting of important board activities are all factors that could increase the effectiveness of outside directors. These reforms marked a change in the corporate governance environment in China by placing more emphasis on interpersonal relationships and market institutions (Mutlu et al.; 2018).

CONCLUSION

In recent years, corporate governance has drawn more attention, especially in the wake of the 1997 Asian financial crisis and the early 2000s corporate scandals. Corporate governance in Asia faces challenges such as family ownership, weak enforcement, lack of independent directors, and shareholder activism. However, opportunities include economic growth and investment potential, modernization and regulatory reforms, increasing environmental, social, and governance (ESG) considerations, increased shareholder activism, and diverse business models. The region's diverse business landscape presents opportunities for innovative governance practices that can adapt to its unique business landscape. However, challenges such as limited transparency, and lack of independent oversight persist, making it crucial for companies to adapt and innovate in the face of these challenges.

Due to its role in fostering trust, stability, and sustainable economic growth, corporate governance is of utmost importance in the Asian market. Effective corporate governance practices guarantee transparency, accountability, and the protection of shareholder rights in a region with a variety of business models, family-owned conglomerates, and state-owned enterprises. These principles not only encourage foreign investment but also risk mitigation, corporate integrity, and ethical business practices. Strong corporate governance serves as a cornerstone for developing resilient and competitive businesses that contribute to the prosperity of the region and to the stability of the global economy as Asia continues to be a global economic powerhouse.

REFERENCES

Abdullah, H., & Valentine, B. (2009). Fundamental and ethics theories of corporate governance. *Middle Eastern Finance and Economics*, *4*(4), 88–96.

Agyris, C. (1973). Some Limits of Rational Man Organizational Theory. *Public Administration Review*, *33*(3), 253–267. doi:10.2307/974803

Alnasser, S. (2012). What has changed? The development of corporate governance in Malaysia. *The Journal of Risk Finance*, *13*(3), 269–276. doi:10.1108/15265941211229271

Aluchna, M., & Idowu, S. O. (Eds.). (2017). *Responsible Corporate Governance: Towards Sustainable and Effective Governance Structures*. Springer International Publishing. doi:10.1007/978-3-319-55206-4

Anon. (2015). *G20/OECD Principles of Corporate Governance 2015*. OECD Publishing.

Balino, T. J. T., & Ubide, A. (1999). *The Korean financial crisis of 1997—A strategy of financial sector reform*. IMF Working Paper WP/99/29.

Chang, S.-J. (2006). Korean Business Groups: The Financial Crisis and the Restructuring of Chaebols. In S.-J. Chang (Ed.), *Business Groups in East Asia: Financial Crisis* (pp. 52–69). Restructuring, and New Growth., doi:10.1093/acprof:oso/9780199287345.003.0003

Chang, S.-J. (Ed.). (2006). Business Groups in East Asia: Financial Crisis, Restructuring, and New Growth. Oxford Academic. doi:10.1093/acprof:oso/9780199287345.001.0001

Chen, Y. S., & Hsu, W. T. (2017). Corporate governance in Asia: A review and research agenda. *Asia Pacific Journal of Management*, *34*(2), 219–243. doi:10.100710490-016-9460-2

Claessens, S., Djankov, S., & Lang, L. H. (1999). *Who Controls East Asian Corporations?* (Vol. 2054). World Bank Publications.

Claessens, S., Djankov, S., & Lang, L. H. (2000). The separation of ownership and control in East Asian corporations. *Journal of Financial Economics*, *58*(1-2), 81–112. doi:10.1016/S0304-405X(00)00067-2

Clarke, T. (2004). *Theories of corporate governance: The philosophical foundations of corporate governance*. Routledge.

Clarkson, M. B. E. (1995). A Stakeholder Framework for Analyzing and Evaluating Corporate Social Performance. *Academy of Management Review*, *20*(1), 92–117. doi:10.2307/258888

Conyon, M. J. (2006). Corporate governance in Singapore: A case study. In International Corporate Governance: A Case Study Approach, Handbook of Partial Least Squares: Concepts, Methods and Applications. Edward Elgar Publishing Limited.

Cyert, R. M., & March, J. G. (1963). *A Behavior Theory of the Firm*. Prentice Hall.

Daidj, N. (2016). The evolution of corporate governance in Japan: The case of vertical keiretsu groups. In *Global Perspectives on Corporate Governance and CSR* (pp. 95–128). Routledge.

Daily, C. M., Dalton, D. R., & Canella, A. A. (2003). Corporate Governance: Decades of Dialogue and Data. *Academy of Management Review*, *28*(3), 371–382. doi:10.2307/30040727

Davis, J. H., Schoorman, F. D., & Donaldson, L. (1997). Toward a Stewardship Theory of Management. *Academy of Management Review*, *22*(1), 20–24. doi:10.2307/259223

DiMaggio, P. J., & Powell, W. W. (1983). The iron cage revisited: Institutional isomorphism and collective rationality in organizational fields. *American Sociological Review*, *48*(2), 147–160. doi:10.2307/2095101

Donaldson, T., & Preston, L. E. (1995). The Stakeholder Theory of the Corporation: Concepts, Evidence and Implications. *Academy of Management Review*, *20*(1), 65–91. doi:10.2307/258887

Echanis, E. S. (2006). Philippine corporate governance: Issues and reforms. *Philippine Management Review, 13*.

Fama, E. F. (1980). Agency Problems and the Theory of the Firm. *Journal of Political Economy*, *88*(2), 288–307. doi:10.1086/260866

Fama, E. F., & Jensen, M. (1983). Separation of ownership and control. *The Journal of Law & Economics*, *26*(2), 301–3025. doi:10.1086/467037

Freeman, R. E. (1984). *Strategic Management: A Stakeholder Approach*. Pitman.

Freeman, R. E. (1999). Response: Divergent Stakeholder Theory. *Academy of Management Review*, *24*(2), 233–236.

Germain, L., Galy, N., & Lee, W. (2014). Corporate governance reform in Malaysia: Board size, independence and monitoring. *Journal of Economics and Business*, *75*, 126–162. doi:10.1016/j.jeconbus.2014.06.003

Gillan, S. L., & Kim, W. (2016). Corporate governance around the world: A look at some of the key issues. *Journal of Corporate Finance*, *39*, 1–33. doi:10.1016/j.jcorpfin.2016.02.008

Globerman, S., Peng, M. W., & Shapiro, D. M. (2011). Corporate governance and Asian companies. *Asia Pacific Journal of Management*, *28*(1), 1–14. doi:10.100710490-010-9240-6

Gutierrez, B. P., & Rodriguez, R. (2013). Diversification strategies of large business groups in the Philippines. *Philippine Management Review, 20*.

Hillman, A. J., Withers, M. C., & Collins, B. J. (2009). Resource dependence theory: A review. *Journal of Management*, *35*(6), 1404–1427. doi:10.1177/0149206309343469

Hunter, W. C., Kaufman, G. G., & Krueger, T. H. (Eds.). (2012). *The Asian financial crisis: origins, implications, and solutions*. Springer Science & Business Media.

Hwang, L., & Kim, Y. (1998). Does the ownership structure of debt and equity affect the agency costs of debt? Japanese evidence. *Journal of Accounting, Auditing & Finance*, *13*(1), 37–67. doi:10.1177/0148558X9801300103

Iskander, M., & Chamlou, N. (2000). *Corporate governance: A framework for implementation*. The World Bank. doi:10.1596/0-8213-4741-1

Jensen, M.C., & Meckling, W. (1976). Theory Of The Firm: Managerial Behavior, Agency Costs And Ownership Structure. *Journal of Financial Economics, 3*, 305-360.

Jiang, F., & Kim, K. A. (2015). Corporate governance in China: A modern perspective. *Journal of Corporate Finance*, *32*, 190–216. doi:10.1016/j.jcorpfin.2014.10.010

Johnson, S., Boone, P., Breach, A., & Friedman, E. (2000). Corporate governance in the Asian financial crisis. *Journal of Financial Economics*, *58*(1-2), 141–186. doi:10.1016/S0304-405X(00)00069-6

Johnston, S., & McAlevey, L. (1998). Stable shareholdings and Japan's bubble economy: An historical overview. *Strategic Management Journal*, *19*(11), 1101–1107. doi:10.1002/(SICI)1097-0266(1998110)19:11<1101::AID-SMJ998>3.0.CO;2-Q

Koike, K. (1993). The Ayala group during the Aquino period: Diversification along with a changing ownership and management structure. *The Developing Economies*, *31*(4), 442–460. doi:10.1111/j.1746-1049.1993.tb00034.x

Liew, P. K. (2007). Corporate governance reforms in Malaysia: The key leading players' perspectives. *Corporate Governance*, *15*(5), 724–740. doi:10.1111/j.1467-8683.2007.00618.x

Limpaphayom, P., & Connelly, J. T. (2004). *Corporate governance in Thailand.* Available at SSRN 965300.

Mallin, C. A. (2017). *Corporate governance*. Oxford University Press.

McGuire, J., & Dow, S. (2009). Japanese keiretsu: Past, present, future. *Asia Pacific Journal of Management*, *26*(2), 333–351. doi:10.100710490-008-9104-5

Meyer, J. W., & Rowan, B. (1977). Institutionalized organizations: Formal structure as myth and ceremony. *American Journal of Sociology*, *83*(2), 340–363. doi:10.1086/226550

Michael, B., & Goo, S. H. (2015). Corporate governance and its reform in Hong Kong: A study in comparative corporate governance. *Corporate Governance*, *15*(4), 444–475. doi:10.1108/CG-09-2013-0109

Milhaupt, C. J., & Pistor, K. (2008). The Livedoor Bid and Hostile Takeovers in Japan: Postwar Law and Capitalism at the Crossroads. In Law and capitalism what corporate crises reveal about legal systems and economic development around the world (pp. 87–108). University of Chicago Press.

Min, B. S. (2013). Evaluation of board reforms: An examination of the appointment of outside directors. *Journal of the Japanese and International Economies*, *29*, 21–43. doi:10.1016/j.jjie.2013.05.001

Min, B. S., & Bowman, R. G. (2015). Corporate governance, regulation and foreign equity ownership: Lessons from Korea. *Economic Modelling*, *47*, 145–155. doi:10.1016/j.econmod.2015.02.030

Monks, R. A. (2002). Creating value through corporate governance. *Corporate Governance*, *10*(3), 116–123. doi:10.1111/1467-8683.00277

Morck, R., & Nakamura, M. (1999). Banks and corporate control in Japan. *The Journal of Finance*, *54*(1), 319–339. doi:10.1111/0022-1082.00106

Mutlu, C. C., Essen, M. V., Peng, M. W., Saleh, S. F., & Duran, P. (2018). Corporate Governance in China: A Meta-Analysis. *Journal of Management Studies*, *55*(6), 943–979. doi:10.1111/joms.12331

Nakamura, M. (2006). Japanese corporate governance practices in the post-bubble era: Implications of institutional and legal reforms in the 1990s and early 2000s. *International Journal of Disclosure and Governance*, *3*(3), 233–261. doi:10.1057/palgrave.jdg.2040081

Nam, S. W., & Nam, I. C. (2004). *Corporate governance in Asia*. Asian Development Bank Institute.

OECD. (1999). *Economic survey*. OECD.

Patrikis, E. T. (1998). Japan's Big Bang Financial Reforms. *Brook. J. Int'l L.*, *24*, 577.

Pound, J. (1988). Proxy contests and the efficiency of shareholder oversight. *Journal of Financial Economics*, *20*, 237–265. doi:10.1016/0304-405X(88)90046-3

Radelet, S., Sachs, J. D., Cooper, R. N., & Bosworth, B. P. (1998). The East Asian financial crisis: Diagnosis, remedies, prospects. *Brookings Papers on Economic Activity*, *1998*(1), 1–90. doi:10.2307/2534670

Roche, J. (2005). Corporate governance in Asia (No. 6). Routledge.

Schipani, C. A., & Liu, J. (2002). *Corporate Governance in China: Then and Now*. SSRN Electronic Journal. doi:10.2139srn.315050

Shleifer, A., & Vishny, R. W. (1997). A Survey of Corporate Governance. *The Journal of Finance*, *52*(2), 737–783. doi:10.1111/j.1540-6261.1997.tb04820.x

Solomon, J. (2012). *Corporate Governance*. Governance, Risk, and Compliance Handbook. doi:10.1002/9781118269213

Solomon, J. F., Solomon, A., & Park, C. (2002, July). The role of institutional investors in corporate governance reform in South Korea: Some empirical evidence. *Corporate Governance*, *10*(3), 211–224. doi:10.1111/1467-8683.00285

Spanos, L. J. (2005). Corporate governance in Greece: Developments and policy implications. *Corporate Governance: The International Journal of Business in Society*, *5*(1), 15-30.

Sundaram, A. K., & Inkpen, A. C. (2004). The Corporate Objective Revisited. *Organization Science*, *15*(3), 350–363. doi:10.1287/orsc.1040.0068

Suzuki, M. (2019). Japanese corporate governance reform: What is required for effective functioning of outside directors? *Yustisia Jurnal Hukum*, *8*(1), 11–29. doi:10.20961/yustisia.v0ixx.29690

Tricker, R. I. (2019). Models of Corporate Governance. In Corporate governance: Principles, policies, and practices (3rd ed., pp. 152–154). Oxford University Press. doi:10.1093/hebz/9780198809869.003.0007

Walker, G., & Fox, M. (2002). Corporate governance reform in East Asia. *Corporate Governance: The International Journal of Business in Society, 2*(1), 4-9.

Wheeler, D., Colbert, B., & Freeman, R. E. (2003). Focusing On Value: Reconciling corporate social responsibility, sustainability and a stakeholder approach in a network world. *Journal of General Management*, *28*(3), 1–28. doi:10.1177/030630700302800301

Chapter 2
Corporate Governance Failure and the Regulatory Fight Against It:
An Examination of Select Instances From India

Vijaya Kittu Manda
https://orcid.org/0000-0002-1680-8210
Independent Researcher, India

Lubza Nihar Khaliq
GITAM School of Business, GITAM University, India

EXECUTIVE SUMMARY

India has recently witnessed several allegations of corporate governance lapses and failure. The alarming situation prompted the government and the regulators to take serious note to make the companies accountable for the allegations and to bring in regulations to contain the policy leaks. The governing body and the board of directors must abide by ethical standards, demonstrating an unwavering commitment to discipline, transparency, fairness, and accountability for their actions. This work uses a case study approach to examine various recent corporate governance failures in India. The examination is made in the following dimensions: accountability, transparency, equitability, responsibility, ethical conduct, board independence, risk management, corporate social responsibility, stakeholder engagement, and regulatory compliance. The study scrutinized various classic and recent corporate governance lapses in established corporate entities and startups and in Indian banks. The measures implemented by regulatory bodies, including the RBI, SEBI, and the MCA, were analyzed.

DOI: 10.4018/978-1-6684-9867-5.ch002

INTRODUCTION

The concept of Corporate Governance encompasses the regulatory and functional dimensions of an organization. Academic researchers examine the various aspects of a corporate company, including accounting, finance, law, management, regulations, and compliance. Corporate governance is a risk mitigation characteristic because corporates with robust governance procedures experience less stress and fewer corporate risks. Some such acclaimed governance practices include higher institutional ownership stakes, concentrated family ownership structures, lower CEO compensation and duality, gender diversity, higher presence of female members in management, and better board dynamics in independent boards (Kalia & Gill, 2023). Good corporate governance, especially in an emerging economy, contributes to business performance and protects shareholder interests (R. K. Singh & Sharma, 2023). Organizations exhibiting sound governance practices are perceived to possess resilient internal control mechanisms, enabling them to achieve superior risk mitigation. Such companies successfully filed reliable financial reporting and monitoring by the Board of Directors (Kanojia et al., 2023). The line between good and bad corporate governance practices is thin, and it is often the minority shareholders who pay the price. India has witnessed some well-known corporate companies have going bankrupt, causing losses to their investors.

The current study adopts a case study approach to examine the events highlighting corporate governance's failure. Secondary data from various verifiable sources are used to understand the happenings.

CORPORATE GOVERNANCE IN INDIAN CORPORATE COMPANIES

The occurrence of corporate governance failure is directly attributable to the actions of the top brass of the company (Sajjad, 2023). Since the Board of Directors oversees corporate governance at the corporate level, the governance activities happen separately and parallel to the company's regular operations. The Indian model of corporate governance is slightly different from that of the Anglo-American, German, and Japanese models (Almaqtari et al., 2020; Jalwani et al., 2022; Natto & Mokoaleli-Mokoteli, 2022). Banks and financial performance are two major well-researched areas (Abhilash et al., 2023).

India has witnessed some major corporate governance failures in recent times. The list of disgraced companies includes Yes Bank, IL&FS, DHFL, Jet Airways, the ADAG group, Zee, and PTC India, amongst others. Central to the issue are two key reasons:

1. Inadequate board-level supervision
2. Nexus between promoters, auditors, rating agencies, and others.

Dish TV

"Entertain-men are back in action" - Dish TV advertisement slogan

In December 2022, Yes Bank invoked the pledge on shares of seven companies, including those of direct-to-home television provider Dish TV, to JC Flowers Asset Reconstruction (ARC) as part of the sale of stressed assets aggregating to Rs. 48,000 crore (Vivek, 2022). The invoked shares constitute 24.19% of the total share capital of DishTV. The forced sale of stressed assets is often the result of corporate defaults on bank loans. The situation also raises a bigger question – potential mismanagement of funds at the company!

Lender invocation of pledged shares in Dish TV is not new. There are several tranches of pledge invocations during 2020-2021(Trendlyne, 2023). Dish TV was under financial stress for a while. Consequently, YES Bank, a key lender, took control of the company from its promoter, Subhash Chandra. After Yes Bank sold shares of the company to JCF ARC, Chandra started attempting to buy shares from the ARC and thereby win control over the company.

On March 1, 2023, minority shareholders began questioning the board's integrity after it found that the company failed to induct four of the six independent directors despite the government approving the appointment. Back on December 26, 2022, the Ministry of Information and Broadcasting (MIB) approved six names for appointment to the Board of Dish TV as proposed between Dish TV and Yes Bank (Livemint, 2023a). The Minority Investors Association of Dish TV conveyed in their letter to the board that the latter's independence was compromised due to the prevalence of members from the promoter group and its affiliated entities. It was alleged that the SEBI regulations about appointing independent directors have not been adhered. More importantly, they alleged that the company had not disclosed material information to shareholders, including the fact that it is facing financial difficulties (Ritu, 2023). The company denied the allegations in its reply on March 6, 2023, and that it complied with applicable regulations. SEBI smelt foul and asked the company to give a detailed response, to which DishTV replied a few days later. With this, SEBI formally started an investigation.

In July 2023, a group of 77 minority shareholders of DishTV who combined hold 10.15% shareholding in the company demanded a probe into the alleged diversion of funds from Dish Infra Services, a wholly-owned subsidiary of Dish TV, to Zee Entertainment Enterprises and a breach of corporate governance (Gopika, 2023). The company denied any wrongdoing and termed the allegations as baseless.

The whole episode is one of several transactions that the securities market regulator is examining as a part of a much bigger probe against Subhash Chandra, founder of Essel Group. In August 2023, SEBI gave its order restraining Subhash Chandra and Punit Goenka from holding any board positions at any listed company (Livemint, 2023b), including in the proposed Zee-Sony merged entity, until further orders. However, the legal fraternity feels that the majority shareholders will put forward their views and decide whether or not the duo should be sitting in a position. Another lesson learned from the episode is that the National Company Law Tribunal (NCLT) clarified that the merger process between Zee and Sony would continue irrespective of the outcome of SEBI barring the duo. The merger process, which started in December 2021, will not be put on hold because doing so will mean sacrificing the interests of shareholders and stakeholders. The overall case highlights the role and power of minority shareholders in ensuring proper governance is in place in the company they invested in.

PTC India Financial Services (PFS)

"Assessing the damage, if any, is a priority. Also, it needs to be assessed whether the allegations are a matter of difference of opinion within the board or of a material lapse in governance." - An unnamed government official.

In January 2022, three independent directors of PTC India Financial Services Ltd (PFS) resigned. They cited concerns about governance and compliance issues. PFS is a Government-owned firm and the financial services arm of PTC India Limited. It is a systematically important non-deposit-taking Non-Banking Finance Company (NBFC) and is classified as an Infrastructure Finance Company by RBI. The company is listed on the Bombay Stock Exchange (BSE) and the National Stock Exchange (NSE). The resignation of three independent directors - Kamlesh Shivji Vikamsey, Santosh B Nayar, and Thomas Mathew T has triggered a corporate governance grenade. The *en masse* resignations alleged that the Chairman and Managing Director (MD) Rajib Mishra and Chief Financial Officer (CFO) Pawan Singh are running the company affairs single-handedly. They were changing the composition of the committees' board and tweaking the loans' terms and conditions without the board's prior approval.

The resignation letters highlighted some critical concerns about the company affairs, particularly the cavalier attitude of the management toward independent directors (Kaushal, 2022). The issue triggered a probe by both the SEBI and RBI independently. SEBI has promptly asked PFS to clarify the happenings at the company. Prima facie found that the Chairman and MD & CFO were responsible for corporate governance failure at PFS. Later, in April 2022, SEBI issued a 72-page show-cause notice to PFS and its management, alleging corporate governance lapses, including:

1. Failing to disclose material information to shareholders
2. Appointing related-party directors to the board
3. Making loans to related parties without proper documentation
4. Failing to maintain proper financial records

The company promptly denied the allegations. However, the board of directors appointed an independent committee to investigate the allegations in June 2022. Later, in July 2022, PFS's auditor, MSKA & Associates, resigned, citing corporate governance concerns. Meanwhile, the independent committee submitted its report to the board of directors, finding that there have been corporate governance lapses at PFS. The report made several recommendations, including removing Rajib Mishra as chairman and managing director.

In August 2022, PFS's board of directors accepted the recommendations of the independent committee and the removal of Rajib Mishra and Pawan Singh from their positions. The Registrar of Companies (RoC) penalized PFS and its MD for not having a functional nomination and remuneration committee.

SEBI found that Rajib Mishra and Pawan Singh were responsible for the failure of corporate governance at the company (Mannu, 2023b). SEBI even questioned the process of appointing Rajib Kumar Mishra for the top job (Rachita, 2023). The RBI directed PFS Chief Pawan Singh to go on permanent leave till his superannuation, which is due October 3, and filled the position by giving additional charge of MD and CEO to its Director-Finance Mahendra Lodha (Mannu, 2023a). The Registrar of Companies (RoC) issued an order penalizing the company for allegedly not having a functional nomination and remuneration committee between early December 2021 and early April 2022. As of August 2023, the crisis-hit company began taking steps for a management overhaul.

The PFS episode highlighted that erratic leaders at the company would be shown the way out, either by the company board or the regulator, sooner or later.

Axis Mutual Fund

"It's bigger than you think." - Axis Smallcap Fund tagline

In May 2022, Axis Mutual Fund was in the middle of a corporate governance failure when a media outlet reported that two fund managers - Viren Joshi and Deepak Agarwal – were indulged in front-running the mutual fund trades on their personal accounts and making illegal personal gains. Viren Joshi is alleged to have tipped off his friends and family about the upcoming trades, allowing them to place their own orders before the orders of the fund house were executed. This allowed them to buy the stocks at a lower price and sell them at a higher price, making a profit at the fund's expense. Front-running is a form of market abuse and is considered illegal.

Fund houses have the fiduciary duty of protecting and safeguarding investor interests, and the fund house had to take the blame for not having adequate risk management practices. The Asset Management Company (AMC) promptly sacked its chief dealer, Viren Joshi. The same month, the Income-Tax Department raided the premises of Joshi. However, in June 2022, Joshi filed a lawsuit against the AMC for wrongful termination. SEBI began investigating the matter in July 2022, and in February 2023, it restrained Joshi and 20 other entities from accessing the capital markets (ET Bureau, 2023). They are also prohibited from associating themselves with the securities market in any way. SEBI directed the impounding of Rs. 30.56 crores in their wrongful gains.

The scandal and the poor performance of several of the funds of Axis MF have resulted in the fund house losing market share. Upon hints from SEBI, the AMC decided to change the leadership and bring in some freshness. It appointed B. Gopkumar as the CEO and Ashish Gupta as the CIO. However, in August 2023, the Head of Equities, Jinesh Gopani, resigned. The company then elevated fund manager Shreyas Devalkar to the role. Considering the scandal and the need to make some fresh appointments, the company decided to make some new appointments – a Chief Risk Officer (CRO), Chief Financial Officer (CFO), and a new Chief Operating Officer (COO).

The Axis Mutual Fund instance shows how companies lose their reputation for lapses in their duties.

Adani Group

"One of the strengths of Adani is that, because we are controlling mines, ships, ports, and logistics, we are the cheapest solution provider for end users." - Gautam Adani

Only 23% of company boards provided information about statutory auditors' independence, competence, and experience as per 2022 statistics. The dispute involving Adani Group and Hindenburg Research (HR), a short seller headquartered in the US, underscored the importance of disclosures to be done by corporate companies, especially those that are publicly listed.

The Adani Group is the third Indian group (after Reliance and Tata) with a market capitalization of $100 billion. It has business interests in port and logistics, agribusiness, energy, defense, and real estate, amongst others (Kumar & Mishra, 2023). In its report released on January 24, 2023, Hindenburg Research made several serious allegations against the Adani Group. The allegations are that the Adani group has indulged in accounting fraud and stock manipulation. It said that the signing partners in the audit team have no significant experience. About 88 allegations are made in its report (Hindenburg, 2023a). The Adani group replied with a 413-page response on January 29, 2023 (Adani Group, 2023). However, Hindenburg rebutted, saying that Adani failed to answer satisfactorily and that the group failed to answer 62 of the 88 questions (Hindenburg, 2023b). Event study analysis showed that the report had a significant impact on the stock prices of the group companies and that the Indian stock markets may not be efficient in its semi-strong form (Mallesha & Archana, 2023).

No wonder sustainability rating companies quickly get their scores reflecting corporate governance lapses. Sustainalytics, for example, downgraded the corporate governance-related scores of Adani Green Energy and Adani Transmission soon after the Hindenburg report was out (Ross & Tommy, 2023). The Adani-Hindenburg saga gave shivers to other listed Indian companies, such as those of the Vedanta group, which share similar characteristics as that of the Adani group (Suresh, 2023).

Issues with the Adani group did not end with the HR report. Global indices took corrective actions. In June 2023, the US regulators began investigating corporate governance failures at the Adani group. The stock market quickly reacted to the news, and investors' wealth of those holding the company shares eroded as the market capitalization began to plummet (Janaki, 2023).

The scholarly community has been tracking the Adani Group for a while. Some prominent studies include the 2015 corporate restructuring (Nidhi & Saurabh, 2016), the cost of non-compliance with regulations (Naeem, 2023), the Market Forces campaign against an Adani coal mine (O'Brien et al., 2022), below-average sustainability integration of its power/energy companies (Sampat, 2022), profitability ratios (S & S, 2021), brand communications done by Fortune oil (Vyas & Bhatt, 2015) amongst others.

Café Coffee Day

"A lot can happen over a cup of coffee." - Café Coffee Day (CCD).

Café Coffee Day (CCD) is a Bengaluru, India-headquartered multinational chain of coffeehouses that has seen its birth, boom, and bounce back under the management of Malavika Hedge, who took the rein after the tragic suicide of her husband and founder Chairman and MD of CCD, Mr. VG Siddartha (Suroju & Disha, 2022).

A few years down the hill, CCD was amidst several allegations, such as siphoning off funds, fund diversion, and mismanagement. As much as Rs. 3,535 crores was found missing from Coffee Day Enterprises Limited (CDEL), the parent company of CCD. CDEL is a listed company; hence, SEBI and stock exchange norms related to compliance and disclosures fall on it.

The money trail showed that seven subsidiary companies were used to make the money finally landed in Mysore Amalgamated Coffee Estates Limited (MACEL), a promoter-led entity. As much as Rs. 2,700 crores were diverted in just four months – between April and July 2019. In return, only Rs. 110 crores was received back by CDEL. The details of the fund transfers came to light from the July 2019 suicide note left by Siddhartha. His note to the Board of Directors said that his teams, auditors, senior management, and even his family were unaware of the transactions and that he alone was accountable for the financial mess. Based on the letter, SEBI began an investigation and found that Siddhartha does several transactions without the board's knowledge. The investigation also found that MACEL was a shell company with no real business operations. The company was essentially used as a conduit to siphon money out of CDEL.

Coffee Day Global (CDGL) is the holding company for the Coffee Day Group's coffee business. During 2019, it was under financial stress, and because of a series of financial irregularities, it eventually collapsed. Overleverage, related-party transactions, misappropriation of funds, and audit failures were the prominent misadventures at the company. After an inquiry, the National Financial Reporting Authority (NFRA) barred auditors ASRMP & Co for two years after finding them guilty of audit lapses and "production misconduct" in FY19. A fine of Rs. 1 crore on the audit firm, Rs. 10 lakhs on one signing partner, and Rs. 5 lakhs each on two other signing partners was imposed (Surabhi, 2023).

On January 24, 2023, SEBI imposed a penalty of Rs. 26 crores on CDEL and asked the company to appoint a reputed law firm in consultation with the National Stock Exchange (NSE) to assist in recovering the outstanding money, constituting an independent board (Jyotindra, 2023). However, the Securities Appellate Tribunal (SAT) stayed the imposition of the penalty till the appeal remains pending before the tribunal (MoneyControl News, 2023).

The CCD scandal highlighted the importance of corporate governance practices, risks of related-party transactions, independent oversight, and the need for whistleblower protection in a company.

Brightcom Group

"It was revealed that Brightcom itself financed the preferential issues by round-tripping funds through subsidiaries and conduit entities." - Enforcement Directorate, Government of India

Advertising technology service provider and new media technology company Brightcom Group Limited became the worst-performing stock of 2022 amongst the BSE 500 companies. It is a darling stock for retail investors after the stock price moved from Rs. 4 in April 2021 to the highs of Rs. 118 in December 2021. Interestingly, the stock is not covered by any leading stockbroker or analyst firm except for a veteran Indian investor despite the stock moving up 2500% in a single year (2021). The stock eventually fell to the low of Rs. 9.35 on April 23, 2023. Not just this instance, but a similar unexplained rise in the share prices of the company was observed in 2019 as well.

Manipulation of financial statements, omission of some financial data from disclosures, complex web of related-party transactions, misappropriation of funds, and, more importantly, non-compliance with regulators led both the SEBI and the Central Bureau of Investigation (CBI) to investigate the affairs of the company. At one point in time, the company's registered address was mentioned as a five-star hotel room on its official website! According to preliminary checks, the profit numbers were inflated, and the company assets and reserves differed from those on the balance sheet. Irregularities are to the tune of Rs. 1,300 crores.

SEBI raised concerns that some of the company's disclosures and financial transactions have been detrimental to investors. In 2021, it appointed Deloitte Touche Tohmatsu India LLP to conduct a forensic audit. SEBI ordered the company directors not to sell, dispose of, or dilute their shareholding. SEBI pointed at audit lapses because auditors failed to issue a qualified opinion. In its interim order in April 2023, SEBI barred the company and its directors from selling, disposing off, or diluting their shareholding in the company. Finally, in August 2023, SEBI gave a detailed 77-page final order detailing the findings of its investigation into the Brightcom Group scam.

Whistleblower Alert at TCS

"A code of conduct violation in a 6-lakh-person organisation is very difficult to detect. Even if I look at all the data in my system, I will not be able to capture it. And because we took action, it came into the public domain, it's not the other way around. Yes, it should not happen. Our core values are very important to us." - CEO, Tata Consultancy Services

In March 2023, a whistleblower message alerted the management of the world's largest IT consulting company about some executives allegedly accepting bribes from staffing firms. The CEO and COO of Tata Consultancy Services (TCS) received the email alleging that ES Chakravarthy, the global head of its resource management group (RMG), was accepting commissions from staffing firms for years. RMG is responsible for allocating available resources to various projects and filling such requirements through contractors in case of any shortfall. It differs from the company's leading talent acquisition group. The management said that the impact arising from the violations, if any, is reported to be minimal.

Leaving no stone unturned, TCS immediately formed an internal committee to investigate the allegations. The internal committee confirmed the allegations to be credible and submitted its report to the management. After the investigation, the management said that the facts and the amount involved were exaggerated in the media. In June 2023, TCS terminated the employment of Chakravarthy and four other executives of RMG. It blacklisted three staffing firms involved in the scandal.

The incident reminded the public of another leading IT company that made headlines in 2005, where a tip-off resulted in an investigation of hundreds of software testers hired illegally. The company not only fired the perpetrator but also retrenched the hired engineers. Bribes and unethical behavior by employees in private despite being decently paid with salaries is not new. Regarding employees' unethical behavior, the United Nations Office on Drugs and Crime reports several reasons, including 'everyone else is doing it,' 'everyone else is doing it,' and 'the end justifies the means' (Krishna Kumar, 2023).

The TCS episode reminds us of the importance and power of whistleblowing in a company and how it can help the management take quick and prompt action against erring individuals.

Other Prominent Mentions

Reliance Industries Limited (RIL)

Even the mighty elephants must face storms and natural calamities. Reliance Industries is the largest listed company in the private sector and has strong leadership across all its business functions. However, there are several instances of corporate governance failures.

In 2005, Anil Ambani, the then Vice-Chairman and Managing Director of RIL, sent a 500-page note on CG to the board, asking them to take appropriate steps in the interest of the company and its shareholders. The report was submitted merely a few days before a Board Meeting on January 21, and the board meeting did not discuss it. A few months down the line, though the Ambani siblings headed towards an agreement later, the MCA still wanted to investigate the CG allegations. Given the Clause 49 regulations being revised, the MCA felt the need to create a database of individuals who can fulfill the requirements of becoming independent directors. Clause 49 required a certain portion of independent directors on their Board from January 2006.

Back in 2007, a fine was imposed on RIL and Mukesh Ambani to the tune of Rs. 25 crores and Rs. 15 crores, respectively, for alleged manipulative trades in Reliance Petroleum Limited (RPL). A fine of Rs. 25 crores was imposed on Mukesh Ambani, Nita Ambani, Anil Ambani, and Tine Ambani for alleged violation of the takeover code regulations in 2000. Surprisingly, the order was passed almost 20 years later. The issue dates to 1994 and relates to the conversion of some warrants. SEBI pointed out that an open offer was not made as per the rules. SEBI imposed a fine of Rs. 30 lakhs on RIL for failing to make disclosures regarding Jio's stake sale to Facebook, Silver Lake, and Vista Equity Partners. The disclosures were made through newspapers rather than the stock exchange route. While the deal happened in March and April 2020, the official corporate disclosure was made on April 22, 2020 (Outlook Business Team, 2020).

Infosys

Sound corporate governance is often believed to be the reason why Infosys enjoyed good valuations despite the company not being the largest nor the fastest-growing Indian IT company when the company went public (Manav, 2023). However, any large corporate company faces governance issues sometimes. Infosys had its fair share of instances of governance lapses. The list included the Infosys acquisition of an Israeli automation company named Panaya in 2015, in which investors questioned the price that Infosys paid for the acquisition. Later, in 2016, the severance packages of $17 million and $12 million given to Rajiv Bansal, the former CFO, and David Kennedy, the former chief legal officer, were criticized as excessive, leading to questions about the company's corporate culture. In 2017, CEO Vishal Sikka had to resign after facing criticism from the company founders for his inability to handle the Panaya and severance package issue properly. An anonymous whistleblower complaint was filed against the company in 2022 about unethical accounting practices.

Satyam Computers Services Limited

Satyam Computer Services Limited (SCSL) is a global IT consulting company and is an icon of Hyderabad, India. It was one of India's largest IT companies in its days. However, in 2009, it was revealed that the company had engaged in widespread corporate governance failures, including inflating its profits and falsifying its accounts (Bhasin, 2016). Acclaimed as India's Enron moment (Madan, 2016), the scandal is well covered in the media and is studied by the academia. The scandal ended with the company's collapse, the arrest of its founder, Ramalinga Raju, and the merger of the company's remaining parts with another IT company - Tech Mahindra Limited.

IL&FS

Infrastructure Leasing & Financial Services (IL&FS), a non-banking financial company (NBFC), defaulted on a loan, triggering a liquidity crisis in the Indian financial system. The government quickly stepped in to bail out the company while the regulators tried to minimize any potential risk propagation. The failure of IL&FS was attributed to several factors, including a lack of independent oversight, weak internal controls, lack of transparency, and related-party transactions (Vijaya Kittu, 2022). The case is a reminder of the importance of corporate governance in businesses of all sizes. Businesses must have strong corporate governance practices to prevent fraud and financial irregularities. Businesses also need to be transparent about their financial dealings to ensure that investors and regulators can track their finances.

Indigo

Indigo, India's largest airliner in terms of passengers carried, had a brief episode of Corporate Governance failure when the promoters had a tussle regarding related party transactions. One of the co-founders of IndiGo Airlines, Rakesh Gangwal, in July 2019 wrote to SEBI, alleging corporate governance lapses at the company (Polisetty & Manda, 2019). SEBI ordered a probe into the allegations, and the company denied any wrongdoing. Gangwal resigned from the board of directors of IndiGo Airlines in October, and the Board of Directors appointed a new Chairman. SEBI preliminary report released in December 2019 finds some prima facie evidence of corporate governance lapses at IndiGo Airlines. The final report was released a month later. The board of directors of IndiGo Airlines accepts the findings of the SEBI report and takes disciplinary action against specific individuals. The story of how Rakesh Gangwal and Rahul Bhatia built a successful airline together and later parted ways will remain an exciting chapter in the history of Indian businesses (ET Online, 2023).

INDIAN STARTUPS AND CORPORATE GOVERNANCE

India is abuzz with startup culture, thanks to the Startup India Initiative proposed by the Government of India in January 2016 (InsightsOnIndia, 2016). India is the world's third-largest ecosystem for startups. The Department for Promotion of Industry and Internal Trade (DPIIT) recognizes over 99,000 startups spanning 670 districts (Kritika & Nayan, 2023).

In the initial years of their establishment, startups typically do not prioritize corporate governance, as their primary focus is on starting well and ensuring their survival. Hence, startups often require customized corporate governance based on their social relationships (David, 2023). Examining a few cases of startup failures mentioned in Harvard Business Review (HBR) highlights the need for a compatible governance structure for startups to grow in the planned path.

Considering the number and gravity of corporate governance failures, the Indian Venture and Alternate Capital Association (IVCA), collaborating with professional services firm Deloitte, has unveiled a framework called '*Startup Governance Playbook*' (Binu, 2023). The startup ecosystem is experiencing turbulence. Venture Capitalists are now seen tightening their norms (Nikhil, 2023). Forensic reviews were called upon for several startups, including BharatPe, Zilingo, Trell, GoMechanic, Broker Network, Infra.Market, and Mojocare.

Governance problems have been abuzzed in the Indian startup ecosystem in the first half of 2023. Nitin Kamath, CEO and co-founder of Zerodha said that while founders often shoulder the blame for corporate governance problems, the venture capital (VC) ecosystem should also share the responsibility. He argued that the overestimation of the size of the Indian markets by both founders and VCs is the root cause of these issues. He said that traditional frauds would be unlikely going forward but would appear rather in misreporting to justify the exaggerated narratives that founders have presented to secure capital (Namit, 2023). Aman Gupta, CMO and co-founder of a successful company, Boat, said that startup founders will be measured based on IQ or EQ and GQ (Governance Quotient) (Hemant, 2023). Following the first-principles thinking approach, the ingredients of good governance are proposed (Manav, 2023):

1. Draft a shareholder's agreement
2. Hold regular board meetings
3. Prioritise statutory compliance
4. Complete book closures and audits promptly
5. Establish revenue recognition and procurement policies from the start

Due to startups ' unique nature, it appears that a separate version of the Companies Act might become necessary. Experts wish that the Company Law Committee (CLC) set up by the Ministry of Corporate Affairs in September 2019 could look into various aspects of the regulator regime of startups.

BYJU's

BYJU'S is an Indian startup that rose to become a global unicorn with its education technology (or etdtech) products that became incredibly necessary for parents to help their children continue education during the pandemic times. BYJU'S went on an inorganic expansion of its business by acquiring competing companies and gaining market share. Much of the funding for the expensive acquisitions came from venture capitalists. However, post-pandemic, sales dropped, and the company was in deep losses. VCs began to worry about company valuations falling at an incredible pace. The company soon began slipping because of its inabilities and lack of sufficient leadership to handle the complexities of the scale and size of its operations and funding.

In late June 2023, the Ministry of Corporate Affairs (MCA) ordered an inspection of the affairs considering significant corporate governance failures (Reetu, 2023). One week after the initiation of the inspection, the statutory auditor, Deloitte, tendered their resignation. This was followed by the resignation of three independent board members who represented three globally renowned investment firms. The probe by the Enforcement Directorate (ED), failure to disclose financial results on time, and call to inspect BYJU'S activities are all dent on the company. BYJU'S, which happens to be a poster boy of the startup community of India, seems to be fading and becoming a bad example.

Mojocare

Bengaluru, India-based healthcare and wellness startup Mojocare started its operations in 2021 and was able to raise $23.7 million in funding. However, it became the subject of a test of its corporate governance practices after financial irregularities surfaced, forcing the company to review its financial statements. The audit's Initial findings exposed issues - overstating revenues and sales, round-tripping of funds, and lack of transparency. So grave is the situation that the company was exploring consolidating its business with a larger player and, in inevitable circumstances, returning money to investors and shut shop! (Kamya, 2023)

BharatPe

Ashneer Grover, the co-founder and former managing director of BharatPe, is sent on leave following allegations of financial irregularities and toxic workplace behavior in March 2022. Later, in April 2022, Grover's wife, Madhuri Jain Grover, was also sent on leave. The allegations against the duo raise questions about the inaction of the board and the lack of proactive measures (Datta & Goyal, 2023).

An independent audit reported in May 2022 that Ashneer and Jain Grover had engaged in financial irregularities, including using company funds for personal expenses and creating fake vendors. Ashneer resigned from BharatPe in June 2022. In July 2022, the company finally filed a police complaint against the duo for alleged financial irregularities and forgery. In August 2022, the Enforcement Directorate (ED) began investigating Grover and Jain Grover for alleged money laundering.

INDIAN BANKS AND CORPORATE GOVERNANCE

Academic research finds that non-duality boards and small-size banks are more adaptable to the governance norms (R. K. Singh & Sharma, 2023). Top executives and chairpersons of some reputed Indian banks, such as ICICI Bank, YES Bank, PMC Bank, and Times Bank, were at the center of various allegations and also suffered arrests at different times.

RBI Regulations

The Reserve Bank of India (RBI) is India's central bank and the banking regulator. RBI constantly examines the conduct of banks and tries to find and bridge gaps in the banking system that can potentially lead to corporate governance failures. RBI observed that banks use smart accounting practices, such as concealing the actual status of stressed loans, to artificially boost financial performance despite issuing guidelines against such practices. These instances can lead to volatility and unwanted risk bubbles in the banking system (PTI, 2023). The RBI Governor has brought up this matter in his address to the Bank boards and management in May 2023. The RBI Governor expressed concern at how banks changed their loan evergreening practices from one form to another after being pointed out by the regulator.

RBI Deputy Director M.K. Jain termed that corporate governance is the root cause of supervisory concerns and suggested that banking supervisors use data analytics to strengthen their supervisory frameworks (Joel, 2023). He stressed the need for an organizational-level compliance culture. The onus to ascertain whether a matter permeates within the institution and gets support from the entity's senior management falls on the supervisors. In another instance, Deputy Governor M Rajeshwar Rao said that boards should set clear expectations regarding risk management and corporate governance and require the management to report regularly (Business Today Desk, 2023).

ICICI Bank

The Videocon loan case is a classic case dating back to 2009 and is a must-read by corporate governance enthusiasts. The sanctioned loans to Videocon Group on the behest of the then Managing Director and CEO Chanda Kochhar. In 2016, Arvind Gupta, a shareholder activist, filed a complaint with the CBI alleging that Chanda Kochhar had abused her position to favor Videocon Group. A CBI case was registered against her. Kochhar resigned from her position. Subsequently, the CBI filed a chargesheet against her.

The Board of ICICI Bank gave sanctions to prosecute Kochhar under the Prevention of Corruption Act (PCA). Other officials involved in the scandal were also prosecuted. The PCA requires approval from the bank's board as the bank employee is held to be a public servant. The bank clarified that no wrongful loss was caused to the bank in the loan transaction.

YES Bank

Yes Bank was growing faster than the banking leaders such as HDFC Bank and Kotak Mahindra Bank at its glorious times. Yes Bank had a market capitalization close to Rs. 1 lakh crores at one point! However, the dream run tumbled when reports emerged that RBI smelled huge divergences of close to 300% between the Non-Performing Assets (NPA) reported by the bank and those identified from the Asset Quality Reports (AQR). There appeared to be underreporting its NPA numbers. The bank has been making profits since its listing in 2004 but reported its first loss in 2018-19, reflecting its poor lending practices. The promoter and CEO made desperate attempts to raise capital. Unhappy depositors began to flee to other banks, worried about potential collapse. The bank's exposure to DHFL, Anil Ambani, and Zee companies is enormous. Money laundering charges were pressed on MD and CEO Rana Kapoor. He was subsequently arrested. However, the bank began losing precious customers. RBI swiftly turned down the board and reconstituted it with its selection, making Prasanth Kumar handle the bank's affairs. SBI and a few other banks have lent capital, thereby averting an almost collapse of the bank. Had the bank collapsed, it would have made a dark picture in the Indian banking history.

SEBI AND CORPORATE GOVERNANCE

Securities and Exchange Board of India (SEBI) is the Capital Market Regulator in India. SEBI has corporate disclosure requirements in the SEBI Listing Obligations and Disclosure Requirements (LODR). The LODR is a comprehensive document that covers a wide range of disclosure requirements, including:

1. Financial statements
2. Material events
3. Corporate governance practices
4. Risk factors
5. Related party transactions
6. Insider trading

SEBI enforces its corporate disclosure requirements through various means, including inspections, audits, and enforcement actions. Companies that fail to comply with the requirements can face penalties, such as fines or suspension from trading.

Corporate disclosures play a vital role in the efficient functioning of the securities market. By ensuring that investors have access to accurate and timely information, corporate disclosures help to promote investor confidence and protect investors from fraud.

Corporate governance in the early days was under the ambit of the Company Act, of 1956. SEBI was given the formal role between 1992 and 2000, thanks to the Companies (Amendment) Act, 2000. Since then, SEBI has remained the gatekeeper of Corporate Governance in India (Gupta & Saxena, 2022), and its need only keeps increasing as public participation in capital markets increases in India over time. SEBI encouraged companies to build and follow best practices in corporate governance and helped listed companies stay as transparent as possible. The MCA and SEBI have constituted various committees to study the system and propose recommendations for world-class standards (Manisha & Anita, 2022). Over time, the voluntary disclosures and passive soft law approach have become increasingly stringent, with SEBI now mandating that certain information be disclosed and provided on time by companies.

Maintaining adequate transparency, timely disclosure, and strict compliance per regulatory and governmental requirements are good steps toward corporate governance. Insufficient disclosures and delayed submissions confuse stakeholders, leaving room for potential ambiguity and leading to chaos in the capital markets. Corporate companies that raise money from the public, whether in the form of equity or debt, must make adequate disclosures so that investors and lenders can understand how safe (or risky) their investment is.

Many Indian corporates have yet to separate the chairperson and managing director posts. While 66 companies have separated the posts, as many as 34 are yet to separate. Reason? The separation of positions is not a mandatory requirement.

Nearly a third of the top 100 companies have permanent board seats, a setup the market regulator plans to eliminate.

The SEBI (LODR) Regulations, 2015 is a formal step towards making corporates disclose. Since then, SEBI released several consultation papers and updates to the regulations (Ranjith & Usha, 2023) to make the level of disclosures and compliance regulations of listed companies to be more transparent (Melissa, 2023).

SEBI often co-ordinates with the Ministry of Finance and the Ministry of Corporate Affairs when strengthening the regulatory landscape. The Ministry is, in general, seen asking SEBI to re-examine norms and take corrective actions that fall within its scope as per the evolving needs.

NSE Colocation and Himalayan Yogi Scam

SEBI's moves to plug loopholes are not just for corporates but also for stock exchanges. The need to investigate a stock exchange arose from a crisis at the National Stock Exchange (NSE).

Moving in line with global trends and practices, NSE introduced the concept of colocation facility in 2009. Traders are allowed to place their servers on the premises of the NSE data center to access stock data feeds faster and take advantage of high-frequency trading (HFT). HFT is a form of algo-trading that allows computers to quickly place buy and sell orders. A few months after this, in December 2009, NSE also began giving access to tick-by-tick (TBT) data. TBT allows brokers to see all buy and sell orders. The combination of colocation servers and TBT is deadly because it allows a granular view of all pending orders and allows them to take advantage by placing orders before others can. Certain stockbrokers reportedly benefited by getting preferential access in the form of early login and split-second access to the trading platform between 2010 and 2015. NSE realized its mistake late but fixed it by introducing a load balancer that allows orders to be automatically allocated to the least crowded server. Similarly, in April 2014, it introduced a multi-broadcast TBT protocol that allows data feeds to be disseminated to all colocation brokers simultaneously instead of the older method of first-come, first-serve. This fixed the advantage earlier taken by those who logged in first.

SEBI received three whistleblower complaints on this in and around December 2015. The complaint mentioned that about Rs. The errand stockbrokers could have made 50 crores to Rs. 100 crores in gains per day. Of course, there are no official figures, as it is impossible to separate genuine orders from orders placed with malice. The then MD and CEO of Chitra Ramkrishna were accused of the transgression of several corporate governance principles. A few years ago, the media acclaimed Chitra Ramkrishna as the 'queen of the bourses', and 'Woman Leader of the Year', and featured her in the 'Hall of Fame' list for being in the list of most influential ladies in India. Chitra Ramkrishna took the role of MD and CEO of NSE in 2013 but had to resign in 2016.

NSE was in a deeper crisis after it was revealed that Chitra Ramakrishna took instructions from a mystic' Himalayan Yogi' (aka Siddha Purusha/Paramhansa) on crucial matters related to the exchange during 2014 and 2016. She stated that she had taken personal and professional guidance from the yogi for over twenty years. Much of her correspondence was to an unknown person who was reached through an Outlook mailbox email. Her appointment as CSO of NSE at a fat salary never heard in the industry was also questioned. Ramkrishna redesignated Anand Subramanian as her advisor and the Group Operating Officer (GOO), but a few months later, no records about his employment could be placed before SEBI. Many of Ramakrishna's emails to the yogi had a cc to Subramanian.

The whistleblower complained as to why Subramanian, who was given so much power and privileges at NSE was never designated to be a Key Management Personnel (KMP) under the Securities Contracts (Regulations) (Stock Exchanges and Clearing Corporations) Regulations, 2012. A forensic investigation conducted by Ernst & Young (EY) suggests that the yogi was none other than Subramanian! An investigation by the Central Bureau of Investigation (CBI) confirmed this. Subramanian's non-co-operation before the investigation agency led to his eventual arrest in February 2022. The Income-tax Department raided the premises linked to Ramakrishnan and her aides on tax evasion charges and financial irregulates. She was eventually arrested on March 6, 2022. She and her aide were granted statutory bail in September 2022. SEBI's investigation later proved that Subramanian, Ramakrishna, and others were guilty and were imposed a penalty. Apparently, the Board of NSE could not detect the wrongdoings (Pattanayak, 2022) until the investigation agencies stepped in. NSE took a whip after it was barred from launching any new product for six months.

Listing Obligations and Disclosure Requirements

SEBI, by way of SEBI (Listing Obligations and Disclosure Requirements) (Second Amendment) Regulations, 2023, tightened the Listing Obligations and Disclosure Requirements (LODR) required by companies. Some salient features of the amendment include:

1. Timely Filling up of Key Managerial Vacancies
2. Disclosures for certain types of agreements binding listed companies
3. Materiality threshold for disclosures
4. Verification of market rumors by listed companies
5. Board permanency
6. Approval of special rights to shareholders:

7. Timelines for disclosure
8. Extension of timelines on the applicability of the Amendment Regulations to high-value listed debt entities ("HVDLEs")
9. Introduction of new disclosure obligations under Schedule III of LODR

Key managerial vacancies that arise in a company are to be filled within three months. This is applicable to the following company positions: Compliance Officer, Chief Executive Officer (CEO), Managing Director (MD), Whole Time Director, Manager, Chief Financial Officer (CFO), and Director. However, any vacancy due to the expiration of any director's term of office must be filled no later than the date such office is vacated.

Corporates, ESG, and Disclosures

Over the years, SEBI has gradually begun making it mandatory for companies to disclose more information than they used to. The idea is to keep enough information on the take so that stakeholders can better understand the company and its situation. While compliance burdens have come down over the years, the need to stay compliant always remains. Despite the burden, ESG compliance helped companies remain transparent and better manage risk. With ESG disclosures, Indian companies were able to improve their reputation and build a sustainability edge at a global level (Dr. Abhay Pandey et al., 2023).

ESG disclosures are found to not only update about the community and societal commitments that the company has made but also build a competitive edge over the long term. Public Sector Undertakings (PSUs), too, began disclosing information. Based on the disclosures available, experts believe that PSUs can improve their ESG image by implementing a coherent legal structure by the Central Government. State Governments should be encouraged to enact bylaws for environment-related issues. Similarly, social accounting should be introduced in enterprises and implement a sound public governance system (Saha Roy, 2023).

While companies disclose their ESG data because of compliance requirements, research showed that six of ten companies picked dipped performance when subjected to an advanced grey prediction model, highlighting the need to improve good governance practices for Indian firms (Rajesh, 2023).

Other topics

1. While green accounting does not affect profitability or market value, it and firm characteristics significantly enhance social responsibility disclosure.

Corporate governance and social responsibility disclosure together impact firm performance and value (Jyoti & NVM, 2023).

2. Integrated Reporting (IR) is believed to be a holistic representation of an organization's financial and non-financial performance (Amit Kumar et al., 2020). Though new in India, early research that went into the adoption of IR by Indian companies shows that the company's size, its structural complexity, and part of the Environmental social governance index affect the adoption of IR (Bhatia et al., 2023).
3. In February 2023, SEBI said it would give more teeth and empower shareholders to improve CG. The market regulator has given retail investors more control over their money by ensuring their funds do not stay with brokers long (ITBD, 2023).
4. In yet another bid to strengthen corporate governance, SEBI directed that listed companies should either confirm or deny any reported event or information in mainstream media that is not general and which indicates that rumors of an impending specific material or event or information in terms of provisions within 24 hours from the reporting of the event. The circular is applicable for the Top 100 listed companies from October 1, 2023, and for the Top 250 companies from April 1, 2024. If the key managerial personnel resigns, the listed entities must inform the exchanges within seven days of resignation. In case a Managing Director or Chief Executive Officer of the listed entity was indisposed or unavailable to fulfill the requirements of the role regularly for more than forty-five days in any rolling period of ninety days, the same, along with the reasons for such indisposition or unavailability shall be disclosed to the stock exchange(s)(Fortune India, 2023).
5. There is an increased need for Indian CEOs to use the power under their control to encourage firms to create ESG committees to enhance ESG disclosure to compete on the world market and reach the United Nations (UN) Sustainable Goal 2030 (Al-ahdal et al., 2023).

MINISTRY OF CORPORATE AFFAIRS

India's Ministry of Corporate Affairs (MCA) has implemented various measures to enhance corporate governance, including the Companies Act 2013, which mandates the appointment of independent directors, the establishment of audit committees, and the disclosure of related-party transactions. The MCA also monitors compliance with these regulations and acts against companies that fail to adhere to them. The MCA's efforts have improved transparency, accountability, and ethical behavior in the Indian corporate sector.

The MCA21 portal is a web-based platform developed by the MCA to provide a single window for all corporate-related services. The portal was launched in 2015 and was subsequently updated to incorporate the changes brought in by the Ministry. The most recent enhancement in the portal is the MCA21 V3, which increases trust-based governance and promotes a balance between productivity and efficiency of capital and human resources (GNConnect, 2023). The portal has a single window for all corporate-related services, supports multiple languages, is available 24/7, has an easy-to-use interface, and becomes a secure and user-friendly platform.

DISCUSSION QUESTIONS

Facilitators and teachers can use the following questions to foster classroom discussion and make the students think better about the subject.

1. **Board Independence and Risk Management**: How does the issue of board independence relate to effective risk management in corporate governance? Can you identify instances where a lack of board independence contributed to risk-taking behavior, leading to corporate governance failures in your country? Discuss strategies for ensuring a balance between board independence and effective risk management.
2. **Accountability and Transparency**: Discuss the significance of accountability and transparency in corporate governance. Can you provide examples of recent corporate governance failures in your country that lacked these qualities? How can companies improve their accountability and transparency?
3. **Ethical Conduct**: Explain why ethical conduct is crucial to corporate governance. What ethical dilemmas have companies faced in recent years, as mentioned in the case study? How can organizations promote and maintain ethical conduct among their leadership and employees?
4. **Regulatory Compliance**: Analyze the role of regulatory bodies such as the central bank and the securities market regulator in addressing corporate governance failures in your country. What specific measures have these regulatory bodies implemented to improve governance practices? Are there any gaps or challenges in enforcing regulatory compliance in the Indian corporate sector?
5. **Stakeholder Impact**: Evaluate the impact of corporate governance failures on various stakeholders, focusing on minority shareholders. How do lapses in accountability, transparency, and ethical conduct affect these stakeholders? What strategies can companies adopt to engage better and protect the interests of all stakeholders?

CONCLUSION

In conclusion, the escalating instances of corporate governance lapses and failures in India have spurred considerable concern over the accountability and transparency of corporate entities. The documented case study analysis unveiled an intricate web of issues encompassing accountability, transparency, equitability, ethical conduct, and regulatory compliance. The pervasive impact of these failures on stakeholders, particularly minority shareholders, underscores the dire need for steadfast commitment to ethical standards, discipline, and fairness within governing bodies and boards of directors. The regulatory actions taken by bodies such as the RBI, SEBI, and MCA are vital steps toward rectifying these lapses. Fostering a culture of effective corporate governance is not merely a choice but an imperative to safeguard shareholder interests and sustain a robust business environment.

REFERENCES

Abhilash, A., Shenoy, S. S., & Shetty, D. K. (2023). Overview of Corporate Governance Research in India: A Bibliometric Analysis. *Cogent Business & Management*, *10*(1), 2182361. doi:10.1080/23311975.2023.2182361

Adani Group. (2023). *Adani Respose*. https://www.adani.com/-/media/Project/Adani/Invetsors/Adani-Response-to-Hindenburg-January-29-2023.pdf

Al-ahdal, W. M., Farhan, N. H. S., Vishwakarma, R., & Hashim, H. A. (2023). The moderating role of CEO power on the relationship between environmental, social and governance disclosure and financial performance in emerging market. *Environmental Science and Pollution Research International*, *30*(36), 85803–85821. Advance online publication. doi:10.100711356-023-28499-5 PMID:37393591

Almaqtari, F. A., Shamim, M., Hattami, H. M. A., & Aqlan, S. A. (2020). Corporate governance in India and some selected Gulf countries. *International Journal of Managerial and Financial Accounting*, *12*(2), 165. doi:10.1504/IJMFA.2020.109135

Amit Kumar, B., Soumya, P., & Meghna, M. (2020). *Integrated reporting in India: Survey on adoption and way forward.* Grant Thornton Bharat. https://www.grantthornton.in/globalassets/1.-member-firms/india/assets/pdfs/integrated-reporting-in-india-december-2020.pdf

Bhasin, M. L. (2016). Fraudulent Financial Reporting Practices: Case Study of Satyam Computer Limited. *The Journal of Economics. Marketing and Management*, *4*(3), 12–24. doi:10.13106/JEMM.2016.VOL4.NO3.12

Bhatia, M., Mehrotra, V., & Thawani, B. (2023). Firm Characteristics and Adoption of Integrated Reporting: An Emerging Market Perspective. *Global Business Review*. Advance online publication. doi:10.1177/09721509231160872

Binu, P. (2023, June 24). *Amid mounting governance issues in start-ups, IVCA and Deloitte launch Start-up Governance Playbook*. https://www.businesstoday.in/entrepreneurship/news/story/amid-mounting-governance-issues-in-start-ups-ivca-and-deloitte-launch-start-up-governance-playbook-386934-2023-06-24

Bureau, E. T. (2023, March 1). Sebi bars 21 entities in Axis mutual fund front-running case. *Economic Times*. https://economictimes.indiatimes.com/markets/stocks/news/sebi-bars-21-entities-in-axis-mutual-fund-front-running-case/articleshow/98313104.cms

Business Today Desk. (2023, June 5). Time right for banks to address gaps in governance framework, says RBI Deputy Guv. *Business Today*. https://www.businesstoday.in/industry/banks/story/time-right-for-banks-to-address-gaps-in-governance-framework-says-rbi-deputy-guv-384213-2023-06-05

Datta, S., & Goyal, S. (2023). The BharatPe debacle: Growth at the cost of governance? *Emerald Emerging Markets Case Studies*, *13*(1), 1–29. doi:10.1108/EEMCS-10-2022-0377

David, R. (2023). Corporate Governance in Indian Startups. *IUP Journal of Corporate Governance*, *22*(1), 39–47.

Debnath, K., & Chatterjee, S. (2023). Corporate Social Responsibility and Role of the Indian State: A Transition Beyond Corporate Philanthropy. In S. K. Msosa, S. Mugova, & C. Mlambo (Eds.), *Corporate Social Responsibility in Developing Countries* (pp. 265–279). Springer International Publishing. doi:10.1007/978-3-031-27512-8_17

Fortune India. (2023, June 16). “Confirm” or “deny” media reports in 24 hrs from October 1: SEBI to top 100 listed cos. *Fortune India*. https://www.fortuneindia.com/enterprise/confirm-or-deny-media-reports-in-24-hrs-from-oct-1-sebi-to-top-100-listed-cos/113075

GNConnect. (2023, June 13). Enhanced MCA21 V3 Portal Paves the Way for Improved Corporate Governance. *Governance Now*. https://www.governancenow.com/views/columns/enhanced-mca21-v3-portal-paves-the-way-for-improved-corporate-governance

Gopika, G. (2023, July 12). *Probe diversion of Dish TV funds, say small investors*. https://www.livemint.com/companies/news/investors-demand-probe-into-alleged-fund-diversion-by-zee-entertainment-from-dish-tv-seek-board-reconstitution-11689100340969.html

Gupta, S., & Saxena, N. (2022). SEBI as a gatekeeper of Corporate Governance in India. *International Journal of Humanities, Law and Social Sciences, 9*(12). https://www.researchgate.net/publication/369542072

Hemant, K. (2023, July 10). *Founders Will Be Measured On Governance Quotient: BoAt's Aman Gupta*. https://inc42.com/buzz/founders-measured-governance-quotient-boat-cmo-aman-gupta/

Hindenburg. (2023a, January 24). *Adani Group: How The World's 3rd Richest Man Is Pulling The Largest Con In Corporate History*. Hindenburg Research. https://hindenburgresearch.com/adani/

Hindenburg. (2023b, January 29). *Our Reply To Adani: Fraud Cannot Be Obfuscated By Nationalism Or A Bloated Response That Ignores Every Key Allegation We Raised*. https://hindenburgresearch.com/adani-response/

InsightsOnIndia. (2016). *Startup India*. https://www.insightsonindia.com/social-justice/welfare-schemes/schemes-under-ministry-of-commerce-industry/startup-india/

ITBD. (2023, March 30). Sebi clears several reforms to empower shareholders, boost corporate governance. *India Today*. https://www.indiatoday.in/business/story/sebi-meeting-new-reforms-empower-shareholders-investors-better-corporate-governance-2353476-2023-03-30

Jalwani, D., Bhura, P. K., & Jha, A. K. (2022). Corporate governance framework in India: An overview. *Asian Journal of Management and Commerce*, *3*(2). https://www.researchgate.net/publication/367177865

Janaki, K. (2023, June 23). Adani Group firms' shares routed, market cap falls below Rs. 10 lakh crores amid US regulatory inquiries. *Business Line*. https://www.thehindubusinessline.com/companies/adani-group-affirms-robust-corporate-governance-amidst-us-regulatory-inquiries/article67001037.ece

Joel, R. (2023, June 15). Corporate governance root of supervisory concerns: RBI deputy governor MK Jain. *Economic Times*. https://economictimes.indiatimes.com/news/economy/policy/corporate-governance-root-of-supervisory-concerns-rbi-deputy-governor-mk-jain/articleshow/101025920.cms

Jyoti, T., & NVM, R. (2023). Impact of Social Responsibility Disclosure on the integration of Green Accounting and Corporate Governance on highly polluted industries in India. *International Journal of Accounting & Finance Review*, 13–24. doi:10.46281/ijafr.v14i2.2027

Jyotindra, D. (2023, January 31). How did INR3,500 crore go missing from the books of Coffee Day Enterprises? Grab your coffee. *Economic Times*. https://economictimes.indiatimes.com/prime/corporate-governance/how-did-inr3500-crore-go-missing-from-the-books-of-coffee-day-enterprises-grab-your-coffee-/primearticleshow/97458468.cms

Kalia, A., & Gill, S. (2023). Corporate governance and risk management: A systematic review and synthesis for future research. *Journal of Advances in Management Research*, *20*(3), 409–461. doi:10.1108/JAMR-07-2022-0151

Kamya, P. (2023, July 7). *Wellness Startup Mojocare Said To Shut Shop Amidst Fraud Allegations: Report*. https://www.medianama.com/2023/07/223-mojocare-shut-shop-fraud-allegations/

Kanojia, S., Lakshmi, V., Sachdeva, S., & Verma, M. (2023). Tensegrity of Internal Control System, Board's Ability and Corporate Governance Practices. *Global Business Review*. Advance online publication. doi:10.1177/09721509231186251

Kaushal, S. (2022, January 20). At PTC India Financial, 3 Independent Directors Resign, Throwing a Corporate Governance Grenade. *The Wire*. https://thewire.in/business/ptc-india-finance-independent-directors-resign

Krishna Kumar, G. (2023, July 9). Corruption in IT sector: Time to strengthen corporate governance. *Deccan Herald*. https://www.deccanherald.com/opinion/panorama/corruption-in-it-sector-time-to-strengthen-corporate-governance-1235462.html

Kritika, N., & Nayan, D. A. (2023, July 5). *Ensuring a Solid Foundation: Corporate Governance for Startups*. Invest India. https://www.investindia.gov.in/team-india-blogs/ensuring-solid-foundation-corporate-governance-startups

Kumar, D., & Mishra, A. K. (2023). The Adani-Hindenburg Saga: A Case Study. *South Asian Journal of Management*, *30*(1), 187–196.

Laskar, S. (2023). Sustainable Corporate Governance and its importance in India. *Indian Journal of Law and Legal Research*, *5*(2). https://www.ijllr.com/post/sustainable-corporate-governance-and-its-importance-in-india

Livemint. (2023a, March 1). *DishTV clarifies on corporate governance breach, calls minority investors allegations "baseless"; stock ends 10% up*. https://www.livemint.com/companies/news/dishtv-clarifies-on-corporate-governance-breach-calls-minority-investors-allegations-baseless-stock-ends-10-up-11677679874563.html

Livemint. (2023b, August 14). SEBI bars Subhash Chandra, Punit Goenka from from holding key positions in Zee; probe to complete in 8 months. *Live Mint*. https://www.livemint.com/companies/news/sebi-bars-subhash-chandra-punit-goenka-from-from-holding-key-positions-in-zee-probe-to-complete-in-8-months-11692029968688.html

Madan, L. B. (2016). Debacle of Satyam Computers Limited: A Case Study of India's Enron. *Wulfenia Journal, 23*(3). https://www.researchgate.net/profile/Madan-Bhasin/publication/299482211

Mallesha, L., & Archana, H. N. (2023). Impact of Hindenburg Research Report on the Stock Prices of Adani Group Companies: An Event Study. *Asia-Pacific Journal of Management Research and Innovation*, *19*(1), 40–46. doi:10.1177/2319510X231169338

Manav, G. (2023, July 8). *Reframing Governance as a lever for Startup Growth and Value Creation*. https://yourstory.com/2023/07/reframing-governance-as-a-lever-for-startup-growth

Manisha, S., & Anita, R. (2022). A Comparative Study of Committee's Reports on Corporate Governance in India. *Journal of Corporate Finance Management and Banking System*, *2*(3). Advance online publication. doi:10.55529/jcfmbs.23.36.51

Mannu, A. (2023a, June 20). RBI sends PFS MD on permanent leave amid governance issue. *ET CFO*. https://cfo.economictimes.indiatimes.com/news/governance-risk-compliance/rbi-sends-pfs-md-on-permanent-leave-amid-governance-issue/101135691

Mannu, A. (2023b, June 23). SEBI finds PTC India Fin Services Chairman, MD responsible for corporate governance failure. *ET CFO*. https://cfo.economictimes.indiatimes.com/news/governance-risk-compliance/sebi-finds-ptc-india-fin-services-chairman-md-responsible-for-corporate-governance-failure/101191927

Melissa, C. (2023, June 22). New Disclosure and Compliance Obligations for Listed Companies in India. *India Briefing*. https://www.india-briefing.com/news/new-disclosure-and-compliance-obligations-for-listed-companies-in-india-28639.html/

MoneyControl News. (2023, March 6). SAT grants stay on SEBI's Rs 26 crore fine on Coffee Day Enterprises. *Money Control*. https://www.moneycontrol.com/news/business/sat-grants-stay-on-sebis-rs-26-crore-fine-on-coffee-day-enterprises-10208241.html

Monish, C. (2023, June 2). India Inc. Focusing on quality over quantity in the search for independent directors. *The Times of India*. https://timesofindia.indiatimes.com/blogs/voices/india-inc-focusing-on-quality-over-quantity-in-the-search-for-independent-directors/

Naeem, A. R. (2023). Navigating the Legal Landscape: Corporate Governance and Anti-Corruption Compliance in the Digital Age. *International Journal of Management and Finance*, *1*(3). https://irshadjournals.com/index.php/ijmf/article/view/39/22

Namit, S. S. (2023, July 3). Zerodha CEO Nithin Kamath Highlights Corporate Governance Issues In Indian Startups. *News18*. https://www.news18.com/business/zerodha-ceo-nithin-kamath-highlights-corporate-governance-issues-in-indian-startups-8212429.html

Natto, D., & Mokoaleli-Mokoteli, T. (2022). External Governance, Corporate Governance, Firm Performance and Economic Growth in the UK and India. *European Conference on Management Leadership and Governance, 18*(1), 482–491. 10.34190/ecmlg.18.1.733

Nidhi, B., & Saurabh, B. (2016). Corporate Restructuring: A Case Study of Adani Enterprises, India. *IRJMSH, 7*(1). http://www.irjmsh.com/abstractview/4136

Nikhil, S. (2023, June 23). *Investor Audit Season For Indian Startups: VCs Tighten The Screw*. https://inc42.com/features/audit-indian-startups-vc-investors-revenue-claims-corporate-governance/

O'Brien, E., Coneybeer, J., Boersma, M., & Payne, A. (2022). Political investorism: Conceptualising the political participation of shareholders and investors. *International Political Science Review*. Advance online publication. doi:10.1177/01925121221098863

Online, E. T. (2023, August 16). Rakesh Gangwal & Rahul Bhatia: How two friends built India's most successful airline and then split ways. *Economic Times*. https://economictimes.indiatimes.com/industry/transportation/airlines-/-aviation/rakesh-gangwal-how-two-friends-built-indias-most-successful-airline-and-then-split-ways/

Outlook Business Team. (2020, June 22). Why Mukesh Ambani's Companies Are Faltering On Corporate Governance To Attract SEBI's Ire. *Outlook*. https://www.outlookindia.com/business/why-mukesh-ambani-s-companies-are-faltering-on-corporate-governance-to-attract-sebi-s-ire-news-203892

Pandey, Tiwari, & Singh. (2023). Environmental Social and Governance Reporting in Indian: An Overview. *EPRA International Journal of Multidisciplinary Research*, 47–51. doi:10.36713/epra14027

Polisetty, A., & Manda, V. K. (2019). Boardroom Battles & Corporate Governance Turbulence at IndiGo. *Journal of Management and Public Policy*, *11*(1), 19. doi:10.5958/0976-0148.2019.00007.6

PTI. (2023, May 29). RBI Found Gaps In Corporate Governance At Banks Despite Guidelines: Das. *Outlook*. https://www.outlookindia.com/business/rbi-found-gaps-in-corporate-governance-at-banks-despite-guidelines-das-news-290404

Rachita, P. (2023, July 13). PTC panel to look into CMD's appointment after SEBI questions process: Sources. *Money Control*. https://www.moneycontrol.com/news/business/economy/exclusive-ptc-panel-to-look-into-cmds-appointment-after-sebi-questions-process-sources-10952101.html

Rajesh, R. (2023). Performance predictions for sustainability governance of firms: Implications to select Indian firms. *Benchmarking*. Advance online publication. doi:10.1108/BIJ-06-2022-0342

Ranjith, K., & Usha, G. S. (2023, July 5). How Sebi's norms for enhanced disclosures promote better governance. *Live Mint*. https://www.livemint.com/money/personal-finance/sebi-introduces-new-amendments-to-listing-regulations-for-better-corporate-governance-and-transparency-in-india-11688497626326.html

Reetu. (2023, June 23). *Ministry of Corporate Affairs ordered inspection into BYJU'S*. https://studycafe.in/ministry-of-corporate-affairs-ordered-inspection-into-byjus-232170.html

Ritu, S. (2023, March 1). Dish TV minority shareholders allege breach in corporate governance, company refutes: Exclusive. *CNBCTV18*. https://www.cnbctv18.com/business/companies/dish-tv-minority-shareholders-allege-breach-in-corporate-governance-exclusive-16067931.htm

Ross, K., & Tommy, W. (2023, February 10). Sustainalytics downgrades three Adani companies' governance scores. *Reuters*. https://www.reuters.com/business/sustainable-business/sustainalytics-downgrades-three-adani-companies-governance-scores-2023-02-09/

S, J. V., & S, V. (2021). A Study on Profitability Position of Ports and Special Economic Zone Limited. *International Research Journal on Advanced Science Hub, 3*(Special Issue 6S), 48–53. doi:10.47392/irjash.2021.164

Saha Roy, S. (2023). An Empirical Evaluation of Environmental, Social and Corporate Governance (ESG) Disclosures on the Select Public Sector Enterprises in India. In *Sustainable Roadmap Development Strategies in India: Paving the Way for a Better Future* (pp. 132–139). Lincoln University College. doi:10.31674/book.2023srdsi011

Sajjad, B. (2023, May 31). Dangers of corporate governance failures. *Greater Kashmir*. https://www.greaterkashmir.com/todays-paper/editorial-page/dangers-of-corporate-governance-failures

Sampat, S. (2022). *Financial performance, moral action & ESG: An integrated approach to sustainability: Through comparative case studies in Indian power generation companies* [Independent thesis Advanced level]. https://www.diva-portal.org/smash/record.jsf?pid=diva2%3A1666463&dswid=-4909

Singh, K., & Rastogi, S. (2023). Corporate governance and financial performance: Evidence from listed SMEs in India. *Benchmarking, 30*(4), 1400–1423. doi:10.1108/BIJ-09-2021-0570

Singh, R. K., & Sharma, S. K. (2023). A non-parametric synthesize measure for corporate governance: Empirical evidence from Indian banks. *International Review of Economics & Finance, 88*, 258–279. doi:10.1016/j.iref.2023.06.019

Surabhi. (2023, April 14). *NFRA bars Coffee Day Global auditor for 2 years*. https://www.financialexpress.com/industry/nfra-bars-coffee-day-global-auditor-for-2-years/3046116/

Suresh, P. I. (2023, March 1). Will Vedanta prove that it will not be the next Adani? *Business Line*. https://www.thehindubusinessline.com/blexplainer/will-vedanta-prove-that-it-will-not-be-the-next-adani/article66566733.ece

Suroju, S. L., & Disha, M. (2022). The Birth, Boom and Bounce Back of CCD. In Management Cases 2022 (pp. 128–132). Academic Press.

Trendlyne. (2023). *Insider Trading & SAST disclosures for Dish TV India Ltd*. https://trendlyne.com/equity/insider-trading-sast/all/DISHTV/335/dish-tv-india-ltd/

Vijaya Kittu, M. (2022). *Lessons from the IL&amp*. FS Financial Crisis., doi:10.17605/OSF.IO/5TZU3

Vikram, S. M. (2023, June 5). New custodians of corporate governance. *The Indian Express*.

Vivek, P. (2022, December 22). Yes Bank Transfers Invoked Shares Of Dish TV, Six Other Firms To JC Flowers ARC. *BQ Prime*. https://www.bqprime.com/business/yes-bank-transfers-invoked-shares-of-dish-tv-six-other-firms-to-jc-flowers-arc

Vyas, P., & Bhatt, F. (2015). Evolution of Fortune Brand Communications of Adani Wilmar. Asian Case Research Journal; Singapore, 19(1).

Chapter 3
Piercing the Gender Prejudice in Corporate Boardroom:
An Exploratory Study of the Approaches for Redressing the Glass Ceiling Phenomenon in Asia

Siddharth Kanojia
https://orcid.org/0000-0002-1479-5292
O.P. Jindal Global University, India

EXECUTIVE SUMMARY

The glass ceiling is a metaphorical concept which represents the invisible barriers and biases that limit the advancement and upward mobility of individuals, particularly women and other underrepresented groups, in their careers. It alludes to the cultural and institutional barriers that keep capable individuals from rising to the top of leadership roles or realising their full potential inside the organisations. Taking cognizance of this matter, various nations around the globe have legislated and recommended gender-based quotas in corporate leadership which inevitably intends to ensure the appointment of women in leadership positions of renowned companies. Accordingly, this chapter intends to explore the factors which contributes to glass-ceiling phenomenon through the empirical survey and compare the affirmative actions implemented by of Asian nations to address the concerns related to glass ceiling. The chapter will also analyse the efficacy of the approaches adopted by China and India in ensuring gender diversity in the boardroom and executive designations.

DOI: 10.4018/978-1-6684-9867-5.ch003

INTRODUCTION

The glass ceiling is a metaphorical concept representing the invisible barriers and biases that limit the advancement and upward mobility of individuals, particularly women and other underrepresented groups, in their careers. It speaks about the cultural and institutional barriers that keep capable people from gaining top leadership positions or realizing their full potential inside organizations. The term implies that the barrier is transparent, making it challenging to identify and address. It suggests that despite qualifications, skills, and aspirations, specific individuals face unspoken limitations that hinder their progress beyond a certain level in the professional hierarchy. These limitations are often rooted in gender, race, ethnicity, age, disability, or other factors that result in discrimination and unequal treatment. The phenomenon of the "glass ceiling" also describes the various barriers that women and people of minorities must overcome to advance in their careers. Many studies that backed the "glass ceiling" theory found that women generally face numerous barriers while choosing their career route (Phillips & Imhoff, 1997).

Additionally, certain unspoken obstacles restrict women from advancing to senior managerial positions in companies. Women face more obstacles than their male counterparts and require unconventional strategies to succeed. It has been observed that women are increasingly playing a significant role in many critical fields, including business, medicine, advocacy, accounting, biomedical, policing, and bureaucracy (Broughton et al., 2009). Hence, their participation and responsibilities have paced at an accelerated rate. Scholars have consensually agreed that the most prominent and influential metaphor to come out of the 20th century is the "glass ceiling." The globe has undergone a tremendous transformation in contemporary technologies in the last few years. However, specific communities persistently need to pay more attention to the concepts of equality and justice. Thus, the "glass ceiling" metaphor is widely used to symbolize invisible barriers that prevent many women, people of colour, and ethnic minorities from reaching and holding onto the most important, influential, and lucrative positions in the workforce (Broughton et al., 2009).

The phenomenon limits career advancement opportunities, preventing qualified individuals from reaching top leadership positions. Consequently, this perpetuates gender inequality and reinforces societal norms that undervalue women's contributions and capabilities. The lack of diversity and inclusion from the glass ceiling restricts access to diverse perspectives, ideas, and experiences, impeding organizational growth and innovation. From an economic standpoint, the glass ceiling contributes to income inequality by perpetuating the gender pay gap and hindering overall economic progress. The unequal distribution of power and influence exacerbates this disparity, impacting productivity and social mobility.

Furthermore, the glass ceiling creates a talent drain as talented individuals may be deterred from pursuing careers in fields or organizations that offer limited opportunities for advancement, leading to a loss of valuable skills and expertise. The presence of the glass ceiling also breeds a negative organizational culture characterized by bias, discrimination and a lack of trust. This toxic environment diminishes employee morale, job satisfaction, and productivity, contributing to higher turnover rates. The glass ceiling also appears in other ways, such as uneven wage structures, low prospects for job progression, exclusion from decision-making processes, and a lack of representation in leadership roles. It is a systemic issue affecting not only the individuals directly impacted but also the organizations and society. The Federal Commission of Glass Ceiling lists a few categories of obstacles for women in progressing to executive positions in organizations (Johns, 2013). The main obstacles are societal, limiting the number of intelligent women qualified for specific jobs. Additionally, the internal structural barriers are the following category of obstacles. Corporate cultures highly influence these obstacles. Accordingly, it is a widely accepted norm that women in positions of authority must exercise caution in how they conduct themselves since they are meant to represent the interest of all women. Hence, women leaders may seek the advice of their mentors, but they frequently lack the success of male leaders owing to gender difficulties. The availability of mentors to assist women employees is one restriction on mentoring for women. If mentors are accessible, the connection between the male mentor and female counterpart becomes the primary concern as they may agonize about how other employees perceive their relationship (Simpson, R., 1997). The pipeline hurdles in the social barrier stand in the way of training and coaching employees in preparation for prospective promotions. Governmental obstacles are described as the third kind of impediment. These impediments include a need for more government oversight of enforcing the applicable law, a failure to collect enough data for in-depth analysis, disagreements, and inadequate divulgence of the presence of a glass ceiling (Townsend, B., 1996).

In the context of two of the world's most populous nations, India and China, examining the presence and effects of this metaphorical barrier takes on particular significance. These countries boast dynamic and rapidly evolving economies. Nevertheless, both continue to grapple with deeply ingrained cultural norms, legal frameworks, and corporate practices that have historically limited access to leadership roles for specific segments of their populations. This comparative analysis explore the application and implication of the glass ceiling phenomenon in India and China, exploring the challenges, opportunities, and transformations within these complex sociocultural and economic landscapes. By dissecting these two nations' unique socio-political and corporate contexts, the chapter aim to shed light on the disparities, advancements, and key considerations related to gender and minority representation in leadership roles. As both of these prominent nations are forging ahead into the global marketplace, understanding the glass ceiling dynamics becomes imperative for regional progress and the broader discourse on gender equality and diversity in the workplace.

LITERATURE REVIEW

Jauhar & Lau (2018) have observed that the glass ceiling impedes the upward advancement of women and underrepresented groups by limiting their access to top leadership positions. However, a former study also revealed a significant disparity in promotions and advancements between genders, with women experiencing barriers related to stereotypes, biases, and exclusion from networking opportunities (Morrison & Glinow, 1990). Additionally, this phenomenon often negatively impacts job satisfaction and the psychological well-being of individuals who face barriers in their career progression. There are numerous instances of these individuals experiencing lower levels of job satisfaction, higher levels of stress, and decreased motivation. This can reduce productivity and increase organizational turnover rates (Yiannakis, 2010). The phenomenon also contributes to the perpetuation of biased and discriminatory organizational cultures. A study has suggest that when women and underrepresented groups are underrepresented in leadership roles, it creates a climate of exclusion, undermines trust, and hampers collaboration and teamwork (Kezar, 2023). This affects overall organizational performance and employee morale.

Moreover, the underrepresentation of women and minority groups in leadership positions limits diverse perspectives, innovative thinking, and the ability to address the needs of a diverse customer base (Kezar, 2020). In contrast, organizations that break the glass ceiling and foster inclusive environments reap the benefits of improved decision-making, creativity, and productivity. Some researchers demonstrate that gender inequality perpetuated by the glass ceiling leads to the gender pay gap and income inequality. This affects individuals' financial well-being and has broader economic consequences, including reduced GDP growth, decreased productivity, and missed opportunities for economic development (Payne, 2005). Consequently, organizations have implemented diversity and inclusion initiatives as a critical strategy to address the glass ceiling. These initiatives include policies that promote equal opportunity, diverse recruitment and retention practices, and mentoring and sponsorship programs. A study have demonstrated that organizations that prioritize diversity and inclusion show improvements in gender representation, career progression, and employee satisfaction (West et al., 2018).

Furthermore, it has been observed that leadership development programs tailored for women and underrepresented groups have emerged as practical tools to address the glass ceiling. These programs focus on building leadership skills, providing mentorship and coaching, and fostering networking opportunities. Studies suggest that such programs enhance participants' self-confidence, networking capabilities, and career advancement prospects (Ziems-Mueller, 2011). Besides, organizations are increasingly investing in bias awareness and training programs to combat unconscious biases contributing to the glass ceiling. These programs aim to educate employees about stereotypes, biases, and their impact on decision-making processes. Accordingly, the concerned studies indicate that raising awareness of biases can lead to fairer evaluations, promotions, and increased representation of women and minority groups in leadership roles. Meanwhile, flexible work policies, such as remote work options, flexible hours, and parental leave policies, play a crucial role in redressing the glass ceiling (Kang & Kaplan, 2019). These policies enable individuals to balance work and personal responsibilities, which positively impacts retention rates and career continuity for women and caregivers. Meanwhile, the efforts to redress the glass ceiling extend beyond organizational initiatives, with advocacy groups and policymakers playing a vital role. These entities work towards influencing policy changes related to pay equity, family-friendly policies, and gender quotas in leadership positions. A study has also indicated that countries with more robust legal frameworks and supportive policies have made remarkable progress in reducing gender gaps and breaking the glass ceiling (Johns, 2013).

Much literature indicates that several Asian countries have adopted gender quotas to address gender disparities in leadership positions. Quota systems vary in design, including reserved seats, party-list systems, and candidate quotas. Some countries have implemented mandatory quotas, while others have adopted voluntary or soft quotas. The implementation of quotas is often influenced by cultural, political, and legal factors unique to each country (Krook et al., 2009). Women are now more frequently seen in corporate leadership positions thanks to gender-based quotas. A study by Heminway (2019) indicated that nations with obligatory quotas have seen appreciable increases in the proportion of women elected to corporate boards and positions in the public sector.

In contrast, the execution of these quotas has come under fire for several reasons. These include resistance from traditional power structures, backlash against perceived "tokenism," and concerns about meritocracy (Klettner et al., 2016). The critics argue that quotas may undermine fairness, perpetuate stereotypes, or create opportunities for political elite families. The effectiveness of quotas in promoting substantive representation and addressing intersectional inequalities is also debated (Newman et al., 2017). Accordingly, some scholars emphasize the importance of intersectionality in quota designs to ensure inclusivity and address multiple dimensions of inequality by recognizing the diversity and experiences of women from various socio-economic backgrounds, ethnicities, and marginalized groups is crucial for meaningful representation and the effectiveness of gender quotas (Sloan et al., 2018). The group of researchers have also focused on the need to go beyond quotas and address underlying structural and cultural barriers to achieve lasting gender equality. Complementary measures, such as gender mainstreaming, political party reforms, capacity-building programs, and changing social norms, are essential for sustaining the progress made through gender quotas (Baksh-Soodeen et al., 2005).

BARRIERS TO PROGRESSION

Barriers might be physical or spiritual, actual or perceived by the recipient. (MaskellPretz and Hopkins 1997). Gender-based prejudices and concerns about gender diversity in corporate boardrooms are intangible hurdles that lead to a consequential negative impact on female employees (MaskellPretz & Hopkins, 1997). The persistent problems with gender discrimination and gender stereotyping that harm women cause the "glass ceiling" effect. Therefore, in actuality, there are significant obstacles (similar to those mentioned earlier) that women still have to overcome to increase their representation at the highest levels of management of businesses, such as organizational, sociological, and psychological Barriers. It is revealed the study by Macarie & Moldovan (2012) that male counterparts actively seek to create barriers to the appointment and progression of women because they cannot accept women's advancement inside the company due to prejudices and preconceived conceptions. As a result, women employees are usually not invited to informal organizational groups and networks, so they do not tend to receive any personal assistance from their male counterparts. Therefore, by excluding women from the strategic decision-making process, their male colleagues purposely

jeer and put up a roadblock to promotion. As a result, women are less likely to progress to positions wherein they are expected to make strategic decisions for the organization.

Further, it has been divulged that women employees experience work-related stress as the day progresses due to pressure from male colleagues, which indirectly impacts their performance (Mukherji et al., 2010). As a result, it would lead to developing an argument to bar them from promotions. These ecosystems can occasionally lead to a loss of encouragement and motivation at the workplace.

Methodology

The study was designed to explore and analyze the numerous causes of gender discrimination in companies that impede the professional advancement of women employees. The research methodology used an exploratory approach. Participants in the survey were determined using a combination of quota sampling and snowball sampling techniques. The quota sampling allowed to collect data from a wide range of participants without the need for a comprehensive list or sampling frame. Whereas, Snowballing technique has assisted in identifying the new samples from the existing members It was acknowledged throughout the preliminary research that it might not be possible to obtain complete information on respondents from which the necessary samples might be chosen. Consequently, the author obtained the referral connections through the preliminary respondents. Thereon, the data was collected through structured questionnaires with multiple choice, closed-ended, and open-ended items, entailing a 100% response rate. Furthermore, since India and China have distinct cultural and social norms. The questions were culturally sensitive and avoided assumptions. The questions were framed to respects cultural nuance. Whereas, understanding the experiences of individuals in their career progression is the core of this study. Hence, the questions were specific to career milestones, promotions, and barriers faced by respondents in their professional journeys. Few questions were kept open-ended to gauge respondents' awareness and acknowledgment of the glass ceiling concept. Likewise, the other open-ended questions allowed respondents to share their personal experiences, challenges, and recommendations related to the glass ceiling.

The author has initiated an empirical survey of Indian and Chinese women by administering structured questionnaires. A total of 40 women across diversified sectors, such as education, healthcare, and corporations, have accepted the invitation to participate in the survey. Of the participants, 32 were married, and the majority were aged 30 to 50. The comprehensive demographic of participants is mentioned in Table 1.

Table 1. Participants' profile (N=40)

Ethnicity	Indian	20	50%
	Chinese	20	50%
Marital Status	Married	32	80%
	Unmarried	8	20%
Age	Below 30	10	25%
	30-50	26	65%
	50 above	4	10%
Industry/Sector	Corporations/MNCs	18	45%
	Education	12	30%
	Healthcare	10	25%

The demographics of participants and other aspects of the factors affecting the career advancement of women employees were studied using the percentage technique. The professional growth of women in corporations was assumed to be constrained by six variables (including three extrinsic and three intrinsic factors), which were identified beforehand. Based on their respective experiences, the respondents were asked to score these variables on a scale of 1 (one) to 10 (ten), with 1(one) being the least important and 10 being the most critical factor. The mentioned variables were ranked on the mean score, and the correlation technique was used to establish the mutuality among the factors. Besides, Cronbach's alpha was used to assess the internal consistency of factors contributing to women's development in the organizations, where a reliability value of 70% (i.e., 0.70) or above denotes reasonably high internal consistency for the variables.

Observations

While interpreting the response, it has been observed that around 65% of the total participants reported the existence of a gender-prejudiced glass ceiling—a total of 6 components, divided into the main categories, i.e., extrinsic and internal factors. The extrinsic factors are those in which the women have no influence. At the same time, they have some influence on intrinsic factors. The responses revealed that cultural and social prejudices in both nations are the main obstacles inhibiting female career advancement in the workplace. The employer's patriarchal policies and the women's family obligations follow them. At the same time, the lack of an appropriate skillset is rated as the prominent intrinsic factor that impedes career progression. A lack of experience and motivation follows this. Therefore, it is apparent from Table 2 that extrinsic factors dominate the intrinsic factors in creating hurdles for women to advance in their profession.

Table 2. Extrinsic and intrinsic barriers to progression

Barriers	Mean	Standard Deviation
Extrinsic Factors		
Cultural and Societal Prejudices	9.50	0.50
Patriarchal ideology and policies of employer	8.00	0.72
Family Obligations	7.60	1.30
Intrinsic Factors		
Lack of Skill and Qualification	5.42	1.35
Lack of Experience	2.60	1.30
Lack of Motivation and Encouragement	1.80	1.00

Extrinsic Factors

From the survey mentioned above, it can be derived that the traditional Asian culture has not been able to liberate itself from the limitations of the antiquated idea of "woman at home." In general, married women are heavily impacted by this issue. As a social institution, marriage places a woman under a societal obligation to care for her spouse, children, and immediate family members. It is a usual belief that male members are the family's primary breadwinners. Contrarily, women have always been seen as home or domestic helpers. Hence, providing primary education to female children should receive little attention from families and society. Consequently, female employees still have to deal with issues related to their dual obligations, i.e., domestic chores and profession (Lachance-Grzela et al., 2010). In recent years, many organizations have offered hybrid working arrangement modes, including work sharing, flex time, and telecommuting.

To allow them to be more flexible. However, according to Anker (1977), women sometimes cannot focus at work because they are obligated to raise their children. Thus, they must take professional sabbatical infinite breaks that prevent them from obtaining executive positions in their firms. In comparison, male employees are often privileged to split their attention between the office and their commitments at home, which allows them to concentrate exclusively on their allotted professional tasks. Despite ideological advancements, the Asian culture expects women to be "excellent mothers." The problem with dual roles is that they are perceived as good moms but inefficient employees if they utilize flexible working arrangements. They risk being perceived as good employees but bad moms if they do not utilize flexible working arrangements, according to Beard et al. (2010).

In addition, because of their spouse's work transfers, women are expected to migrate along with them, forcing them to give up potentially lucrative careers to uphold this societal norm. Moreover, Asian cultures sometimes perpetuate workplace stereotypes and discrimination against women. Traditional beliefs regarding women's roles as subordinate to men, limited intellectual capabilities, and emotional instability contribute to gender bias and hinder women's career progress. Such stereotypes result in a lack of opportunities, lower wages, and limited representation of women in leadership positions. In some Asian countries, women face restricted access to education and skill development opportunities, limiting their employment prospects and career growth. Deep-rooted gender biases often prioritize male education, resulting in limited resources and opportunities for women to acquire the necessary qualifications and skills. Women struggle to compete in the job market without access to quality education and professional development. As a result, some Asian countries lack comprehensive workplace policies that can address the specific needs and challenges working women face. For instance, the maternity leave policies are inadequate, and the absence of paternity leave often reinforces traditional gender roles. Hence, the absence of these policies supporting work-life balance, flexible working arrangements, and equal pay further impedes women's progress in the workplace.

Focussing on the specific cultural norms, the Chinese culture with its rich heritage and traditions, plays a noteworthy role in shaping societal norms and values. The country has made remarkable economic progress in the past couple of decades—nevertheless, certain aspects of its cultural heritage challenge women's career progression. The Chinese culture has traditionally accentuated distinct gender roles by assigning women primary responsibilities for household duties and caregiving. These expectations often lead to a societal perception that women's primary role is to be wives, mothers, and caretakers (Horta & Tang, 2023). Subsequently, hindering women's pursuit of professional careers as they face pressure to prioritize family over personal ambitions.

Further, Confucianism, a philosophical system that has profoundly influenced Chinese culture, places urgency on hierarchical relationships, filial piety, and harmony within the family. While these values are often valued and respected, they can reinforce gender stereotypes and expectations. The emphasis on filial piety often places additional responsibility on women to care for elderly parents, limiting their time and energy for career development (Kim, 2007). Furthermore, the pursuit of work-life balance poses quirky challenges for women in Chinese culture. The expectations of being both successful professionals and dedicated caregivers can be overwhelming. Traditional cultural norms and limited support structures, such as affordable childcare, contribute to women shouldering a disproportionate burden in balancing work and family responsibilities.

Nevertheless, It is essential to recognize that Chinese culture is changing, and there are encouraging signs of advancement as more Chinese women pursue higher education and work there. The government has implemented policies to promote gender equality and support women's career development. The organizations are also recognizing the value of gender diversity and implementing initiatives to address gender imbalances in leadership positions. Likewise, The patriarchal social structure of India places males in positions of power and authority. Traditional conventions and practices frequently reinforce Male dominance and control, which perpetuate gender inequality. This often leads to biases and discrimination against women in the workplace, hindering their career progression and access to leadership positions (Habiba & Ashfaq, 2016).

Furthermore, Indian culture is also characterized by prevalent gender biases and stereotypes. Deeply ingrained societal beliefs perpetuate the notion that men are more suitable for specific roles or industries. These biases are manifested in hiring decisions, performance evaluations, and career advancement opportunities (Amis et al., 2020). Consequently, women face greater scrutiny, lower expectations, and biases regarding their ability to balance work and family responsibilities. Nonetheless, government initiatives, such as skill development programs and gender-specific policies, are challenging cultural norms, fostering supportive work environments, and promoting gender equality. India is intensely moving towards unlocking its women's immense potential and paving the way for their meaningful contribution to the nation's progress.

AFFIRMATIVE ACTION

Gender-based quotas are hotly contested to be an effective way to improve the distribution of talent on the job market, particularly in situations where underlying issues with discrimination and inequities have resulted in the severe underrepresentation of women in positions of power. Quotas may also have good unintended consequences since they encourage more women to seek their educational, professional, and leadership potential by serving as role models, inspiration, and motivators. From an equitable standpoint, quotas can directly raise the appointment of women in corporate boardrooms. They can lead to broader organizational effects, such as a trickle-down effect that makes it easier to attract and keep women in senior management roles (ILO - Promoting women in business and management). Several studies in Asia have observed the combined shreds of evidence of the relationship between gender variety in the boardroom and the company's overall performance. The research by Caspar Rose (2007) divulges that female representation on boards has no substantial link with the company's overall performance as measured using Tobin's Q. Likewise, the observation of Companies by Chapple and Humphrey in 2013 took an aggregate method to evaluate the overall performance of portfolios of corporations with gender-diversified boardrooms and found no proof of affiliation among variety and overall performance19. Conversely, the observation of corporations by Campbell and Mínguez-Vera (2007) uncovers a tremendous impact of the proportion of women on board on company value 20. Similarly, the evaluation by Liu, Wei, and Xie of corporations in China in 2014 found a tremendous and substantial relationship between board gender variety and the company's overall performance. Correspondingly, the observation of corporations in Hong Kong, Singapore, Malaysia, and South Korea by Low, Daniel & Roberts, Helen & H. Whiting, and Rosalind (2015) showed that the increasing appointments of female directors in the boardrooms had a positive effect on the success of the business as a whole. They also convey how this relationship is moderated by the nation's attitude towards women in the workforce. Concerning legislative actions, few Asian nations have adopted a stringent approach to the glass ceiling. India has implemented several legislative actions to address gender inequality in the workplace. These include the Companies Act of 2013, which requires specific categories of companies to appoint at least 1 (one) woman director in their respective boardrooms. The Maternity Benefit (Amendment) Act of 2017 has endeavoured to extend the duration of maternity leave from 12 weeks to 26 weeks while mandating the employer to provide crèche facilities at the premises. The Sexual Harassment of Women at Workplace (Prevention, Prohibition, and Redressal) Act of 2013 has mandated establishing internal organizational committees to address and prevent sexual harassment. Japan has also taken some measures to promote gender equality in the workplace as they have introduced legislation on the Promotion of Women's Participation and Advancement in the workplace. This act aims to promote women's participation and advancement in the workplace by encouraging companies to set numerical targets for female representation and report their progress. In addition, Japan has legislated the Act on securing equal opportunity and treatment between men and women in employment. This act prohibits gender-based discrimination in employment and provides measures to ensure equal treatment and opportunities for men and women. South Korea, on the other hand, has legislated the Act on equal employment and support for work-family reconciliation. This act intends to enhance gender equality in employment and support work-family reconciliation by providing varied measures such as parental leave, childcare support, and flexible working arrangements. Likewise, Malaysia has also implemented the Employment Act 1955, which provides provisions against discrimination in employment based on gender, including equal pay for work of equal value. At the same time, the present Malaysian government has drafted. The Gender Equality Bill aims to eliminate gender discrimination and promote gender equality in various aspects of society. (Sundara Raja & Devadasan 2014). The details of affirmative actions by the Asian Nations are listed in Table 3.

FINDINGS

The majority of countries on the Asian continent have taken the same stance on the problem of the underrepresentation of women in corporate top management. The results observed in certain countries with mandatory quotas show that legislation, fines, and other penalties may effectively bring more female candidates to the debate table. However, only some countries that have chosen the voluntary and discretionary path have also demonstrated that supporting bottom-up corporate activities may lead to meaningful development. Employers and business organizations are crucial in communicating with government agencies, statutory bodies, and their people. In contrast, legal statutes and exemplary initiatives are being drafted and implemented regardless of the course taken (Langevoort, 2017). Hence, to create a pipeline of skilled and experienced female candidates that can fill the need for the position in corporate boardrooms and help the business develop and flourish thanks to the variety of perspectives they provide. Accordingly, corporate leaders should implement the recommended quotas and be proactive in initiating the process of appointment of women to leadership positions.

Table 3. Countries with quota or recommendation for the appointment of women in boardrooms

S No.	Country	Legislated Quotas	Other Recommendations
1	China	No gender quotas for women	
2	Hong Kong	No gender quotas for women	Disclose board diversity policy or explain
3	India	One Women Director Companies Act 2013	
4	Indonesia	No gender quotas for women	
5	Japan	No gender quotas for women	Disclose - % of women
6	Korea	No gender quotas for women	Bill – 30% of women in senior management
7	Malaysia	30% women mandatory for more than 250 employees	-
8	Singapore	The Singaporean Law has not reserved quotas in place for women serving on boards in Singapore.	Under the applicable Singapore's Code of Corporate Governance, the The boardroom of categorized companies is expected to have a suitable mix of skills and experience, including diversity of gender and age.
9	South Korea	The applicable law requires boards of certain public companies to have at least one a female member	Companies are required to file an annual report to the minister of economy and finance on whether they have established and met the quotas
10	Taiwan	There are no gender quotas for women in publicly listed companies	State-owned and legal foundations, at least 1/3rd of women on board

Though the development of the Asian-Pacific region in terms of gender equality has been gradual, women now hold 20% more management roles than they did 20 years ago. The region that has made the most progress is Eastern Asia, where the percentage of women managers climbed from 18% to 28% between 2000 and 2019. Nonetheless, the majority of nations in the area still need parity. Worryingly, just 17% of middle and senior executive designations in the region are held by females, eventually leading to the proportion of women in these positions being considerably lower. According to the regional survey by Deloitte (*See* Table 4), the appointment of women in the boardroom has steadily grown to 11.7% in 2021 from 7.8% in 2016. The appointment as chairman of the board has also seen slow growth from 2.6% in 2016 to 5.4% in 2021. On similar lines are the appointment of women as CEO & CFO, i.e., marginal growth from 2.9% in 2016 to 4.1% in 2021.

Table 4. Appointment of women in boardrooms and executive positions in Asia

Asia				
Participation	**Year**	**2016**	**2018**	**2021**
Women Board Member		7.8%	9.3%	11.7%
Women – Chair of Board		2.6%	4.2%	5.4%
Women - CEO		2.9%	3.4%	4.1%
Women - CFO		NA	16%	19.8%

China

Even though companies are pushed to pick directors with certain professional credentials and establish specific rules for appointing directors, China has no laws requiring boardroom gender diversity. The second Board Diversity Conference was only attended by 12 investment institutions and 11 publicly traded firms from the Shenzhen region up until this point, and it was organized by the Shenzhen Research Association of Corporate Governance in late 2020. The critical elements of this initiative are (i) Investors will use board gender diversity as a significant success metric for evaluating the efficacy of governance in corporations, (ii) the establishment of investment funds which primarily shall focus on businesses with significant numbers of females in executive and directorship positions (iii) By the end of the year 2021, companies which have approached the investment funds must have at least one women director and at least 20% women representation in senior executive positions; Whereas, by the end of year 2023, they must have kept at least one female director on board and raised the proportion of women in senior executive roles by 10%, or to 30%.

According to Dennis Chow (2022), gender diversity in Mainland China has significantly improved over the previous ten years. Nonetheless, the Nankai University's Centre for Research in Corporate Governance found that there are, on average, just 1.3 women directors among the more than 3,000 public businesses as of November 2020. It implies that there is still much space for improvement. Further, we can observe from Table 5 that there is an inevitable increase in the participation of women in the boardroom and executive positions from 2016 to 2021. Thus, it can be construed that there is a historical trend where many listed businesses believe in fostering the development of gender-diversified corporate cultures, even though there is no mandate for ensuring the quota for women serving in boardrooms as the directors or particular legislative mandate and obligation on boardroom diversity in the Mainland China. Women directors can provide alternative viewpoints and opinions while making decisions.

Table 5. Appointment of women in boardrooms and executive positions in China

China				
Participation	**Year**	**2016**	**2018**	**2021**
Women Board Member		10.7%	10.6%	13.1%
Women – Chair of Board		1.9%	6.4%	10.3%
Women - CEO		2.3%	5.8%	6.4%
Women - CFO		NA	24.3%	25.8%

India

According to the Companies Act of 2013, major public limited companies and listed firms in India must nominate at least one woman to their boardroom. According to the concerned provision, a female director must replace a vacancy on a board of directors that she previously held within one quarter after the vacancy or before the next board meeting, whichever comes earlier. As of April 2020, the boards of the largest 1000 publicly listed companies, based by market capitalization, must include at least one woman independent director, according to the Securities and Exchange Board of India (SEBI) listing requirement. Companies who violate these rules shall be imposed with a pecuniary acceptable amount of INR 5,000 per day till the listing requirements are fully complied with. In addition to the pecuniary sanctions, the S.E.B.I. also implemented a listing requirement for companies to publish in their annual reports, which shall include a matrix outlining the skill set, experience, and competencies of the board to improve diversity in Indian corporate boards.

Furthermore, the Comprehensive Companies Act of 2013 also mandated that insurance company's boards have at least one female member, which is reiterated by the IRDA, i.e., the Insurance Regulatory Authority of India's governance standards. This comprises unlisted insurance businesses whose principal regulating authority is the IRDA. Consequently, the effect of this legislative and regulatory mandate can be seen in Table 6.

Table 6. Appointment of women in boardrooms and executive positions in India

India				
Participation	**Year**	**2016**	**2018**	**2021**
Women Board Member		12.4%	13.8%	17.1%
Women – Chair of Board		3.2%	4.5%	3.6%
Women - CEO		6.6%	3.4%	4.7%
Women - CFO		NA	2.5%	3.9%

There is an apparent inclination in appointing women directors in the boardroom, i.e., from 12.4% in 2016 to 17.1% in 2021. However, the increment in the appointment as chair of the board is not that significantly similar to that of appointment in executive roles. Thus, it is appropriately interpreted by Atul Dhawan (2022) that the Indian regulatory authorities have established a comprehensive framework to promote the presence of women in senior positions in corporations; the data indicate a significant disconnect between the intended measures and actual conditions. Given the current speed of change, the need for diverse boards that collaborate for the same goal is more significant than ever. Now, it is a time for Indian corporations to pay greater attention to gender diversity and gender equity.

CONCLUSION

There is a widespread belief that the phenomenon of the glass barrier is one of the foremost reasons for this perplexed situation of women's professional advancement. To address this concern, various forms of mandates have been utilized to reduce workplace inequality. However, its desired results have yet to be achieved, demonstrating how difficult it is to apply and enforce laws. It can be inferred from the observations (in Table – 2) and comparative data that a glass ceiling exists in corporations hailing from nations from the Asian continent. Thitherto, it is manifested that an invisible barrier is restricting women from moving up in their careers and workplaces beyond a certain level. The primary noteworthy elements contributing to this invisible barrier are the disparate treatment of men and women because of the portrayed justification that male counterparts are viewed as superior to women in the workplace. This subsequently leads to the situation wherein the female counterparts do not have equal standing with men. This situation needs to be addressed, and the only way to do it with constructive social improvements is through the modernization of organizational management thought processes. Every organization should put its employees' abilities first to further its development and that of society. Instead of concentrating on "man resource" or "woman resource" individually, every company should concentrate on "human resource." Nothing can grow if it is out of balance; therefore, everything should be balanced. There are certain efforts for women, such as a women's bank and a women's police station, which women run.

While India and China have made significant economic strides on the global stage, they continue to grapple with gender disparities in leadership roles and the challenges posed by their respective cultural norms, corporate practices, and legal frameworks. Hence, addressing the glass ceiling is a matter of social justice and has profound implications for economic growth and productivity. India should strengthen its anti-discrimination laws, ensuring they explicitly address gender-based discrimination in the workplace. Clarity in legal provisions can facilitate more straightforward litigation for victims of discrimination. A robust enforcement mechanism should be established to monitor compliance and investigate discrimination claims. Indian public and private sector organizations should be obliged to disclose diversity metrics such as gender representation at different levels of leadership. This transparency can drive accountability and encourage organizations to adopt inclusive hiring practices. While, China should continue to refine and strengthen its anti-discrimination laws to address gender-based discrimination besides considering to implement quotas for gender representation in leadership roles within state-owned enterprises. Hence, implementing comprehensive legal frameworks, targeted initiatives for education and skill development, and promoting inclusive workplace practices are vital steps toward dismantling the glass ceiling and creating more equitable and prosperous societies in India and China.

REFERENCES

Amis, J. M., Mair, J., & Munir, K. A. (2020). The organizational reproduction of inequality. *The Academy of Management Annals*, *14*(1), 195–230. doi:10.5465/annals.2017.0033

Anker, R. (1977). The effect of group-level variables on fertility in a rural Indian sample. *The Journal of Development Studies*, *14*(1), 63–76. doi:10.1080/00220387708421662

Baksh-Soodeen, R., Etchart, L., Onubogu, E., & Johnson, T. (Eds.). (2005). *Gender mainstreaming in conflict transformation: Building sustainable peace*. Commonwealth Secretariat.

Broughton, A., & Miller, L. (2009). Women in senior management: Is the glass ceiling still intact? *ISGUC The Journal of Industrial Relations and Human Resources*, *11*(5), 7–24. doi:10.4026/1303-2860.2009.0122.x

Campbell, K., & Mínguez-Vera, A. (2008). Gender diversity in the boardroom and firm financial performance. *Journal of Business Ethics*, *83*(3), 435–451. doi:10.100710551-007-9630-y

Cicchiello, A. F., Fellegara, A. M., Kazemikhasragh, A., & Monferrà, S. (2021). Gender diversity on corporate boards: How Asian and African women contribute to sustainability reporting activity. *Gender in Management*, *36*(7), 801–820. doi:10.1108/GM-05-2020-0147

Habiba, U., Ali, R., & Ashfaq, A. (2016). From patriarchy to neopatriarchy: Experiences of women from Pakistan. *International Journal of Humanities and Social Science*, *6*(3), 212–221.

Heminway, J. M. (2019). Me, Too and# MeToo: Women in Congress and the Boardroom. *Geo. Wash. L. Rev.*, *87*, 1079.

Horta, H., & Tang, L. (2023). Male and female academics' gendered perceptions of academic work and career progression in China. *Higher Education Quarterly*, *77*(3), 515–536. doi:10.1111/hequ.12419

Jain, N., & Mukherji, S. (2010). The Perception of 'Glass Ceiling' in Indian Organizations: An Exploratory Study. *South Asian Journal of Management*, *17*(1).

Jauhar, J., & Lau, V. (2018). The 'Glass Ceiling' and Women's Career Advancement to Top Management: The Moderating Effect of Social Support. *Global Business and Management Research*, *10*(1).

Johns, M. L. (2013). Breaking the glass ceiling: Structural, cultural, and organizational barriers preventing women from achieving senior and executive positions. *Perspectives in Health Information Management*, (Winter).

Kang, S. K., & Kaplan, S. (2019). Working toward gender diversity and inclusion in medicine: Myths and solutions. *Lancet*, *393*(10171), 579–586. doi:10.1016/S0140-6736(18)33138-6 PMID:30739693

Kezar, A. J. (Ed.). (2020). Rethinking leadership in a complex, multicultural, and global environment: New concepts and models for higher education. Stylus Publishing, LLC.

Kezar, A. J. (Ed.). (2023). *Rethinking leadership in a complex, multicultural, and global environment: New concepts and models for higher education*. Taylor & Francis. doi:10.4324/9781003446842

Kim, K. H. (2007). Exploring the interactions between Asian culture (Confucianism) and creativity. *The Journal of Creative Behavior*, *41*(1), 28–53. doi:10.1002/j.2162-6057.2007.tb01280.x

Klettner, A., Clarke, T., & Boersma, M. (2016). Strategic and regulatory approaches to increasing women in leadership: Multilevel targets and mandatory quotas as levers for cultural change. *Journal of Business Ethics*, *133*(3), 395–419. doi:10.100710551-014-2069-z

Krook, M. L., Lovenduski, J., & Squires, J. (2009). Gender quotas and models of political citizenship. *British Journal of Political Science*, *39*(4), 781–803. doi:10.1017/S0007123409990123

Lachance-Grzela, M., & Bouchard, G. (2010). Why do women do the lion's share of housework? A decade of research. *Sex Roles*, *63*(11-12), 767–780. doi:10.100711199-010-9797-z

Langevoort, D. C. (2017). Cultures of compliance. *The American Criminal Law Review*, *54*, 933.

Low, D. C., Roberts, H., & Whiting, R. H. (2015). Board gender diversity and firm performance: Empirical evidence from Hong Kong, South Korea, Malaysia and Singapore. *Pacific-Basin Finance Journal*, *35*, 381–401. doi:10.1016/j.pacfin.2015.02.008

Macarie, F., & Moldovan, O. (2012). Gender discrimination in management: Theoretical and empirical perspectives. *Transylvanian Review of Administrative Sciences*, (35E), 153–172.

Maskell-Pretz, M., & Hopkins, W. E. (1997). Women in engineering: Toward a barrier-free work environment. *Journal of Management Engineering*, *13*(1), 32–37. doi:10.1061/(ASCE)0742-597X(1997)13:1(32)

Morrison, A. M., & Von Glinow, M. A. (1990). Women and minorities in management. American Psychological Association.

Newman, C., Chama, P. K., Mugisha, M., Matsiko, C. W., & Oketcho, V. (2017). Reasons behind current gender imbalances in senior global health roles and the practice and policy changes that can catalyze organizational change. *Global Health, Epidemiology and Genomics, 2*, e19.

Pajo, K., McGregor, J., & Cleland, J. (1997). Profiling the pioneers: Women directors on New Zealand's corporate boards. *Women in Management Review*, *12*(5), 174–181. doi:10.1108/09649429710182341

Payne, D. C. (2005). *The Glass Ceiling Ten Years Later: A Study of the Professional Woman's Perception of Success in Corporate America* [Doctoral dissertation]. Capella University.

Phillips, S. D., & Imhoff, A. R. (1997). Women and career development: A decade of research. *Annual Review of Psychology*, *48*(1), 31–59. doi:10.1146/annurev.psych.48.1.31 PMID:9046555

Rantanen, J., Muchiri, F., & Lehtinen, S. (2020). Decent work, ILO's response to the globalization of working life: Basic concepts and global implementation with special reference to occupational health. *International Journal of Environmental Research and Public Health*, *17*(10), 3351. doi:10.3390/ijerph17103351 PMID:32408597

Rose, C. (2007). Does female board representation influence firm performance? The Danish evidence. *Corporate Governance*, *15*(2), 404–413. doi:10.1111/j.1467-8683.2007.00570.x

Schwartz, F. N. (1989). Management women and the new facts of life. *Women in Management Review*, *4*(5). Advance online publication. doi:10.1108/EUM0000000001789

Simpson, R. (1997). Have times changed? Career barriers and the token woman manager. *British Journal of Management*, *8*(s1), 121–130. doi:10.1111/1467-8551.8.s1.10

Sloan, L., Joyner, M., Stakeman, C., & Schmitz, C. (2018). Critical multiculturalism and intersectionality in a complex world. Oxford University Press.

West, M. A., Hwang, S., Maier, R. V., Ahuja, N., Angelos, P., Bass, B. L., Brasel, K. J., Chen, H., Davis, K. A., Eberlein, T. J., Fong, Y., Greenberg, C. C., Lillemoe, K. D., McCarthy, M. C., Michelassi, F., Numann, P. J., Parangi, S., Reyes, J. D., Sanfey, H. A., ... Wren, S. M. (2018). Ensuring equity, diversity, and inclusion in academic surgery: An American Surgical Association white paper. *Annals of Surgery*, *268*(3), 403–407. doi:10.1097/SLA.0000000000002937 PMID:30004923

Yiannakis, C. (2010). *The moderating role of self-directedness in a Job Demands-Job Resources Model for working women*. University of Johannesburg.

Ziems-Mueller, W. J. (2011). *A Qualitative Inquiry of Barriers Facing Female Faculty Desiring Career Progression into Higher Education Administration* [Doctoral dissertation]. University of Phoenix.

ADDITIONAL READING

Arora, A. (2022). Gender diversity in boardroom and its impact on firm performance. *The Journal of Management and Governance*, *26*(3), 735–755. doi:10.100710997-021-09573-x

De Jonge, A. (2014). The glass ceiling that refuses to break: Women directors on the boards of listed firms in China and India. *Women's Studies International Forum*, *47*, 326–338. doi:10.1016/j.wsif.2014.01.008

Duppati, G., Rao, N. V., Matlani, N., Scrimgeour, F., & Patnaik, D. (2020). Gender diversity and firm performance: Evidence from India and Singapore. *Applied Economics*, *52*(14), 1553–1565. doi:10.1080/00036846.2019.1676872

Kanojia, S. (2020). Appointment of Women Directors: An Overview of South Asian Nations. *New Paradigms In Business Management Practices*, *2*, 285.

Khaw, K. L. H., Liao, J., Tripe, D., & Wongchoti, U. (2016). Gender diversity, state control, and corporate risk-taking: Evidence from China. *Pacific-Basin Finance Journal*, *39*, 141–158. doi:10.1016/j.pacfin.2016.06.002

Saeed, A., Yousaf, A., & Alharbi, J. (2017). Family and state ownership, internationalization and corporate board-gender diversity: Evidence from China and India. *Cross Cultural & Strategic Management*, *24*(2), 251–270. doi:10.1108/CCSM-11-2015-0159

Sharma, S., & Sehrawat, P. (2014). Glass ceiling for women: Does it exist in the modern India. *Journal of Organization & Human Behaviour*, *3*(2-3), 9–15.

Sial, M. S., Zheng, C., Cherian, J., Gulzar, M. A., Thu, P. A., Khan, T., & Khuong, N. V. (2018). Does corporate social responsibility mediate the relation between boardroom gender diversity and firm performance of Chinese listed companies? *Sustainability*, *10*(10), 3591. doi:10.3390u10103591

KEY TERMS AND DEFINITIONS

Affirmative Action: A set of State's policies and programs designed to address historical discrimination and promote equal opportunities for individuals from underrepresented or disadvantaged groups.

Filial Piety: Concept and virtue which emphasizes the respect, loyalty, and obedience that children are expected to show to their parents and elders.

Gender Mainstreaming: A strategy adopted by the state to promote gender equality and address the issues of gender disparities.

Meritocracy: A social philosophy or system in which people's advancement and success are primarily determined by their respective abilities, talents, and skills.

Quotas: A specific quantity or limit that is set for allocating resources.

Tobin's Q: A concept to assess whether a company's market value is overvalued or undervalued relative to the replacement cost of its assets.

Tokenism: Practice of making a superficial effort to include members of underrepresented groups in order to give the appearance of diversity and inclusivity, without genuinely addressing issues of discrimination or inequality.

Trickle-Down Effect: Policies of the state that primarily benefit the wealthy and businesses will ultimately lead to benefits "trickling down" to the broader population.

Chapter 4
Luckin Coffee:
A Look at Corporate Governance in the Chinese Market

Yiqian Zhang
Coventry University, UK

Iberedem Obot
AML/CFT Resources Nigeria Limited, Nigeria

EXECUTIVE SUMMARY

The Luckin Coffee case presents an opportunity for an important analysis of corporate governance challenges of Chinese businesses and regulators because of the 2020 scandal and the fact that it carries on business in China and is a publicly traded company in the US. In the past, company failures have led to local and sometimes global queries about the processes through which companies' objectives are set and pursued. The regulatory changes ensuing from corporate scandals can be far-reaching, controversial, and leading to global regulatory contagion. In the Luckin scandal, its real and potential implications involved two of the world's dominant economies. The concerns from the Luckin scandal are the issues on which this chapter is focused. The chapter explores the concepts and regulatory solutions that are relevant to the Luckin scandal. The dynamics of the Chinese market and the consequences of the scandal are explored in the chapter. Ultimately, the need for caution in the discourse on regulatory response to scandals such as the Luckin case is articulated in the chapter.

DOI: 10.4018/978-1-6684-9867-5.ch004

INTRODUCTION

Corporate and accounting scandals have often caused public concern about the processes through which companies' objectives are set and pursued in the context of the social, regulatory and market environment. Scandals such as the Luckin Coffee (LK) accounting fraud case have been no different. (Stevenson & Wong, 2020) The potential challenge of the public concern for the causes of these scandals has often been that they put pressure on regulatory bodies who in turn could and, at times, do institute regulations that are controversial at best. For instance, in 2001, the Chinese government came under increasing public pressure to improve its policy towards corporate governance structures because of scandals involving listed companies in China such as Guanxia Industry Co. Ltd, Macat Optics and Electronics Co. Ltd, Sanjiu Pharmaceutical Co. Ltd and Lantian Co. Ltd. (Shan & Round, 2012, p. 1317) A popular example of the global repercussions of company failures is in how the scandals involving large corporations such as Enron and WorldCom led to enactment of regulation that would be a model for regulators seeking to interfere with the governance of corporations in several jurisdictions, including Japan. (Suzuki, n.d.) The scandal led to the creation of the Sarbanes–Oxley Act of 2002 (SOX) (USA) and other similar legal documents such as the Financial Security Law of France 2003, German Corporate Governance Code 2002 were also promulgated in response to the perception that stricter rules on the governance of corporations was required in various parts of the world. Following the passing into law of the SOX, it became an example of how corporate governance reforms could reignite the age-old quandary about the consequence of government interference in business boardroom decisions. Its passing into law in the US spurred up an appetite or calls for similar laws to be passed in other parts of the globe.[1] (Lin, 2004, pp. 11-15) (Nwogugu, 2019, p. 544) (Bhabra & Hossain, 2018, p. 1034) At the same time, the SOX was being criticized for reasons such as the widely touted view that the Act was dissuading foreign companies from entering the U.S capital market. (Colon, 2005) It was opined that some of the very aspects of SOX that have been the most criticized are also the most widely copied. (Loewenberg, 2008) In Canada, the SOX influenced model of corporate governance regulation was adopted by enacting Bill 198 2002 (which is commonly referred to as C-SOX) was criticized for being politically motivated and not based on empirical facts or a critical evaluation of the local environment. (Bhabra, Hossain, & Karmakar, 2020, pp. 262-263) Therefore, some stakeholders have expressed criticisms about the necessity and consequence of the regulatory reaction to corporate governance scandals. Alongside the detractors of the SOX 2002, there are proponents that have countered any negative sentiments about the Act by highlighting its positive impact. (Peregrine, 2021) Consequently, the objective of this chapter is not based on the need to duel on the propriety or otherwise of any corporate governance regulation, instead, the motivating factor is the knowledge that the response to scandals can be controversial and far reaching. This chapter is predicated on the need for adequate dissemination of knowledge on corporate governance concepts or solutions that are relevant to the scandals that can invoke public sentiments about the need for stricter rules. Especially because there is some level of global convergence that has usually trailed regulatory reactions to corporate governance scandals, (Liang & Useem, 2009, p. 169) it is imperative that interested members of the public are able to understand and consider existing cooperate governance mechanisms before clamouring for wholesale regulatory redesigns.

Consequences of The Scandal

The Luckin Coffee accounting scandal in 2019 resulted in severe financial consequences for the company, its investors and the broader market. The revelation of fabricated transactions amounting to approximately $310 million severely tarnished the company's reputation and triggered a sharp decline in its share price (Peng, et al., 2022). Following the scandal, the company's stock was delisted from the Nasdaq, which significantly reduced its market value and led to a loss of confidence among investors. The delisting also impeded Luckin's ability to raise capital in the global market, which is crucial for a growth-oriented firm. The financial consequences extended to legal and regulatory fines, as the company had to settle with the U.S. Securities and Exchange Commission (SEC) for a substantial amount (Coley, 2020). The financial distress also compelled Luckin to restructure its operations and cut costs, impacting its growth trajectory and competitive standing in the coffee retail sector.

On the non-financial front, the scandal profoundly impacted Luckin's brand image and trustworthiness among customers, suppliers, and business partners. Being embroiled in such a scandal painted the company as unreliable and dishonest, which could have long-term repercussions on customer loyalty and supplier relationships.

The Fraud of Luckin Coffee

Luckin Coffee's first store was opened in Beijing in October 2017 by Jenny Zhiya Qian. The company, known for its minimalist, cashless stores, expanded rapidly, reaching 4,507 Chinese locations by the end of 2019, quickly overtaking Starbucks, which has opened over 4,200 stores in China since entering the country in 1999. The company adopted a business strategy of burning through cash in a bid to grab market share. The company's stock was reported to have steadily risen from its May 2019 IPO, partially due to its reported growth in sales (Wang, 2020). Before Luckin was hit by the accounting scandal, its IPO price of $17 per share had nearly tripled to an all-time high of $50.02 per share on 17 January 2020.

Public consciousness of the LK scandal began on 31 January 2020 when a short selling investment fund name Muddy Waters Research received and published an unattributed report on the fraud (Muddy Waters Research, 2020). LK's stock would eventually fall by as much as 27% after Muddy Waters announced that it had sold short the shares of the Chinese challenger to Starbucks because of a report questioning the financial dealings of the coffee chain. (Ahmed, 2020) By February 2020, about 30% of LK's available shares have been reportedly sold short, with the dollar value of these bearish bets at $951 million. Obviously, this action by Muddy Waters and other short sellers was predictable because their business model is to borrow shares and sell same at current value to other investors in the hope of purchasing the borrowed shares when its value drops at a later date. (Ahmed, 2020) LK's fraudulent activities that were being exposed and its market valuation of 12 billion in January of 2020 made it an attractive option for short sellers. (Xi & Huang, 2021) The company discredited the report released by Muddy Waters Research but in April 2020 it announced that an internal investigation had found its chief operating officer to be culpable for overstating its 2019 sales by about 2.2 billion yuan ($310 million). (Ahmed, 2020) (Lucas, 2020) In a consequent Securities and Exchange Commission (SEC) investigation it was revealed that in the period of April 2019 through to at least January 2020, the company had fabricated sales figures after failing to meet its performance predictions and the markets high expectation for revenue and growth. (Securities and Exchange Commission vs Luckin Coffee, Inc., 2020, p. 6 & 9) LK engaged in fraudulent actions such as publishing revenue that was realized from fake orders by individual and corporate customers who did not actually redeem the coupons that were on offer to the public. (Securities and Exchange Commission vs Luckin Coffee, Inc., 2020, p. 7) LK's bank statements were also altered to make funds that came from seven third party entities that were controlled by or associated with its employees look like they came from fictitious agents. The funds from the third-party entities were used for a scheme where employees of LK would generate fake coupons and fabricate coupon sales to the fictitious agents. Afterwards, fake orders by individual customers who had purportedly bought coupons from the fictitious agent were created by LK and recorded as part of its revenue for the period. (Securities and Exchange Commission vs Luckin Coffee, Inc., 2020, p. 8) While the scheme of fake coupon sale was ongoing, LK made transfers back to the third-party entities through bank transfers and fabricated expense payments to donors. During the period, LK staff inflated their costs to amounts that were consistent with the companies inflated revenue and consequently, they were afforded the funds that were paid back to the third-party entities. (Securities and Exchange Commission vs Luckin Coffee, Inc., 2020, pp. 9-10) The SEC investigation established that

LK fraudulently incorporated the fraudulent sales transaction into its records and intentionally and materially overstated its reported revenue in its publicly available financial statement. LK also intentionally and materially understated its net loss during the relevant period. (Securities and Exchange Commission vs Luckin Coffee, Inc., 2020, p. 1) The SEC surmised that LK's lack of adequate internal accounting controls allowed the fraudulent activities to be undetected for at least nine months. (Securities and Exchange Commission vs Luckin Coffee, Inc., 2020, p. 14) The scandal was publicised by some politicians as another example of how the extant regulations were not extensive.[2] (Stevenson & Wong, 2020) Therefore, was LK's internal controls failures an indication of the need for regulatory overhaul as a remedy to the dire weaknesses of extant cooperate governance mechanisms.

The Corporate Governance Failures of Luckin Coffee

Corporate governance has been described as entailing all the laws, regulations, codes, and practices that define how a company is administrated. It refers to the mechanisms put in place to determine the rights and responsibilities of all long-term active agents that attract talent and financial capital, boost internal efficiency, and provide economic value to stakeholders of an organization. (SpriggHR, n.d.) It has also been described as the framework of policies and guidelines that inform a company's conduct, decision-making and practice. (University of Lincoln, 2022) Another useful definition of corporate governance is that it generally refers to the set of mechanisms that influence the decisions made by managers when there is a separation of ownership and control. (Larcker, Richardson, & Tuna, 2005) From these definitions it is clear that the decision making of business entities is the focus of corporate governance. It seeks to influence how business objectives are set and achieved, how risks are monitored and assessed, and how internal performance is optimized. Invariably, good corporate governance is said to be practiced in business institutions where managers and agents are influenced by relevant mechanisms to promote smoother running of operations and adopt processes that are compliant with regulation, cost effective and ensure visibility of errors. (SpriggHR, n.d.) The notion of accountability, transparency, fairness and responsibility are principles that all corporate governance compliant institutions must apply in their decision-making and practice. (University of Lincoln, 2022) Therefore, the principles and practice of corporate governance are important for protecting shareholders' interest. Incidences such as the Luckin scandal have often been a catalyst for the conversation on whether to make widely accepted corporate governance best practices into the status of hard law. To be specific, the Luckin confession that was made on April 2020 spurred swelling disbelief on U.S.-listed Chinese firms, which culminated in the passing of the Holding Foreign Companies Accountable (HFCA) Act on 20 May

2020. In December 2020, the HFCA Act was signed into law, and in effect, it gave US-listed Chinese companies three years to comply with the US audit requirements, or to give up their US listings. However, the notion that the Luckin scandal was justification for instituting more regulations has remained contentious. One study showed that the Luckin coffee board's low level of independence made it an outlier case and not a normally among other NASDAQ-listed Chinese companies. In other words, their study underscored a reason for caution to be associated with the idea that the Luckin scandal was representative of all US-listed Chinese companies (Xi & Huang, 2021). Xi and Huang's underscoring of the independence of Luckin's board is instructive because it connects the scandal to the controversial corporate governance concept of CEO duality. The fraud perpetrated in Luckin suggests that CEO duality could have been an issue that impacted on the ability for corporate governance structures to ensure transparency. Therefore, the following subsections will look at the relationship between Luckin Coffee, CEO duality and disclosures in the Chinese market.

Luckin Board Structure

The examination of Luckin Coffee's board structure during the 2019 accounting scandal reveals significant deviations from ideal governance practices, especially for a U.S. listed company. Unlike the U.S. listing rules advocating board independence, Luckin's governance leaned heavily towards insider dominance with six insiders and two outsiders (independent directors) on the board (Vagle, et al., 2021). This setup likely hindered objective oversight and increased conflict of interest risks due to pre-existing affiliations between insider directors and UCAR Inc., owned by the chairman.

The failure to detect or address fabricated transactions and overstated revenues reflects a possible ethical shortfall and a culture of complacency. The audit committee, tasked with ensuring financial integrity, fell short of its mandate, delegating crucial responsibilities to management, thereby undermining necessary checks and balances. Even when faced with apparent unethical practices, there was a notable silence from the audit committee and the board, highlighting a lack of transparency and communication breakdown. These governance flaws played a part in, or worsened, the accounting scandal, emphasizing the need for a balanced, independent board and an effective audit committee to uphold financial integrity and ethical conduct within an organization.

Transparency in Luckin and the Chinese Market

Transparency is an important component and principle of corporate governance. It is observed to entail a corporation must exercise openness and willingness to disclose truthful, accurate and timely information regarding the company's financial, social and political position to shareholders, stakeholders, consumers and the wider community (University of Lincoln, 2022). Under good corporate governance culture, organisations are expected to have routine external audits an effective and independent internal audit function that has the respect, confidence and cooperation of both the board and the management (National Committee On Corporate Governance, n.d.). Consequently, the Luckin scandal raises concerns about cooperate governance failures because it was the companies lack of adequate internal controls that allowed the fraud to continue, without detection, for at least nine months (Securities and Exchange Commission vs Luckin Coffee, Inc., 2020, p. 14). Expectedly, there has been a lot of focus on the causes and lessons to be taken from the Luckin affair. The role of the regulators in China and the US has been a prominent part of the conversations about the scandal. One of the issues raised is that some foreign firms accessing U.S. capital markets were using foreign auditors from their home countries to audit their financial records (Gnanarajah, 2020). The use of non-US auditing firms was problematic for the Public Company Accounting Oversight Board (PCAOB) which was mandated to provide independent oversight of audits of public companies by US law.[3] The SEC had sought to remedy this challenge by either entering into multilateral or bilateral agreements with various foreign regulators, but they faced limitations with regulators in China (Gnanarajah, 2020). At the time, a rule that was reversed in 2023, prohibited all Chinese companies listed overseas from sharing their financial documents with foreign regulators and auditors due to national security concerns.[4] In the Luckin case, the auditing firm was registered with the PCAOB, but it was never subjected to a Board inspection before the scandal occurred (Mahoney, 2020). The scrutiny of Luckin's auditor was exacerbated because of strong and growing opposition against the fact that the PCAOB could not inspect audit work and practices done on US reporting companies by PCAOB-registered accounting firms in China. These barriers were touted as hindrances to the fair and transparent financial reporting culture of the US capital markets (Bu, 2021, pp. 508-509). Some commentators expressed concerns about whether the regulators could have confidence in the processes of a firm it had not inspected for more than a decade (Mahoney, 2020). A curious action by Luckin's auditor was the fact that it had written a private letter to a number of investment banks stating that it did not have any issue with the financial performance of Luckin in the first three quarters of 2019. The reality was that Luckin's auditor was not liable in the scandal because they did not audit the 2019 financial statements that were used to deceive the general public. Unlike what is required for annual reports, the sort of letter written by Luckins auditor are part of the standard due diligence conducted by underwriters prior to securities offerings, when companies' financial statements have not been audited (Yang, 2020). The letter was useful because the quarterly financial statements for companies listed in the U.S. are not required by law to be audited, but the statements must be reviewed by a certified public accounting firm to ensure accuracy and completeness. Reviews are substantially narrower in scope than an audit and they provide only limited assurances because they do not include an investigation of the listed company's internal controls or risk of fraud. The low cost of a review, when compared to an audit, make it a less burdensome option for companies. Therefore, without foresight or knowledge of the financial misdealing in Luckin, the public and regulators were justifiably not alarmed by Luckin's use of a comfort letter by its auditor. A cause for liability would have arisen if an audit was conducted and a positive report was given for the fraudulent statements. It is only through conjecturing and using unverifiable claims that any sort of unethical conduct can be ascribe to Luckin's auditing firm. Ultimately, Luckin's auditing firm was not found to be liable by US or Chinese regulators (Shicong, Auditor EY Denies Liability for Luckin Coffee's Financial Scandal, 2020). Consequently, there is reason to contend that the high level of focus on the connection between China and Luckin's auditing firm and an assumed auditing impropriety in the scandal was not the best way to avoid a reoccurrence in the future. There is no reason to conclude that there was collusion between Luckin and its auditing firm. It is incomprehensible that a fee arrangement for public offer would have incentivized the auditor to collude with Lucking to commit fraudulent issuance of securities when it was aware of the legal requirement for the annual filling of an audit report with the SEC. An upside (rise in value) of stock leading to a large financial gain could have been an incentive for Lucking's management team but for the auditing firm to help conceal fraud would be akin to a large reputational gamble because the annual filling of audit is useful for identifying any misdealing. Failure to identify the fraud during auditing would be opening audit firm to criminal and reputational damage that is not justifiable. Therefore, the management team, and not the auditors, are the factors to be looked in the quest to avoid a reoccurrence and protect investors.

As a business domiciled in China but publicly traded in the US, Luckin's scandal cast the spotlight on US-listed Chinese firms. The mantra of how US-listed Chinese companies were not playing fair was prominent in the reportage of the Luckin affair. The not playing fair tag was largely a result of the long-standing view that China was substantially subsidizing its state-owned enterprises (SOEs) and this constituted unfair competition with their foreign counterparts (Bu, 2021, pp. 513-514). With the playing unfair moniker being associated with the scandal, it would be easy for less informed people to conclude that a large segment of US-listed Chinese firms was seeking to gain advantage over their foreign contemporaries by engaging in deliberate financial opaqueness. Unbeknownst to a lot of people, most of the US-listed Chinese companies that are not SOEs are not exactly Chinese, legally speaking. The setup of elaborate corporate structure known as variable interest entity (VIE) or Sina-model structure in which a typical arrangement would involve Mainland registered entities having complicated ownerships that enable them to also have a listing entity (whose stocks are held by global investors) registered in an offshore location. The VIE structure is used by a large portion of Chinese companies to circumvent a Chinese government prohibition of foreign funded investments in industries such as financial services and internet information and services. It is trite that the US securities market has been an attractive destination for Chinese companies because of China's stringent listing standards, frequent regulation change and long waiting time for IPO approval in the domestic market (Peng, Yang, & Wu, 2022). The ease of access and deregulation in the US securities market has been an important attraction for most of the Chinese companies listed therein. Before 2020, the use of VIE structures by Luckin and many other U.S listed companies like Alibaba and Baidu meant that their listing entities were not subject to China's securities market regulator, the China Securities Regulatory Commission (CSRC) (Penga & Yang, 2020, p. 5). In effect, the Luckin fraud was ongoing at a time when disclosure requirements were lax for foreign companies in the US and at the same time, it was an overseas-listed company that the CSRC was not empowered to regulate. The lax reporting requirement in the US was remedied by passing the HFCA in the aftermath of the scandal. Conversely, in the month before Luckin acknowledge the fraud, China amended its Securities Law to afford it a Long-arm jurisdiction to hold accountable any overseas-listed company that its regulators deem to have to have disrupted the Chinese market and acted against the interest of investors.[5] The amended securities law was the basis on which the Chinese regulators reviewed Luckin finances immediately after the company admitted to the fraud (Shicong, China Sends Team to Luckin Coffee to Probe Accounting Fraud, 2020). The Chinese securities regulator concluded that Luckin violated Chinese laws on inappropriate competition by inflating its operational data, and also misled the public with faked statistics between August 2019 and April 2020. Two Luckin entities and 43 other companies were fined by China's securities regulator for their role in the scandal (Lee & Yu, 2020). In the US, Luckin agreed to a settlement, including permanent injunctions and paying USD180 million in monetary penalties after the SEC concluded its investigation.

The institution of a legal basis for the Chinese authority to impose accountability on overseas listed companies negatively impacting their local market is useful for influencing these businesses with the knowledge that infringements could attract investigation and sanction by regulators in China. In the context of the corporate governance, the usefulness of the changes to the disclosure requirements in the US and China's review of its confidentiality law is not substantial. Yes, the regulatory changes promote transparency but they are not going to stop a management team that is willing to publish fraudulent financial figure like Luckin did. In hindsight, the expectation that the fraud would not be discovered at the point of yearly fillings with the SEC is indicative of a lack of awareness or understanding of the regulatory environment. Therefore, the lessons and subsequent changes derived from the Luckin episode should be about why the management team or board did not stop the fraud happening.

CEO Duality and the Luckin Scandal

The concept of CEO duality has been a part of corporate governance discuss on what an appropriate management structure is (Ali, et al., 2022, pp. 3-4). It refers to the situation where the roles of the Chairman of the Board and the CEO are held by the same individual. CEO duality used to be common in businesses but there has been a move away from the practice in recent times. In China and the US several rules encourage businesses to separation of the Chairman and CEO roles. In the US the SEC does not mandate a specific structure but it emphasizes the importance of independent board oversight. Some stock exchanges require companies to have independent directors on their boards and disclose their reasons if the roles of CEO and Chairman are combined. The approach to a transition away from CEO duality has generally not been mandatory in China or the US. This maybe because there is yet to be definite evidence for or against it. The mostly non-mandatory approach that has been adopted in the regulation of CEO duality maybe because there have been both negative and positive findings in research on its impact in China (Ali, et al., 2022, p. 4) and in the US (Abels & Martelli, 2013, pp. 137-138). From a theoretical perspective, the proponents of agency theory assert that CEO duality weakens the trusteeship duties of the board of directors. On the other hand, stewardship theorists contend that the merging of duality roles institutes a harmony between the board of directors, managers and shareholders, which is more efficient and effective in order to reach the goals of increasing sales and profit maximization within organizations (Abels & Martelli, 2013, p. 137). In discussions on the Luckin scandal, the actions of the management and board present a twist to the typical theoretical analysis of CEO duality. Firstly, the notion and importance of duality in the Luckin scandal arises because there is reason to conclude that the chairman and CEO were colluding. It has been reported that the chairman, Charles Zhenyao Lu, sent emails instructing colleagues to commit fraud and some of the external companies that helped to facilitate the scheme have ties to him (Coley, 2020) (Martinez, 2020). The CEO, Jenny Zhiya Qian, participated in fabricated transactions and is a long-term work subordinate of the chairman. At the minimum, there was a desertion of the agency theorist's expectation that through a separation of roles, the CEO managing the corporation would be held accountable to shareholders though the Chairman and the board of directors. It would seem that the chairman and CEO were allied in the goal of fabricating financial information and so their relationship possessed the harmony expected in the duality arrangement promoted by the stewardship theory (Abels & Martelli, 2013, p. 137). The management team being long-term lieutenants of the chairman was not ideal for promoting good corporate governance but to regulate what management and board relationship is permissible would be draconian and unnecessary. History has shown that business people always find ways to promote their interest while claiming to complying with the laws or guidance. For instance, in China, board of supervisors and external directors were introduced to monitor management, financial affairs and business activities on behalf of shareholders. However, in the selection process, the management usually chose independent directors who share common views with the board of directors. Consequently, it is not surprising that in practice the board of supervisors and the independent directors are observed to have only provided nominal checks on management (Jiao, 2020). Similarly, the reputational cost that may or may not be associated with practicing duality is avoided by the appointment of a CEO that is subservient to the chairman. Moreover, Luckin coffee has shown that it practiced a purported separation of management and ownership during the period of disclosure failures but it adopted CEO duality after the scandal period. Under a CEO duality regime, the company improved on its disclosure mechanisms and eventually achieved its objective of surpassing its biggest rival in total Chinese sales. Accordingly, the Luckin Coffee story has demonstrated that individual human frailties must not be overlooked in the discourse on corporate governance regulation. Therefore, instead of putting all the focus on the governance failure in the scandal, the emphasis should be on the fact that the management team was willing to risk violating law such as the Chinese accounting law against production of false accounting reports.[6] The availability of laws do not stop criminality because offenders ill-advisedly believe they can get away with the crime. With the same logic, there were mandatory and nonmandatory corporate governance mechanisms and criminal law mechanisms that should have influenced the management team to not commit fraud. Their decision to misrepresent their true financial position must be viewed as an action for which there is ample deterrent regulation.

CONCLUSION

The chapter analysed the dynamics of corporate governance in China through the lens of the Luckin scandal. The scope for analysing corporate governance is wide and so the geographical location of Luckin coffee, the 2020 scandal and the structure of its business presents an opportunity for a bespoke look at important challenges that can shape the global regulatory environment. The exploration in this chapter shows that transparency and board independence failures led to the scandal but they did not occur because of a lack of substantial regulatory safeguards. It is essential that regulatory change is carried out with an understanding of the tendency for business people to look for loopholes and the potential for government intrusion to stifle economic growth.

The Luckin Coffee scandal serves as a stark reminder of the implications of financial misconduct and the importance of adhering to ethical practices and financial regulations to build and maintain trust with stakeholders. The scandal spotlights some lessons that must be adopted to avoid similar occurrences. For instance, having stringent financial controls and oversight mechanisms to detect any discrepancies or fraudulent activities at an early stage and implementing robust internal audit functions and employing external auditors with strong reputations for integrity can be beneficial. Companies should also have clear policies and protections in place for whistle-blowers. Ensuring that employees feel safe when reporting unethical behavior or financial discrepancies is key to uncovering potential issues early. Other practices to be imbibed by companies are transparency and accurate reporting, fostering strong ethical culture, ensuring regulatory compliance, implementing thorough risk management process and there must be open, honest, and regular communication with investors and other stakeholders. Crucially, companies can learn from the mistakes of others by analyzing the causes and consequences of high-profile scandals like Luckin Coffee's, and taking steps to ensure they don't repeat the same errors.

Discussion questions:

1. How critical are board independence and transparency to preventing financial misconduct in corporations, and what measures can be instituted to ensure adherence?
2. How can companies establish robust audit mechanisms to deter or detect financial misconduct at early stages?
3. How can organizations foster a safe and supportive environment for reporting financial discrepancies or other unethical behaviors?
4. What steps can companies take to rebuild trust and ensure transparent communication with investors and other stakeholders post-scandal?

REFERENCES

Abels, P. B., & Martelli, J. T. (2013, April 5). CEO Duality: How Many Hats Are Too Many? *Corporate Governance, 13*(2), 135–147. doi:10.1108/14720701311316625

Ahmed, S. I. (2020, February 4). *Luckin Coffee share price may nearly double to $60 on U.S. exchanges: Hedge fund Citron Capital.* Retrieved June 19, 2023, from Reuters: https://www.reuters.com/article/us-luckin-coffee-stock-citron-idUSKBN1ZY2EK

Ali, S., Naseem, M. A., Jian, J., Rehman, R. U., Malik, F., & Ahmad, M. I. (2022, August 9). "How" and "When" CEO Duality Matter? Case of a Developing Economy. *Sage Journals*, 1–15.

Bhabra, H., & Hossain, A. T. (2018). SOX vs C-SOX: Which one works better? *Managerial Finance, 44*(8), 1031–1046. doi:10.1108/MF-03-2018-0097

Bhabra, H. S., Hossain, A. T., & Karmakar, V. R. (2020). An overview of C-SOX and directions for future research. *Managerial Finance, 46*(2), 254–266. doi:10.1108/MF-10-2018-0530

Bu, Q. (2021, September 03). The anatomy of Holding Foreign Companies Accountable Act (HFCAA): A panacea or a double-edge sword? *Capital Markets Law Journal, 16*(4), 503–527. doi:10.1093/cmlj/kmab022

Coley, B. (2020, December 17). *Luckin Coffee Agrees to Pay $180 Million Fine for Fraud Scandal.* Retrieved July 23, 2023, from QSR: https://www.qsrmagazine.com/finance/luckin-coffee-agrees-pay-180-million-fine-fraud-scandal

Colon, D. (2005). The Foreign Bank Exemption to the Sarbanes-Oxley Prohibition on Loans to Directors and Officers. *Journal of International Business and Law, 4*(1), 123–151.

Gnanarajah, R. (2020). Introduction to Financial Services: Accounting and Auditing Regulatory Structure, U.S. and International. Congressional Research Service. Congressional Research Service.

Jiao, L. (2020, July 14). *Pinduoduo and Luckin Coffee Show China's Corporate Governance Dilemmas.* Retrieved July 24, 2023, from Nikkei Asia: https://asia.nikkei.com/Opinion/Pinduoduo-and-Luckin-Coffee-show-China-s-corporate-governance-dilemmas

Larcker, D. F., Richardson, S. A., & Tuna, I. (2005, May 16). *How Important is Corporate Governance?* Philadelphia: The Wharton School University of Pennsylvania.

Lee, S. Y., & Yu, S. (2020, September 22). *China fines Luckin Coffee and linked firms a total of $9 million* (M. Anantharaman, & R. Gopalakrishnan, Eds.). Retrieved July 22, 2023, from Reuters: https://www.reuters.com/article/luckin-coffee-investigation-fine-idINKCN26D07O

Liang, N., & Useem, M. (2009). Profiles of Corporate Governance in Leading Countries: China. In A. Burmajster & A. Jolly (Eds.), *The Handbook of International Corporate Governance: A Definitive Guide* (2nd ed., pp. 167–175). Kogan Page Ltd.

Lin, T. W. (2004). Corporate Governance in China: Recent Developments, Key Problems, and Solutions. *Journal of Accounting and Corporate Governance*, *1*(1), 1–23.

Loewenberg, S. (2008, February 26). *SOX's outside reach a model for foreign markets*. Retrieved June 19, 2023, from Politico: https://www.politico.com/story/2008/02/soxs-outside-reach-a-model-for-foreign-markets-008678

Lucas, A. (2020, April 2). *Shares of China's Luckin Coffee plummet 80% after investigation finds COO fabricated sales*. Retrieved June 18, 2023, from CNBC: https://www.cnbc.com/2020/04/02/luckin-coffee-stock-plummets-after-investigation-finds-coo-fabricated-sales.html

Mahoney, J. P. (2020, April 17). *Inspection of PCAOB-Registered Chinese Auditor*. Retrieved July 21, 2023, from Harvard Law School Forum on Corporate Governance: https://corpgov.law.harvard.edu/2020/04/17/inspection-of-pcaob-registered-chinese-auditor/

Martinez, I. (2020, June 16). *Luckin Coffee Delays Publishing 2019 Annual Report Over Fraud Probe*. Retrieved July 23, 2023, from S&P Global Market Intelligence: https://www.spglobal.com/marketintelligence/en/news-insights/latest-news-headlines/luckin-coffee-delays-publishing-2019-annual-report-over-fraud-probe-59058938

Muddy Waters Research. (2020, January 31). *MuddyWatersResearch @ muddywatersre*. Retrieved June 19, 2023, from Twitter: https://twitter.com/muddywatersre/status/1223274746017722371

National Committee On Corporate Governance. (n.d.). *The 8 Corporate Governance Principles*. Retrieved 2023 July, from National Committee On Corporate Governance: https://nccg.mu/8-corporate-governance-principles

Nwogugu, M. I. (2019). *Complex Systems*. Multi-Sided Incentives and Risk Perception in Companies.

Peng, Z., Yang, Y., & Wu, R. (2022, June). The Luckin Coffee scandal and short selling attacks. *Journal of Behavioral and Experimental Finance*, *34*, 34. doi:10.1016/j.jbef.2022.100629

Penga, Z., & Yang, Y. (2020, November 13). A Ripple in the Muddy Waters: The Luckin Coffee Scandal and Short Selling Attacks. *SSRN*.

Peregrine, M. W. (2021, December 20). *The Lasting, Positive Impact of Sarbanes-Oxley*. Retrieved June 18, 2023, from Harvard Law School Forum on Corporate Governance: https://corpgov.law.harvard.edu/2021/12/20/the-lasting-positive-impact-of-sarbanes-oxley/

Securities and Exchange Commission vs Luckin Coffee, Inc., 1:20-cv-10631 (United States District Court Southern District of New York December 16, 2020).

Shan, Y. G., & Round, D. K. (2012). China's Corporate Governance: Emerging Issues and Problems. *Modern Asian Studies*, *46*(5), 1316–1344. doi:10.1017/S0026749X1200008X

Shicong, D. (2020, July 16). *Auditor EY Denies Liability for Luckin Coffee's Financial Scandal*. Retrieved July 22, 2023, from Yicai Global: https://www.yicaiglobal.com/news/auditor-ey-denies-liability-for-luckin-coffee-financial-scandal

Shicong, D. (2020, April 27). *China Sends Team to Luckin Coffee to Probe Accounting Fraud*. (P. Thomas, Editor) Retrieved July 24, 2023, from Yicai Global: https://www.yicaiglobal.com/news/china-sends-team-to-luckin-coffee-to-probe-accounting-fraud

Sprigg, H. R. (n.d.). *The Importance of Corporate Governance*. Retrieved may 27, 2023, from SpriggHR: https://sprigghr.com/blog/board-management/the-importance-of-corporate-governance/

Stevenson, A., & Wong, E. (2020, April 30). *Chinese Coffee Chain's Scandal Renews U.S. Calls for Oversight*. Retrieved June 17, 2023, from The New York Times: https://www.nytimes.com/2020/04/30/business/luckin-coffee-china-fraud-wall-street.html

Suzuki, K. (n.d.). *Japan exercises US-style control*. Retrieved June 20, 2023, from Mori Hamada & Matsumoto Japan: https://www.mhmjapan.com/content/files/00014813/20071019suzuki.pdf

University of Lincoln. (2022, June 16). *What are the Core Principles of Corporate Governance?* Retrieved July 21, 2023, from University of Lincoln: https://online.lincoln.ac.uk/what-are-the-core-principles-of-corporate-governance/

Wang, J. (2020, May 13). *Fall From Grace: Luckin Coffee's Former Billionaire CEO Fired Amid Fraud Scandal.* Retrieved July 12, 2023, from Forbes: https://www.forbes.com/sites/jenniferwang/2020/05/13/fall-from-grace-luckin-coffees-former-billionaire-ceo-fired-amid-fraud-scandal/

Xi, C., & Huang, Y. (2021, July 8). *Are US-Listed Chinese Firms a Minefield? A Board Perspective.* Retrieved July 19, 2023, from Oxford Business Law Blog: https://blogs.law.ox.ac.uk/business-law-blog/blog/2021/07/are-us-listed-chinese-firms-minefield-board-perspective

Yang, J. (2020, July 16). *Ernst & Young Says It Isn't Responsible for Luckin Coffee's Accounting Misconduct.* Retrieved July 22, 2023, from Wall Street Journal: https://www.wsj.com/articles/ernst-young-says-it-isnt-responsible-for-luckin-coffees-accounting-misconduct-11594909084

ENDNOTES

1. C-SOX - Canadian equivalent of Sarbanes–Oxley Act, Financial Security Law of France ("Loi sur la Sécurité Financière") - 2003 French equivalent of Sarbanes–Oxley Act, J-SOX - 2006 Japanese equivalent of Sarbanes–Oxley Act and TC-SOX 11 Turkish equivalent of Sarbanes–Oxley Act.
2. The scandal became one of the factors used to promote the bill title the Ensuring Quality Information and Transparency for Abroad-Based Listings on our Exchanges Act (EQUITABLE Act).
3. The Public Company Accounting Oversight Board (PCAOB) which was created by congress for public companies in the Sarbanes-Oxley Act of 2002 (P.L. 107- 204).
4. the Rules on Strengthening the Confidentiality and Archives Administration of Overseas Securities Offering and Listing by Domestic Enterprises (Regulation 29 (2009), issued by the CSRC on October 20, 2009. This rule has been superseded by the revised Provisions on Strengthening Confidentiality and Archives Administration of Overseas Securities Offering and Listing by Domestic Companies (Regulation 44 (2023)). The Provisions contain the rules that companies must follow if their overseas listing requires the disclosure of state secrets or information jeopardising national security or public interest. Where overseas authorities conduct inspections of a domestic company, the Provisions provide that such inspections will be enabled by a "cross-border regulatory cooperation mechanism.

5 The change was made in paragraph 4, Article 2 of the Securities Law of the People's Republic of China that was amended on March 1, 2020.

6 In China, companies that produce false accounting reports and those who instruct them to do so will face charges if their misconduct constitutes a crime.

Chapter 5
Ayondo Ltd. Corporate Governance Issues of First FinTech Company Listed on the Catalist Board of Singapore Exchange

Paul N. C. Tiong
https://orcid.org/0000-0003-3569-4922
Coventry University, UK

EXECUTIVE SUMMARY

Ayondo Ltd. (Ayondo) (now known as RSQ Technology Ventures GmbH) was the first financial technology (fintech) company to be listed on the Catalist Board of the Singapore Exchange (SGX) on 23 March, 2018. However, the company was suspended from trading on 1 February, 2019, less than a year after listing. This case highlights corporate governance issues related to Ayondo, and also, fintech companies in general, in the context of Singapore. Examples of issues discussed are the roles of (a) board of directors; (b) sponsor in listing; (c) auditors; (d) regulatory bodies; (e) investors. These issues have ramifications for stakeholders. This case also includes lessons gleaned from the corporate governance issues and some actionable recommendations. This case study covers only the corporate governance issues of Ayondo in the period leading up to its listing and shortly thereafter. It does not include other ongoing issues subsequent to the listing.

DOI: 10.4018/978-1-6684-9867-5.ch005

INTRODUCTION TO AYONDO

Ayondo was founded in 2008 in Frankfurt, Germany by Thomas Winkler (Chairman) and Robert Lempka (Chief Executive Officer) (CEO). The substantial shareholders of the company were Luminor Capital Pte. Ltd. (Luminor Capital), a private equity group in Singapore, which held a 19.85% stake in the company; and Thomas Winker, who owned 5.66% (Pillai, 2019b).

The company provides a brokerage platform for users to conduct social trading to optimise their returns on investment, by copying the trades of top traders on the platform (Hans, 2018). This social trading platform has won many national and international awards, with more than 250,000 users from over 100 countries using it (RSQ Technology Ventures GmbH, 2023).

Ayondo's brokerage platform is a fintech disruptor of traditional online brokerage. It leverages on the emerging trend of social trading. "Social trading" enables users to conduct trades by replicating the portfolios of top traders, on a real time basis. The trades are transacted on Ayondo's WeTrade platform. Users could also trade independently, i.e., "self directed" trading, by transacting on the company's TradeHub platform. All the products offered to users are contracts for differences (CFD). They include stock indices, foreign currency, commodities, equities, fixed income, ETFs and cryptocurrencies (Stocksbnb, 2018).

The company earns revenue from CFD spreads. When a customer transacts, Ayondo will take one of the following positions: (a) hedge out the position to other financial institutions to minimise the financial risks but earns a smaller spread; (b) keep the position and bear the financial risks; (c) balance off the position with a trade on the opposite side. Besides revenue from CFD spreads, Ayondo also earns financing income from interest charged on margins that customers utilise to purchase the CFD products (Stocksbnb, 2018).

Ayondo became the first fintech company to be listed on the SGX in 2018. The company decided to get listed in Singapore because of the country's good reputation. Moreover, SGX was developing the fintech sector at the time and Ayondo wanted to benefit from the support provided (Leow, 2018b).

For the financial year ended 31 December, 2018, the board of directors of Ayondo comprised of Thomas Winkler (Non-Executive Chairman), Foo Fatt Kah (Non-Executive Director), Foong Daw Ching (Lead Independent Director), Chan Heng Toong (Independent Director) and Lam Shiao Ning (Independent Director) (Ayondo Ltd, 2018a). At the time of listing in March 2018, members of the management team were Robert Lempka (Executive Director and CEO), Rick Fulton (Chief Financial Officer) (CFO), Edward Drake (Chief Operating Officer) (COO), Sarah Brylewski (Chief Marketing Officer) (CMO), Angela Sadler (Chief Talent Officer and General Counsel) (CTO/GC) and Raza Perez (Chief Product Officer) (CPO) (Ayondo Ltd, 2018c).

As at 31 December, 2018, Ayondo's registered office was at 20 Collyer Quay #01-02, Singapore 049319. However, the company's principal place of business was at 10th Floor, Linen Court, 10 East Road, London N1 6AD, United Kingdom (Ayondo Ltd, 2018a). The company also had other offices in Germany, Spain and Switzerland (Ayondo Ltd, 2018c).

BIOGRAPHY OF THE DIRECTORS OF AYONDO

On listing date, Ayondo provided the biography of the directors of the company in its offer document (Ayondo Ltd, 2018c), extracts of which, are summarised as follows (pp. 191-193):

Thomas Winkler is the Executive Chairman and the co-founder of the Group. Thomas Winkler has more than 24 years of working experience in the European banking, investment and securities trading industries. He is responsible for the formulation of the Group's strategic business directions and managing the Group's external relationship with key shareholders and investors. He is also responsible for overseeing the implementation of the business goals and objectives of the Group, and identifying new strategic business opportunities and directions to augment existing operations. He completed his commercial apprenticeship at Swiss Bank Corporation in 1983 and subsequently attended one year at the Höhere Wirtschafts- und Verwaltungsschule (HWV), a Swiss economic school in Zurich in 1989.

Robert Lempka is the Executive Director and CEO and co-founder of the Group. Robert Lempka has more than 24 years of working experience in the European banking, investment and securities trading industries. Robert Lempka graduated from University of Trier, Germany in September 1993 with a Master of Science. He also attended Dublin City University, Ireland for nine months on scholarship and another six months of scientific visit in University of California, USA.

Foo Fatt Kah is the Non-Executive Director. Foo Fatt Kah has more than 25 years of experience in investment banking, venture capital and private equity investments. He is also the managing director and co-founder of Luminor Capital Pte. Ltd., a private equity fund management firm based in Singapore since 2008. Foo Fatt Kah obtained his degree in Medicine from Queen's University, UK in 1984 and subsequently obtained his Masters in Business Administration from Queen's University in 1987.

Foong Daw Ching is the Lead Independent Director. Foong Daw Ching has more than 30 years of audit experience. Foong Daw Ching is also an independent director of Starland Holdings Limited, Travelite Holdings Ltd. and Suntar Eco-City Limited.

Foong Daw Ching was awarded the Public Service Medal (Pingat Bakti Masyarakat) by the President of Singapore in 2003 and a Merit Service Award by the Institute of Certified Public Accountants of Singapore in 2000. He is a Fellow of the Institute of Chartered Accountant in England and Wales, a Fellow of the Institute of Singapore Chartered Accountants (formerly known as Institute of Certified Public Accountants in Singapore), and a Fellow member of CPA, Australia.

Chan Heng Toong is the Independent Director. Chan Heng Toong has more than 17 years of experience in investment banking. He obtained a Bachelor of Engineering (Honours) from the University of Singapore in 1973 and Masters of Business Administration (Finance) from the University of British Columbia in Canada in 1979.

Lam Shiao Ning is the Independent Director. She has more than 20 years of experience as a corporate lawyer in Singapore. Lam Shiao Ning obtained a Bachelor of Laws (Honours) from the University of Hull, United Kingdom in 1995 and was called to the bar of England and Wales in July 1996. She was admitted as an advocate and solicitor of the Supreme Court of Singapore in March 1998. Lam Shiao Ning is a member of The Law Society of Singapore, the Singapore Academy of Law and the Inquiry Panel of the Law Society of Singapore. She also holds a Diploma in Financial Management from the Association of Chartered Certified Accountants, United Kingdom. Lam Shiao Ning is a senior teaching fellow at the Singapore Institute of Legal Education and an adjunct lecturer at the Singapore Management University's law faculty.

Corporate Governance Specifics

Attempted Listing on SGX via Reverse Takeover

On 20 June, 2016, Starland Holdings Limited (Starland) (now known as Luminor Financial Holdings Limited) (Luminor Financial) announced that it entered into an agreement with Ayondo to purchase a 100% stake in the company for S$157.5 million (P. C. Lee, 2016). The company said that this would provide it with the opportunity to diversify into the fintech business. Starland is a Singapore property developer of residential and commercial properties in the Peoples' Republic of China and in Singapore (Luminor Financial Holdings Limited, 2023). It was a subsidiary of GRP Limited (GRP) (with an 82.91% stake), an industrial products company, listed on the Mainboard of SGX. Upon the completion of the acquisition of Ayondo by Starland, it would also result in a reverse takeover of Starland by Ayondo. This enabled Ayondo to get listed on the SGX via an alternative pathway instead of the traditional route by an initial public offering (IPO), given the volatility of the financial markets at that time and the higher listing costs of an IPO (Ayondo Ltd, 2016). After the reverse takeover, the consolidated group had a market capitalisation of S$210 million with Ayondo shareholders owning 75% of the group. A listing on the SGX allowed Ayondo to access funds from the capital market which the company hoped to use to accelerate the growth of its business by investing in enhanced mobile technology. It acquired TradeHero, a stockmarket simulation app, in November, 2016.

Failed Reverse Takeover

On 25 September, 2017, Starland announced that the conditions precedent for the reverse takeover deal with Ayondo had not been fulfilled or waived by the long-stop date on 23 September, 2017. Consequently, the reverse takeover of Starland by Ayondo failed to materialise (J. Lee, 2017).

Due to the failed reverse takeover, Starland decided not to convert a S$1.027 million loan into new ordinary Ayondo shares. Instead, the company decided that the redeemable convertible loan and the accrued interest be repaid in cash (Leow, 2018c).

Subsequent Listing via an IPO

On 16 March, 2018, Ayondo announced that it had registered offer documents for listing on the Catalist Board of SGX, via an IPO. UOB Kay Hian was appointed as the Sponsor of the IPO. The offer price for the shares was S$0.26 per share. 80.77 million shares were available for the IPO, of which, 8.9 million shares were offered to the public while the remaining shares were for private placement. Ayondo expected to raise about S$18.5 million from the IPO. The company intended to use around half of this amount for loan repayment. S$5.25 million would be spent on marketing and another S$2.1 million on platform enhancement. The remaining S$2.6 million would be used as general working capital (Leow, 2018b).

Ayondo's IPO was fully subscribed at about 1.3 times. 571 applicants were successful in subscribing the public shares. As for the placement shares, 270 placees were successful. Kwan Chee Seng, the founder and executive director of Luminor Capital, took up another 3.75 million placement shares, which increased his stake in Ayondo to 21.6% (Leow, 2018a). Luminor Capital had been Ayondo's largest shareholder since 2014 (Mui, 2018).

Ayondo made its debut on the SGX on 26 March, 2018. Its shares opened at 24 cents each, which was, below the IPO price of 26 cents (Mui, 2018).

Ownership After Listing

After Ayondo was listed on SGX, the directors and management team of the company would have held the following stakes (the total of direct interest and deemed interest) in the company: Thomas Winkler (7.1%), Foo Fatt Kah (19.2%), Foong Daw Ching (0.1%), Chan Heng Toong (0.1%), Lam Shiao Ning (0.1%), Robert Lempka (6.4%), Rick Fulton (0.7%), Edward Drake (0.7%), Sarah Brylewski (1.1%), Angela Sadler (0.4%) and Raza Perez (0.6%). The controlling shareholders (other than directors) and their associates were: Luminor Pacific Fund 1 Ltd. (10.1%) and Luminor Pacific Fund 2 Ltd. (7.9%) (Luminor Funds), Kwan Chee Seng (21.6%), Kwan Yu Wen (daughter of Kwan Chee Seng) (18.0%), GRP (1.2%) and Starland (1.2%) (Ayondo Ltd, 2018c).

With Kwan Chee Seng and his daughter, Kwan Yu Wen, being controlling shareholders of the company, there were questions on whether the board of directors of the company could exercise independence and make decisions in the best interests of the company.

At the time of listing, Kwan Chee Seng was a director and shareholder of Luminor Capital, the company that managed the Luminor Funds. By virtue of Section 4 of the Securities and Futures Act 2001 (Securities and Futures Act), he was deemed to have an interest in the shares of the company held by Luminor Funds. Similarly, by virtue of Section 7 of the Companies Act 1967 (Companies Act), Kwan Chee Seng was deemed to be interested in all the shares held by GRP and Starland: He had a 32.5% shareholding interest in GRP, which owned 100% of GRP Land Pte. Ltd. (GRP Land) which, in turn, owned 100% of GRP Chongqing Land Pte. Ltd. (GRP Chongqing Land) which, in turn, owned 83.2% of Starland (Ayondo Ltd, 2018c).

Appointment of Peter Moe as an Independent Director of GRP by Kwan Chee Seng

On 3 September, 2013, Peter Moe was appointed as an independent director of GRP (Chua, 2013). He was appointed by Kwan Chee Seng. SGX had made a query to GRP (where Kwan Chee Seng was a substantial shareholder) on the suitability of Peter Moe as a director. He was previously disqualified from acting as a director due to a criminal conviction for breach of duties as a director under the Companies Act and was fined the maximum amount of $5,000. Furthermore, there were civil proceedings against him relating to a complaint to the Law Society for misrepresentation and misuse of position, which were later withdrawn after mediation. On 9 September, 2013, GRP issued a response to SGX. GRP said that its board of directors and nominating committee (NC) were not concerned about Peter Moe's criminal conviction and civil proceedings. They were of the view that the conviction did not involve "moral turpitude" and that it "will make Mr Moe a more experienced person" (Mak, 2013). Mak (2013) opines that this view lowers the bar for qualifying as a director by considering legal actions as a director as a "positive attribute." He suggested for SGX to query GRP further to determine whether Peter Moe was nominated by a substantial shareholder(s).

Resignation of Robert Lempka

After listing, on 9 May, 2018, Ayondo released its audited financial statements for the year ended 31, December, 2017. The company announced a loss for the year net of tax of CHF (Swiss francs) 9.760 million, which was less than the loss in 2016 of CHF10.434 million, by 6.5% (Ayondo Ltd, 2018b). On the same day, Ayondo also released its unaudited financial statements for the first quarter ended 31 March, 2018. The company reported a loss for the period net of tax of CHF6.306 million, which was worse than the loss for the same quarter in 2017 of CHF2.795 million, a decrease by 125.6% (Ayondo Ltd, 2018d). On 23 January, 2019, Ayondo announced the resignation of Robert Lempka as Executive Director and CEO of the company, which was less than a year after he was appointed (Singapore Exchange Limited, 2019a). On 17 April, 2019, Ayondo announced that it had received a letter of demand from Robert Lempka, in relation to his resignation, of S$165,800 (Ayondo Ltd, 2019b).

Disagreements Over the Calculation of the Common Equity Tier 1 (CET1) Ratio of Ayondo Markets Limited

In 2019, Ayondo owned 99.97% of Ayondo Holding AG (Ayondo Holding), which owned 99.91% of Sycap Group (UK) Limited (Sycap Group) which, in turn, owned 100% of Ayondo Markets Limited (Ayondo Markets) (Ayondo Ltd, 2019d). Ayondo Markets was regulated by the Financial Conduct Authority (FCA) in the United Kingdom (UK). The FCA required Ayondo Markets to maintain a prescribed CET1 ratio, in line with The Basel Framework (Basel Committee on Banking Supervision, 2023).

In January 2019, one of Ayondo Group's employees provided feedback on the calculation of the CET1 ratio. Subsequently, KPMG LLP (KPMG) in the UK was engaged to assess whether Ayondo Markets' accounting and regulatory treatment of certain items in the calculation of its CET1 ratio was appropriate and in compliance with the International Financial Reporting Standards (IFRS) and FRS 102, the financial reporting standard applicable in the UK and Republic of Ireland (FRS 102). The statutory auditors of Ayondo Markets' financial statements were Ernst & Young LLP (EY), who issued an unqualified opinion on them. However, KPMG disagreed with Ayondo Markets' treatment of two items, namely, technology software expenditures and inter-company balances and transactions. If KPMG's views were adopted instead, there would be a negative impact on the CET1 ratio. The directors of Ayondo Markets decided not to adopt KPMG's views. They reasoned that EY had opined that the company's financial statements gave a true and fair view of the state of the company's affairs. In addition, the directors said that the CET1 ratio had been submitted to the FCA, like what it had done in the past, for more than five years, and the FCA did not raise any concerns about the company's calculation of the ratio (Ayondo Ltd, 2019e).

Applications for Extension to Release the Financial Statements for 2018 and 2019

Ayondo announced on 1 March, 2019 that it had applied to the Singapore Exchange Securities Trading Limited (SGX-ST) for an extension of time by one month to (1) release the company's unaudited financial statements for the year ended 31 December, 2018 (FY2018); (2) hold annual general meeting (AGM) for FY2018; (3) release the company's unaudited financial statements for the quarter ended 31 March, 2019 (1Q2019). The reason given was the expending of resources and personnel to respond to queries from the FCA relating to the compliance with regulatory requirements (Mak, 2019).

On 6 March, 2019, Ayondo submitted an application to the Accounting and Corporate Regulatory Authority (ACRA) for an extension of time of 60 days to convene the AGM for FY2018; that is, by 29 June, 2019 (Ayondo Ltd, 2019a). ACRA approved Ayondo's application on 3 April, 2019 (Ayondo Ltd, 2019c).

On 29 March, 2019, Ayondo made an application for a further extension of time by an additional month (i.e., two months altogether) to (1) release the company's unaudited financial statements for FY2018 (by 1 May, 2019); (2) hold AGM for FY2018 (by 30 June, 2019); (3) release the company's unaudited financial statements for 1Q2019 (by 15 July, 2019). The grounds for the request for a further extension of time were (1) the auditors, EY, needed more time to audit the financial statements for FY2018 due to the complexity of the outstanding audit matters; (2) as a result of (1), the auditors' report would be delayed, and therefore, the AGM for FY2018 would have to be postponed; (3) again, due to (1), the preparation of the financial statements of 1Q2019 would also be delayed, and so, the deadline for them would need to be extended too (Ayondo Ltd, 2019a). SGX-ST approved Ayondo's application for a further extension of time on 18 April, 2019 (Lam, 2019).

Sale of Ayondo Markets to BUX Holding B.V.

On 8 May, 2019, Ayondo announced that it had entered into an agreement to sell Ayondo Markets to its key partner, BUX Holding B.V. (BUX), a fintech company registered in the Netherlands, for £5.7 million. The sale would be carried out by the disposal of Sycap Group's 100% stake in Ayondo Markets to BUX. Most of the sale proceeds would be used to pay the £5.9 million debt owed by Ayondo and its three units to Ayondo Markets, as at 31 December, 2018. Ayondo said the rationale for the sale was that it faced working capital deficiency as a result of continued losses. The losses were mainly due to regulatory changes on products imposed by European and UK regulators and unfavourable trading conditions in the CFD markets in 2018 (V. Tay, 2019). The sale would be subject to the approvals of regulatory authorities and shareholders (NS Banking Staff Writer, 2019).

Notification by SGXRegco to Put on Hold the Sale of Ayondo Markets

Singapore Exchange Regulation Pte Ltd (SGXRegco), on 15 March, 2019, informed Ayondo to put on hold the sale of Ayondo Markets to BUX until the FCA had clarified Ayondo Markets' compliance with capital adequacy requirements, and also, after Ayondo had ascertained its financial situation. More specifically, SGXRegco required the following conditions to be met before the sale could proceed: (a) confirmation from FCA on Ayondo Markets' compliance with CET1 requirements and the amount of shortfall in capital; (b) completion and release of the audited financial statements for FY2018; (c) SGXRegco's clearance of the circular relating to the sale before it could be dispatched to shareholders to get their approval of the sale at an Extraordinary General Meeting; (d) shareholders' approval of the sale; (e) regulatory approvals, including from FCA and SGX. Additionally, SGXRegco required Ayondo to disclose the following in its circular to the shareholders: (a) rationale of the sale of Ayondo Markets and justifications on why it was in the best interests of the Group and shareholders; (b) explanation of the developments of the Group since listing in March 2018 which led to the sale; (c) the Group's business plans and future directions (Singapore Exchange Regulation Pte Ltd, 2019). On 8 May, 2019, Ayondo announced the confirmation that Ayondo Markets' CET1 ratios had been calculated in line with market practice and reported to the FCA quarterly in the past and noted that the FCA had not raised any concerns on the calculation of the ratio (V. Tay, 2019). Later, Ayondo managed to obtain the approval of shareholders to dispose off Ayondo Markets. On 6 June, 2019, the company announced the completion of the sale (Pillai, 2019a).

Resignations From the Leadership Team

Sean Downey was appointed as CFO of Ayondo on 20 July, 2018. He resigned on 15 February, 2019. He left the company because of differences with management over the sale of Ayondo Markets. Moreover, he had a difference of opinion relating to the required change of Ayondo Markets' calculation of the CET1 ratio to the method suggested by KPMG and the timing for that change. He also expressed "discontent with treatment and (the) working relationship" at the company (Pillai, 2019a).

After the resignation of Robert Lempka, Richard Mark Street was appointed as the interim CEO. On 27 June, 2019, Ayondo announced his resignation to "pursue other career opportunities and for personal reasons" (Jye, 2019).

On 28 June, 2019, Ayondo announced the retirement of Chan Heng Toon as an independent director "due to personal time commitment" (Singapore Exchange Limited, 2019b). On the same day, Mita Natarajan (Chief Business Development Officer) and Raza Perez (CPO) also resigned from the company. The reasons for their departure could not be ascertained (H. M. Tay, 2019).

Lessons Gleaned From Corporate Governance Issues

The corporate governance issues faced by Ayondo provide important lessons for various stakeholders; including, companies, regulatory bodies, investors, academics/researchers, corporate governance consultants and students. The ramifications of the issues on stakeholders are discussed further in the sub-sections below.

Repercussions for Companies

After Ayondo's listing, Kwan Chee Seng and his daughter, Kwan Yu Wen, held 21.6% and 18.0% stakes in the company, respectively. Being the controlling shareholders of the company, there were concerns on whether the board of directors could exercise independence and make decisions in the best interests of the company. One view is that, as professionals, the directors will exercise professional judgement in their decisions to ensure that the interests of the company are protected. The other view is that the controlling shareholders could interfere or be perceived to interfere with the decisions of the board of directors, and therefore, the board cannot exercise all decisions in the best interests of the company. In other words, some decisions made by the board may be in the interests of the controlling shareholders rather than the company. To allay concerns of board independence, the best practice for companies is to disclose the following information in the annual report, in compliance with SGX-ST's Rules (Singapore Exchange Limited, 2023): (a) identification of the director it considers to be independent; (b) at least one-third of the board is made up of independent directors; (c) the Chairman is an independent director, is also not the CEO, is not part of the management team and the Chairman and CEO are not immediate family members and that they do not have close family ties with each other.

In 2013, Peter Moe, who had a criminal conviction and civil proceedings against him, was appointed as an independent director of GRP by Kwan Chee Seng, a substantial shareholder of GRP. SGX had queried GRP on the suitability of Peter Moe as a director. GRP had responded that its board of directors and NC were not concerned about the legal actions against him. SGX's appointment template requires companies to disclose their "search and nomination process." GRP did not do so in its original announcement and in its response to SQX (Mak, 2013). The best practice would be for GRP to fully disclose how Peter Moe was appointed as a director.

Repercussions for Regulatory Bodies

In the above discussion, it was noted that, after Ayondo had listed, Kwan Chee Seng and his daughter, Kwan Yu Wen, held substantial stakes in the company, and therefore, were controlling shareholders of the company. Their large ownership of the company raised questions on the ability of the board of directors to exercise independent judgement and make decisions that are in the best interests of the company. The concerns were that the father and daughter could interfere or be perceived to interfere with the decisions of the board of directors. To mitigate these concerns, SGX should ensure that companies provide the information on board independence that is required to be reported by SGX-ST's Rules, as listed above, in the annual reports and that these requirements are complied with.

As described above, Peter Moe was appointed as an independent director of GRP by Kwan Chee Seng, a substantial shareholder of the company, despite having a criminal conviction and civil proceedings against him. Although, SQX had queried GRP on the suitability of Peter Moe as a director, Mak (2013) suggested that SGX queried GRP further to establish whether Peter Moe was nominated as a director by a substantial shareholder(s).

Repercussions for Investors

It was highlighted above that Ayondo's brokerage platform is a fintech disruptor of traditional online brokerage because it leverages on the emerging trend of social trading, which enables users to conduct trades by replicating the portfolios of top traders on a real time basis. The company earns revenue from CFD spreads and from interest charged on margins that customers utilise to purchase the CFD products. When investors make decisions on where to invest, they should carefully consider the investment risks. Companies listed on the SGX Catalist Board have higher investment risks compared to companies listed on the Mainboard. There are two primary reasons: (a) companies may list on the Catalist Board without a track record of profitability; (b) there is no assurance that there will be a liquid market for trading the shares after listing. If investors are not careful, they could lose all or part of their investments. When in doubt, investors should consult their legal, financial, tax or other professional adviser(s).

As pointed out above, one of the conditions set by SGXRegco for the sale of Ayondo Markets to BUX was that Ayondo must seek the approval of its shareholders first before the sale could go ahead. SGXRegco required Ayondo to disclose the following in its circular to the shareholders relating to the sale: (a) rationale and justifications for the sale; (b) explanation of developments which led to the sale; (c) its business plans and future directions. This requirement is in line with Principle 11 of the Code of Corporate Governance (Monetary Authority of Singapore, 2018), which recommends that companies give all their shareholders "a balanced and understandable assessment of its performance, position and prospects" so that they can make informed decisions. Thus, shareholders should be aware of their right to information that is necessary for them to assess the company.

Repercussions for Academics/Researchers

Academics and researchers could conduct further research on the factors affecting corporate governance in Asia and offer some recommendations for improvement. For example, in Singapore, researchers could find out answers to the following questions: (a) why did some of the companies listed on the SGX collapsed?; (b) how could SGX and sponsors scrutinise companies deeper before they are allowed to list?; (c) what more could auditors do to ensure that financial statements show a true and fair view of the company's affairs?; (d) who should be held accountable for errors, omissions and unethical conduct?.

Repercussions for Corporate Governance Consultants

Ayondo opted to get listed on the Catalist Board of the SGX via a reverse takeover of Starland rather than by way of the traditional IPO. The reasons for selecting this option as provided by the company were that the financial markets were volatile at the time of listing, and that, an IPO would have caused it to incur higher listing costs. Corporate governance consultants may advise companies that intend to get listed on SGX (or other capital markets in Asia or elsewhere) to consider the reverse takeover pathway instead of an IPO, if the market was volatile and/or the company would like to reduce the costs of listing. This route will reduce the risks of the company trading its shares at a market price that is lower than the IPO price and it also allows the company to take advantage of the lower listing costs.

Repercussions for Students

It is essential for students to learn about corporate governance, including the unique issues and challenges that businesses face in Asia due to the different cultures, laws and regulations, listing rules, codes of corporate governance and other requirements in different countries. Corporate governance becomes more complex when there are mergers and acquisitions of companies in different countries. Hence, it is important for students to understand the international dimension of corporate governance.

Actionable Recommendations

As a result of the lessons learned from the corporate governance issues discussed above, some recommendations that could be actioned include (a) enhancing board supervision; (b) fostering transparency and accountability; (c) encouraging ethical conduct/business practices within companies. These are discussed further below.

Enhancing Board Supervision

SGX should ensure that when companies fill out the appointment template, they disclose their "search and nomination process" fully so that it is clear how a director was appointed. If a company did not disclose the process fully, SGX should query the company further to ensure that a director, particularly, one that has legal actions against him, was not nominated by a substantial shareholder(s).

Fostering Transparency and Accountability

When a company appoints a director, it should be completely transparent about its "search and nomination process" to the SGX and stakeholders of the company. They should be clear that a director, especially a person with legal actions against him, was not nominated by a substantial shareholder(s).

Encouraging Ethical Conduct/Business Practices Within Companies

Ayondo permitted one of the employees in January 2019 to provide feedback on the calculation of the CET1 ratio. The company should continue to encourage employees to provide feedback and suggestions, whether good or bad, and on all aspects of the business so that improvements can be made. Ideally, the company should not reprimand employees for giving negative and unfavourable comments. The company should have a whistleblowing policy and clearly communicate to its employees the procedures for raising any concerns safely.

CONCLUSION

Ayondo Ltd was the first fintech company to be listed on the Catalist Board of the SGX. The company was a fintech disruptor of traditional online brokerage by leveraging on the emerging trend of social trading. Its brokerage platform won many national and international awards. There were many users from all over the world. However, Ayondo was suspended from trading less than a year after listing. This case reveals that an innovative business model is not sufficient for fintech companies to succeed. A high level of corporate governance is also essential. To achieve this, the involvement of all stakeholders is paramount. The board of directors, sponsors in listing, auditors, regulatory bodies, investors and corporate governance consultants have extremely important roles to play. It is vital for academics and researchers to continue their research on corporate governance issues in Singapore, and in Asia in general, so that corporate governance can be improved further. It is also crucial for students to learn and understand the scope and complexities of corporate governance around the world so that they are better prepared for the workplace.

DISCUSSION QUESTIONS

1. A fintech company wish to get listed on the Singapore Exchange. Should it opt to get listed via a reverse takeover or an initial public offering (IPO)? Why?
2. After Ayondo's listing, Kwan Chee Seng and his daughter, Kwan Yu Wen, held 21.6% and 18.0% stakes in the company, respectively; and so, were controlling shareholders of the company. Could the board of directors exercise independence and make decisions in the best interests of the company?
3. Peter Moe had a criminal conviction and civil proceedings against him. However, Kwan Chee Seng, a substantial shareholder of GRP, appointed him as an independent director of the company. Were GRP's board of directors and nominating committee (NC)'s objectivity influenced by Kwan Chee Seng? In what way(s)?
4. Why is it risky for investors to invest in companies going to list or are listed on the SGX Catalist Board? How can investors minimise their potential risks of losing their investments?
5. How could companies encourage ethical conduct/business practices?

6. When Ayondo Markets Limited was sold to BUX Holding B.V., the sale was subject to the approvals of regulatory authorities and shareholders. Was it necessary to obtain the approval of shareholders? Why?
7. Is there a potential conflict of interest between SGX's role as a regulatory body and its commercial role to develop the fintech sector? Why?

REFERENCES

Ayondo Ltd. (2016). *FinTech and Social Trading Pioneer ayondo aims for Singapore listing* [Press release]. Retrieved from https://links.sgx.com/FileOpen/Ayondo_PressRelease_20160413_Final.ashx?App=ArchiveAnnouncement&FileID=398927&AnncID=03JWW0J6EA8WSLHO

Ayondo Ltd. (2018a). *Annual Report 2018*. Retrieved from https://links.sgx.com/FileOpen/ayondo_Annual%20Report%20FY2018.ashx?App=Announcement&FileID=563273

Ayondo Ltd. (2018b). *Audited Financial Statements for the Financial Year Ended 31 December 2017*. Retrieved from https://links.sgx.com/FileOpen/ayondo_FY2017%20results%20_090518.ashx?App=Announcement&FileID=504781

Ayondo Ltd. (2018c). *Offer document dated 15 March 2018* [Press release]. Retrieved from https://boersengefluester.de/wp-content/uploads/assets/annuals/2016/A2JG3A.pdf

Ayondo Ltd. (2018d). *Unaudited Financial Statements for the First Quarter ended 31 March 2018*. Retrieved from https://links.sgx.com/FileOpen/ayondo_1Q2018%20results_090518.ashx?App=Announcement&FileID=504782

Ayondo Ltd. (2019a). *Application to the Singapore Exchange Securities Trading Limited for further extensions of time to (I) Release the company's unaudited financial statements for the financial year ended 31 December 2019 ("FY2018"), (II) Hold Annual General Meeting ("AGM") for FY2018, and (III) Release the company's unaudited financial statements for financial period ended 31 March 2019 ("1Q2019")* [Press release]. Retrieved from https://links.sgx.com/FileOpen/ayondo%20-%20Further%20Extension%20of%20Time%20for%20FS%20and%20AGM_Final_290319.ashx?App=Announcement&FileID=549439

Ayondo Ltd. (2019b). *Receipt of Letter of Demand* [Press release]. Retrieved from https://links.sgx.com/FileOpen/ayondo_Receipt%20of%20Letter%20of%20Demand_Final_170419.ashx?App=Announcement&FileID=553766

Ayondo Ltd. (2019c). *Results of application to the Accounting and Corporate Regulatory Authority ("ACRA") for extension of time to hold Annual General Meeting ("AGM") for the financial year ended 31 December 2018 ("FY2018")* [Press release]. Retrieved from https://links.sgx.com/FileOpen/ayondo-%20Results%20of%20ACRA%20Application%20for%20EOT_Final_030419.ashx?App=Announcement&FileID=550163

Ayondo Ltd. (2019d). *Sale And Purchase Agreement In Relation To The Disposal Of The Entire Issued Shares Of Ayondo Markets Limited* [Press release]. Retrieved from https://links.sgx.com/FileOpen/ayondo_Announcement%20on%20the%20BUX%20SPA_Final_080519.ashx?App=Announcement&FileID=558337

Ayondo Ltd. (2019e). *Update pursuant to rule 703(1) of Section B: Rules of Catalist of the Listing Manual of the SGX-ST: A. Update on Ayondo Markets Limited B. Heads of Terms with BUX Holding B.V.* [Press release]. Retrieved from https://links.sgx.com/FileOpen/ayondo%20-%20Update%20Announcement_Final_140219.ashx?App=Announcement&FileID=543645

Banking Staff Writer, N. S. (2019). Ayondo explores sale of UK subsidiary to Dutch fintech BUX. *NS Banking*. Retrieved from https://www.nsbanking.com/news/ayondo-markets-sale-bux/

Basel Committee on Banking Supervision. (2023). *The Basel Framework*. Bank for International Settlements.

Chua, T. (2013). GRP appoints Peter Moe as director. *Singapore Business Review*. Retrieved from https://sbr.com.sg/manufacturing/people/grp-appoints-peter-moe-director

Hans, D. B. (2018). SGX to see first fintech listing on Catalist board with Ayondo. *Reuters*. Retrieved from https://news.finchcapital.com/post/102ernp/sgx-to-see-first-fintech-listing-on-catalist-board-with-ayondo

Jye, N. R. (2019). Ayondo interim CEO to quit after less than 6 months on the job. *The Straits Times*. Retrieved from https://www.straitstimes.com/business/companies-markets/ayondo-interim-ceo-to-quit-after-less-than-6-months-on-the-job

Lam, F. (2019). Ayondo gets statutory demand of payment for S$165,800; gets nod to delay FY2018 results, AGM. *The Business Times*. Retrieved from https://www.businesstimes.com.sg/companies-markets/ayondo-gets-statutory-demand-payment-s165800-gets-nod-delay-fy2018-results-agm

Lee, J. (2017). Starland's S$158m RTO with fintech firm Ayondo lapses. *The Business Times*. Retrieved from https://www.businesstimes.com.sg/companies-markets/starlands-s158m-rto-fintech-firm-ayondo-lapses

Lee, P. C. (2016). Fintech Ayondo to list on SGX through $158 mil reverse takeover of Starland. *The Edge Malaysia*. Retrieved from https://theedgemalaysia.com/article/fintech-ayondo-list-sgx-through-s158-mil-reverse-takeover-starland

Leow, A. (2018a). Ayondo's IPO sees public applications come in at four-and-half times the number of offer shares. *The Business Times*. Retrieved from https://www.businesstimes.com.sg/companies-markets/ayondos-ipo-sees-public-applications-come-four-and-half-times-number-offer-shares

Leow, A. (2018b). Fintech Ayondo registers offer documents for Catalist listing. *The Business Times*. Retrieved from https://www.businesstimes.com.sg/companies-markets/fintech-ayondo-registers-offer-documents-catalist-listing

Leow, A. (2018c). Starland decides not to convert S$1.03 million loan into Ayondo shares; will be repaid in cash after IPO. *The Business Times*. Retrieved from https://www.businesstimes.com.sg/companies-markets/starland-decides-not-convert-s103-million-loan-ayondo-shares-will-be-repaid-cash

Luminor Financial Holdings Limited. (2023). *About Us*. Retrieved from https://www.luminorfinancialholdings.com/aboutus

Mak, Y. T. (2013). *GRP should clarify board appointment*. Retrieved from https://governanceforstakeholders.com/2013/09/29/grp-should-clarify-board-appointment/#:~:text=SGX%20should%20query%20GRP%20further,by%20the%20board%20and%20NC

Mak, Y. T. (2019). *No sign of governance*. Retrieved from https://governanceforstakeholders.com/2019/03/03/no-sign-of-governance/

Mui, R. (2018). Ayondo, Singapore's 1st listed fintech firm, opens trading debut at 24 cents. *The Straits Times*. Retrieved from https://www.straitstimes.com/business/companies-markets/ayondo-opens-on-trading-debut-at-s024#:~:text=Home-,Ayondo%2C%20Singapore%27s%201st%20listed%20fintech%20firm%2C%20opens,trading%20debut%20at%2024%20cents&text=SINGAPORE%20%2D%20Global%20fintech%20group%20Ayondo,listed%20on%20the%20Singapore%20bourse

Pillai, S. (2019a). Ayondo CFO quits in under a year over 'differences with management'. *The Business Times*. Retrieved from https://www.businesstimes.com.sg/companies-markets/ayondo-cfo-quits-under-year-over-differences-management

Pillai, S. (2019b). Ayondo shareholders vote to dispose UK unit. *The Business Times*. Retrieved from https://www.businesstimes.com.sg/companies-markets/ayondo-shareholders-vote-dispose-uk-unit

RSQ Technology Ventures GmbH. (2023). *About Us*. Retrieved from https://ayondo.com/en/about-us

Singapore Exchange Limited. (2019a). *Ayondo Ltd - Change - Announcement of Cessation: Resignation of Executive Director and Chief Executive Officer*. Author.

Singapore Exchange Limited. (2019b). *Ayondo Ltd - Change - Announcement of Cessation: Retirement of Independent Director* [Press release]. Retrieved from https://links.sgx.com/1.0.0/corporate-announcements/QKOCQXS97KFR3FIN/a13d4038e33c996cad1268f40a24d7be11716a4e399bcb39b4e5264f9c337a60

Singapore Exchange Regulation Pte Ltd. (2019). *Ayondo Ltd - Notice of Compliance* [Press release]. Retrieved from https://links.sgx.com/FileOpen/Notice%20of%20Compliance-ayondo-16April2019.ashx?App=Announcement&FileID=553554

Stocksbnb. (2018). *Ayondo Ltd: The alternative asset management platform*. Retrieved from https://www.stocksbnb.com/reports/ayondo-ltd-the-alternative-asset%20-management-platform/

Tay, H. M. (2019). Fintech firm Ayondo stares at a spate of resignations from its top brass. *Deal Street Asia*. Retrieved from https://www.dealstreetasia.com/stories/ayondo-resignations-142505/

Tay, V. (2019). Ayondo inks deal to sell UK unit for £5.7m. *The Business Times*. Retrieved from https://www.businesstimes.com.sg/companies-markets/ayondo-inks-deal-sell-uk-unit-ps57m

Chapter 6
Nominee Directors and Performance Evidence From Indian State-Owned Enterprises

Archana Goel
Chitkara Business School, Chitkara University, Punjab, India

Kiran Mehta
Chitkara Business School, Chitkara University, Punjab, India

Renuka Sharma
https://orcid.org/0000-0002-6514-3411
Chitkara Business School, Chitkara University, Punjab, India

EXECUTIVE SUMMARY

The effectiveness of board characteristics on the financial organization's performance has been examined in several studies. Studies that looked into the characteristics of the boards of state-owned enterprises (SOEs) are scarce. Therefore, this chapter aims to scrutinize how nominee directors and Indian SOEs' perform. The findings consider that nominee directors raise the performance of the SOEs utilizing a variety of performance parameters and control variables. The research backs up agency theory. The conclusions have specific ramifications that the government and decision makers must address.

DOI: 10.4018/978-1-6684-9867-5.ch006

INTRODUCTION

The directors play a major part in resolving the agency issues between investors and managers. While the existing literature has examined the influence of board features that uphold the shareholders' interests by endorsing corporate strategies and optimising shareholders' value (Dalton et al.,1999); most of these researchers have primarily focused on the listed financial companies. Only a few studies have investigated the board characteristics in SOEs. This study concentrates on the board characteristics of Indian SOEs, especially the role of outside directors, including representatives of government, lenders, and investors, known as nominee directors. More specifically, this study has attempted to explore the interface between nominee directors and Indian SOE performance.

The study of SOEs in India is motivated by several factors. Few studies examined how SOEs and nominee directors perform (Nachane et al., 2005; Jayadev M., 2016). According to numerous research, SOEs struggle with a lack of competitiveness and conflicting goals. Additionally, ministries and bureaucrats intervene politically with SOEs by focusing on their immediate political objectives (Thompson et al., 2019), which lowers profitability and creates slack (Peng et al., 2016). Government subsidies and significant borrowing backed by the government have been used to repair this drop in profitability (Srivastava & Kathuria, 2020). As a result, a country's financial burden is ultimately caused by SOEs' poor performance.

SOEs Gross Domestic Product (GDP) provide about fifty per cent of the world's GDP. As per the Public Enterprises Survey 2022, 248 State-Owned Enterprises (SOEs) were operational during the fiscal year of 2021-22, with only 188 reporting profitability. The cumulative revenue generated by these profitable SOEs amounted to Rs. 2,64,000 crores. With a 38% increase, the aggregate debt of SOEs rose from Rs 11,73,000 crore in 2020-21 to Rs 1897,000 crore in 2021-22. The huge financial support these SOEs get from the government will reduce in the upcoming year. This makes it essential to look at these SOEs in the context of India and highlight measures that can enhance their operational efficiency.

Numerous earlier studies have emphasized the Board's prominent role in improving the outcome of SOEs Many prior studies have highlighted the prominent role of the Board in upgrading the performance of Indian SOEs (Mbo & Adjasi, 2017; Madaan et al., 2022). The public interest must be considered when the SOE boards carry out their responsibilities, ensure transparency, and protect the stakeholders (Peng et al., 2016). However, political meddling limits their ability to make decisions. This study focused on the function of nominee directors on Indian SOEs' boards. The government, the lender, or the staff may choose nominee directors. Instead of being involved in the business's daily operations, they actively participate in the board meetings. They ensure that the laws and regulations are in force within the organization. If any violations come to the knowledge of the nominee directors, the matter should be taken at the board meetings, and the nominating institute should be informed about such developments (Kaul & Agarwal, 2022; Salleh et al., 2021)

Nevertheless, there is a long-lasting controversy about the fiduciary responsibilities of 'nominee directors.' Should such a director be loyal to a nominator, keeping in mind his duty to do what is best for the entire company? Are these nominated directors ever free to pick the latter over the former when their duty to the nominator and their duty to the firm conflict?'

The issue of nominee directors serving on the company's boards is controversial. The information hypothesis emphasises that the nominating institute has simple access to information when nominee directors are appointed to the Board, which is not otherwise conceivable. It allows the business to easily acquire debt financing at low rates, which lowers agency issues and eventually improves business performance. Similarly, nominee directors are likewise outsiders and possess professional experience, according to the monitoring hypothesis. They guarantee that organizational policies have been properly implemented and facilitate the boards' effective operation (Ghosh, 2018). It results in improved management oversight and decreased agency issues, improving business performance. As against this, the debt-equity agency hypothesis posits that the nominee directors lower the company's valuation as they engender conñicts between equity holders and financiers. It might be because the lenders' nominee directors favour less risky business models, which would result in smaller investments and payouts for those companies.

These differing theoretical arguments have been mirrored in the available empirical literature. While some studies found evidence favouring the nomination of nominated directors, other researchers did not. The prior studies did not address the effects of nominee directors on the SOEs' boards, particularly in India. In Indian SOEs, the government or other SOEs appoints nominee directors. The maximum number of nominee directors may be appointed is two, according to the Department of Public Enterprises. It is necessary to determine whether these nominee directors influence SOE performance.

In light of this, the current study intends to look into how nominated directors have affected the performance of 19 well-run Indian SOEs over 18 years. It gauges efficiency utilizing accounting-based indicators, like ROA. The study has made several contributions. The study attempted to scrutinise the interface between the SOEs' performance and nominee directors. Second, the study looked at the linkage over a long period—specifically, 18 years.

Review of Literature

The prior literature investigating the liaison between nominee directors and corporate performance is less and mainly concerns the role of nominee directors on firm value. In the Japanese banks, Morck and Nakamura (1999) and Kaplan and Minton (1994) found that companies with poor performance have more nominee directors as they restrict the private benefits extracted by the managers in these companies. In the U.S., Kroszner and Strahan (2001) showed that commercial bankers on boards are usually not from "associated" (i.e., banks with which the company has a lending relationship) banks and are less frequent in ðrms with a higher probability of conñict (e.g., smaller ðrms). These represent legal constraints such as doctrines of lender liability and equal subordination, which limit the position of nominee directors on the boards. It explains why Booth and Deli (1999) do not find support on boards of the borrowing firms for a constructive position for associated commercial bankers.

Banaji (2004) conducted 160 interviews between April 1998 and January 2000 and highlighted the vital role of the nominee in the Indian boards. In opposition to this, Levine (2004) claimed that nominee directors on company boards do not bring technical knowledge and, as a result, little to the boards' deliberation. Nachane et al. (2005) examined how 1157 public and private manufacturing businesses in India performed when nominee directors were in place. They discovered that, instead of playing a watchdog function, bank nominee directors share their expertise on the boards of non-financial companies. As measured by ROCE and MBVR for 2002-2003, nominee directors adversely impacted the performance of 195 Indian businesses, according to Dwivedi (2007). Dittman et al. (2010) opine that bank nominee directors on German boards promote their corporations as the lenders and reduce the corporation's market value. Bubna and Gopalan (2012) examined how 238 Indian companies performed when bank nominee directors were present. They found that these businesses performed poorly, had high leverage levels, and paid fewer dividends. Similarly, Shukla (2017) discovered that nominated directors adversely impacted the performance of 30 listed Indian corporations from 2011 to 2016. Panicker et al. (2019) opined that nominee directors negatively influenced the internationalisation of 764 Indian companies for the period 2006-17. Additionally, these directors affirmatively moderate the association between family ownership and internationalisation and adversely moderate the association between foreign institutional investors and internationalisation. According to Bhatia and Gulati (2020), nominee directors negatively impacted Indian banks' performance from 2005 to 2017. Medina-Salgado et al (2020) also posited that the presence of nominee directors is adversely related to the propensity to cooperate in 126 Spanish firms. Nominee directors adversely impact the performance of Indian public sector banks between 2009 and 2017, according to Gupta et al. (2021). Jadiyappa et al. (2022)

observed the adverse influence of bank-appointed nominee directors on the stock volatility of 228 Indian firms from 2007 to 19. This implies that companies with bank nominee directors do not invest in risky projects. Shekhar and Lukose (2022) examined the impact of bank-appointed nominee directors on the debt-equity choice of the companies and observed that these directors support equity over debt. Such firms can easily get credit during periods of constrained external funding. In contrast to these studies, Chada and Banerjee (2023) assessed the impact of bank-appointed nominee directors on the chances of financial distress of 2811 Indian companies. They found an affirmative association between the two. Jayadev M (2016) also examined the results of businesses with bank nominee directors on their boards. The findings imply that nominee directors on boards have a considerable, favorable impact on both ROA and Tobin's Q. Empirically, Kiranmai and Mishra (2019) did not observe any influence of nominee directors on the performance of 42 listed Indian SOEs throughout 2012–2017.

According to the discussion above, there are opposing claims about how nominee directors perform on corporate boards. However, the role of nominated directors in State-owned Enterprises is hardly covered except by Kiranmai and Mishra (2019). Therefore, it is important to investigate how nominee directors' performance and that of State-owned Enterprises are related.

THEORETICAL FRAMEWORK

Agency theory has been widely utilised to study principal-agent dynamics (Thompson et al., 2019). According to agency theorists, a perpetual conflict exists between principals and agents, leading to agency problems. The principal-agent dilemmas are comparatively more pronounced in State-Owned Enterprises (SOEs). Initially, it is noteworthy that the bureaucrats hold a distinctive position in State-Owned Enterprises (SOEs), which could potentially impact the motivation of directors and shareholders to engage in monitoring activities. In contrast, the absence of incentives provided by bureaucrats is a demotivating factor for managers, hindering their ability to achieve higher performance levels. Furthermore, it has been argued that these bureaucrats' business acumen and resources are insufficient to effectively oversee and regulate the agents of each state-owned enterprise, as noted by Peng et al. (2016) and Mehta and Sharma (2016). The exacerbation of information asymmetries causes deviation from state-owned enterprises' goals, as Peng et al. (2016) noted.

Thus, agency theory in support of the information and monitoring hypothesis argues that nominee directors favourably influence the performance of SOEs. The reason for this could be that the appointment of these directors on the board provides easy access to the information to the nominating institute, which is not possible otherwise, which can reduce agency problems and ultimately upgrade the performance. Moreover, these directors are also outsiders and have professional expertise. They facilitate the boards' adequate functioning and ensure the organisational policies and plans have been appropriately implemented (Ghosh, 2018). It leads to improved manager supervision and fewer agency issues, enhancing firm performance.

Hypothesis Development

Nominee directors, selected by entities such as the government, employees or lenders, are considered external to the organisation and possess specialized knowledge in their respective fields. According to Ghosh (2018), their role involves facilitating the effective functioning of the boards and ensuring the implementation of organisational plans and policies. According to Nachane et al. (2005), nominee directors can facilitate the exchange of information between a company and its nominator. The facile dissemination of information among executive directors fosters a rapport that empowers state-owned enterprises to petition the government for financial backing. Conversely, certain authors contend that a proximate association between said directors and the organization may result in a monopoly based on information (Rajan, 1992).

Previous studies examining the nominee directors and performance linkages have yielded mixed findings. For example, Dwivedi (2007), Dittman et al. (2010), Bubna and Gopalan (2012), Shukla (2017), Panicker et al. (2019), Bhatia and Gulati (2020), Medina-Salgado et al. (2020), and Gupta et al. (2021) have provided unfavorable outcomes while studying the association of nominee directors with the performance of companies. However, Chada and Banerjee (2023) and Jayadev M (2016) found favorable outcomes while studying nominee directors with financial distress and company performance, respectively. Researchers such as Kiranmai and Mishra (2019) observed no relationship between the two variables.

Aligned with the agency theory and prior research, this study anticipates a favorable impact of these directors on the performance of state-owned enterprises. Following is the hypothesis:

H_1: The nominee directors favorably impact the SOE's performance.

RESEARCH METHODS

Sample and Data Sources

Initially, 61 SOEs registered on BSE were chosen for this study These SOEs represented around 8% of the entire market capitalisation in February 2020. The study has solely considered the top 24 State-Owned Enterprises (SOEs) based on their market capitalisation. After the commencement of the study, five State-Owned Enterprises (SOEs) were excluded from the original dataset of 24 SOEs due to their non-inclusion for the entire study duration. The ultimate sample com prises 19 SOEs. These entities comprise 7 Maharatnas, 8 Navratnas, and 4 Miniratnas. According to the Public Enterprises Survey of 2019, Maharatnas, Navratnas, and Miniratnas have been assigned exceptional corporate governance ratings and granted significant authority by the government to their respective boards. It considers the 18-year period starting in April 2001 and ending in March 2019. Since clause 49 went into force in 2001, the sample begins in 2001 and ends in 2019, representing the most recent year for which data is available. The final sample comprises 342 observations from 19 companies during 18 years. Data on the nominee directors, control factors, and performance variables were gathered from the SOE websites, annual reports and the Bloomberg database.

Variables

This study employs ROA, ROE, and TQ as the dependent variables to assess the linkages between nominee directors as well as company performance, building upon prior research conducted by Kao et al. (2019), Mishra (2020), and Heo (2018). The ROA parameter quantifies how profitable a company is in proportion to the deployment of assets. Therefore, a higher ratio indicates superior performance, while a lower ratio indicates inferior performance. According to the tenets of agency theory, managers have the potential to misuse profits, resulting in diminished returns for shareholders. The ROA is closely linked to managerial proficiency in efficiently leveraging the organisation's resources, which ultimately pertain to the stakeholders. The values have been selected from the prowess database. The ROE quantifies the earnings generated by a company utilising shareholder funds. A higher ratio corresponds to superior share performance. The ROE values are sourced from the prowess database. TQ represents the discounted value of anticipated future earnings derived from shareholders' asset investments. When the TQ value exceeds one, investors anticipate the firm to generate greater future earnings utilising its current resources. In contrast, companies with less than one TQ ratio indicate suboptimal resource utilisation, resulting in reduced future income generation from available resources. As per Kao et al. (2019), the aforementioned variable is measured by a formula involving the ratio of the equity market value and aggregate liabilities scaled by the assets book value.

The study's independent variable pertains to nominee directors. The nominee directors are evaluated based on their percentage. These directors are appointed by either the government or other state-owned enterprises in Indian state-owned enterprises. The Department of Public Enterprises has implemented a policy limiting the employment of nominee directors to a maximum of two. Consistent with the works of Heo (2018), Shawtari et al. (2017), and Kiranmai and Mishra (2019), this study employs four control variables, namely, firm age, firm size, leverage, board size, CEO Duality and sales growth, as presented in Table 1.

Table 1. Variables of the study

Variable Name	Variable Description	Measure
Dependent Variable		
ROA	Return on Assets	Collected from Prowess database
ROE	Return on Equity	Collected from Prowess database
TBQ	Tobin's Q	Equity market value + total liabilities over the assets book value
Independent Variable		
PND	Nominee directors	% Age of Nominee directors on the Board
Control Variables		
FS	Firm Size	Natural log of the market capitalization
FA	Firm Age	Log of the present year – incorporation year
LEV	Leverage	Total outside liabilities/ Total Assets
SG	Sales growth	Current year sales minus last year sales over the last year sales
BS	Board size	Aggregate number of directors in the board
CEOD	CEO duality	1 if Chairman of the board and managing director are same person and O otherwise

Source: Author's Self compilation

Consistent with previous research, the measurement of firm size is determined by taking the natural logarithm of the market capitalisation. Large firms' presence may adversely impact smaller companies' performance due to increased bureaucratic oversight, elevated agency costs, and reduced prospects for growth. In many organisations, it is common for senior executives to relinquish their oversight, which can lead to implementing suboptimal strategies. The potential absence of transparency could potentially increase the expenses associated with monitoring. Contrary to the opposing viewpoint, as Heo (2018) posited, the present study anticipates a favourable impact on the performance resulting from the presence of large firms. This is attributed to the advantages of economies of scale, which serve as a barrier to entry for new firms and the employment of skilled personnel, ultimately leading to improved company performance. Furthermore, it is feasible for individuals to secure financing at a lower cost and potentially achieve increased portfolio diversification.

The quantification of another control variable, namely firm age, has been accomplished by taking the log of the difference between the current yearend of the company and the year it got incorporated. Although established companies possess greater proficiency and revenue, resulting in economies of scale, they have already attained the maturity phase of the product life cycle and face limited opportunities for expansion. In contrast, emerging enterprises must establish their reputation within the industry and incur substantial expenses. This study posits that the State-Owned Enterprises (SOEs) performance is adversely affected by the age of the firm.

Leverage is identified as the third control variable. It is derived by dividing the aggregate external liabilities by the aggregate assets. The augmentation of leverage indicates that external funds are being utilized, heightening the company's risk and capital cost. Thus, the company is pressured to improve its performance to offset costs. Additionally, it enhances equity shareholders' profitability by trading on equity. According to Jensen and Meckling's seminal work in 1976, the presence of debt holders can effectively reduce conflicts between shareholders and managers by creating the threat of bankruptcy and providing oversight and monitoring. Consequently, the research anticipates a favorable influence of leverage on the efficacy of State-Owned Enterprises (SOEs).

The sales growth is assessed by differencing the present year's and last period's sales, then dividing it by the sales from the last year. According to agency theory, managers pursue growth to achieve personal objectives such as increased compensation and job security. Furthermore, firms prioritising growth are more likely to invest in profitable projects that increase their earnings and overall firm value. It is anticipated that there will be a positive impact on corporate performance. Among the governance variables, board size and CEO duality have been employed. Board size is assessed by the aggregate of the total directors on the board. According to agency theory, appointing more directors on the board leads to better monitoring of the managers, improving the companies' performance (Sharma et al., 2022). CEO Duality is a dummy variable with value one if the Chairman and CEO are the same person and O if they are different persons. Agency theory claims that CEO duality hurts company performance because it gives the CEO greater authority. He may put his ambitions over stakeholder expectations. This will worsen agency issues by pitting the CEO against stakeholders (Goel, 2021).

Empirical Model and Estimation Technique

The study makes use of the following models to scrutinise the linear interface between the Indian SOEs' performance and nominee directors:

Model 1

$$\boldsymbol{ROA_{it}} = \alpha_0 + \beta_1 \boldsymbol{PND} + \beta_2 \boldsymbol{FS} + \beta_3 \boldsymbol{FA} + \beta_4 \boldsymbol{LEV} + \beta_5 \boldsymbol{SG} + \beta_6 \boldsymbol{BS} + \beta_7 \boldsymbol{CEOD} + \omega_{it}$$

Model 2

$$ROE_{it} = \alpha_0 + \beta_1 PND + \beta_2 FS + \beta_3 FA + \beta_4 LEV + \beta_5 SG + \beta_6 BS + \beta_7 CEOD + \omega_{it}$$

Model 3

$$TBQ_{it} = \alpha_0 + \beta_1 PND + \beta_2 FS + \beta_3 FA + \beta_4 LEV + \beta_5 SG + \beta_6 BS + \beta_7 CEOD + \omega_{it}$$

The data includes both companies and period, therefore panel data is the most suited. Panel data has fixed, random, and pooled OLS models. Hausman test selects the fixed effect model over the random effect (Baltagi, 2008) ($\chi^2 = 16.47$; $d_f = 5$; $p < 0.01$). Further, Heteroskedasticity and serial correlation also affect OLS Regression outcomes. If these data issues persist, regression coefficient standard errors will be inaccurate (Baltagi, 2008). The study applies the White Heteroskedasticity Test and LM Test. The White Heteroskedasticity Test reject the null hypothesis ($\chi 2=44$; p=0.000). The LM Test also the null hypothesis ($\chi 2 = 2$; p=0.000). It suggests the issue of heteroskedasticity and serial correlation in the data. Therefore, the study adopts a fixed-effect panel regression with clustered standard errors throughout.

RESULTS AND ANALYSIS

Descriptive Statistics

Table 2 depicts the descriptive statistics for each variable under study. ROA ranges from -21.11 to 41.14, averaging 7.76. ROE ranges from 110 to -336.5, averaging 13.73. TQ ranges from 16.4 to 0.33 with a mean of 1.36. The highest and lowest nominee director rates are 0 and 91, respectively. Firm size ranges from 3.51 to 6.47, averaging 5.01. The firm age ranges from 0.95 to 1.85, averaging 1.58. Leverage ranges from 0.65 to 37.81, with an average of 4.56. Sales growth ranges from -1.00 to 1.56, averaging 0.12. Board size ranges from 4 to 22 averaging at 12. CEO duality ranges from 0 to 1

Pearson Correlation

Table 3 shows Pearson correlation results. The correlation coefficients among all variables vary from -0.446 (CEO Duality and nominee directors) to 0.684 (ROA and ROE). A correlation value below 0.80 indicates no multicollinearity among the variables (Baltagi, 2008).

Table 2. Findings of descriptive statistics

	Mean	Maximum	Minimum	Std. Dev.	Median
ROA	7.76	41.14	-21.11	9.01	6.87
ROE	13.73	110	-336.5	34.60	15.49
TBQ	1.36	16.4	0.33	1.45	0.97
PND	21.44	90.91	0.00	16.93	17
FS	5.01	6.47	3.51	0.67	5.03
FA	1.58	1.85	0.95	0.18	1.64
BS	12.06	22	4	3.46	12
CEOD	0.69	1	0	0.46	1
LEV	4.56	37.81	0.65	5.34	2.57
SG	0.12	1.56	-1.00	0.23	0.1

Source: Author's self-compilation

Table 3. Pearson correlation results

	PND	BS	CEOD	Q	ROA	ROE	FA	LEV	SG	FS
PND	1									
BS	-.313**	1								
CEOD	-.446**	.098	1							
Q	-.126*	.008	.025	1						
ROA	.030	.008	-.199**	.272**	1					
ROE	.016	.074	-.141**	.114*	.684**	1				
FA	-.175**	.161**	.190**	.086	-.116*	.051	1			
LEV	-.087	-.038	.116*	.146**	.428**	.154**	-.117*	1		
SG	.110*	.101	-.049	.039	.129*	.088	-.085	.002	1	
FS	-.221**	.221**	.110*	.272**	.043	.068	-.110*	.147**	.080	1
**. Correlation is significant at the 0.01 level (2-tailed).										
*. Correlation is significant at the 0.05 level (2-tailed).										

Panel Regression

This study conducts panel regression with a fixed-effect model and clustered standard errors to order to examine the validity of hypothesis H_1. Model, 1-3 of Table 4, depicts the regression findings for estimating the nominee directors and SOEs performance linkages by using the different dependent variable.

Table 4. Fixed-effect regression results

Variables	Model 1	Model 2	Model 3
(Constant)	28.17 (4.61) *	89.20 (2.51) **	-2.43 (-1.64) **
PND	0.06 (2.47) **	0.25 (1.89) ***	-0.01 (-0.16)
FS	5.99 (7.15) *	30.67 (6.51) *	2.28 (11.30)*
FA	-33.57 (-7.40) *	-149.82 (-5.87) *	-4.67 (-4.31)*
LEV	0.29 (3.47) *	0.44 (0.92)	-0.04 (-2.04)**
SG	2.92 (2.46) **	4.35 (0.65)	0.24 (0.86)
BS	0.27 (2.52) **	0.56 (0.93)	-0.01 (-4.22)
CEOD	-5.22 (-4.08) *	-5.86 (-0.82)	-0.01 (-0.03)
R^2	0.74	0.45	0.41
Adjusted R^2	0.72	0.40	0.37
F statistic	36.43*	10.23*	8.95*
D-W statistic	0.79	1.59	1.38
Number of observations	342	342	342

This table reports fixed effect panel regressions for model 1, 2 and 3 to establish the relationship between nominee directors and various SOEs performance parameters measured via ROA for model 1, ROE for model 2 and Tobin's Q for model 3. The details related to all the variables are defined in Table 1 above. D-W: Durbin Watson. T- statistics values are in parentheses. *,** and *** denote significance at the 1, 5, and 10% level, respectively

Source: Author's self-compilation

In model 1, ROA is our dependent variable. Concerning nominee directors, the adjusted R^2 of 0.72 depicts that nearly 72% of the variance in ROA is described by the model. Nominee directors show a positive association with firm performance measured via ROA (β_1=0.06; $p < 0.05$), supporting hypothesis H_1. It depicts that higher proportion of nominee directors is favorably correlated with ROA. The findings of the study are in conformity with the studies conducted by Nachane et al. (2005) and Jayadev M (2016) and is inconsistent with the results reported by Dwivedi (2007); Dittman et al. (2010); Bhatia and Gulati (2020) and Gupta et al. (2021).

In model 2, ROE is our dependent variable. The adjusted R^2 of 0.40 depicts that the model describes nearly 40% of the variance in ROE. Nominee directors depict a positive association with firm performance measured via ROE (β_1=0.25; $p < 0.10$), supporting hypothesis H_1. It illustrates that positive linkages exist between nominee directors and ROE. The present argument aligns with the findings of Nachane et al. (2005) and Jayadev M. (2016). It is incongruent with the results of Dwivedi (2007), Dittman et al. (2010, Bhatia and Gulati (2020) and Gupta et al. (2021).

In model 3, TQ is the dependent variable. The adjusted R^2 of 0.37 depicts that the model describes nearly 37% of the variance in TQ. Nominee directors depict an inverse but insignificant linkage with firm performance measured via TQ (β_1=-0.01), thereby not supporting hypothesis H_1. It is that nominee directors do not affect the market performance of the SOEs. The argument is in accordance with the findings of Kiranmai and Mishra (2019), while it is not in agreement with the research conducted by Dwivedi (2007) and Dittman et al. (2010).

In models 1-3, firm size affirmatively influences SOE performance (Model 1-β = 5.99; $p < 0.01$; Model 2- β= 30.67; $p < 0.01$; Model 3- β= 2.28; $p < 0.01$) The firm age had an inverse and substantial effect on SOE performance in models 1-3 (Model 1-β= - 33.57; $p < 0.01$; Model 2-β= -149.82; $p < 0.01$; Model 3-β= -4.67; $p < 0.01$) The third control variable leverage affirmatively effect SOE performance in Model 1 (Model 1-β= 0.29; $p < 0.01$); positive but not significant in Model 2; and adverse and significant in Model 3 (β= -0.04; $p < 0.05$). In Model 1, the Sales Growth improves Indian SOE performance (Model 1- β= 2.92; $p < 0.05$), but it is insignificant in Models 2 and 3. The fifth control variable, Board size is positive and significant in Model 1(Model 1- β= 0.27; $p < 0.05$), and insignificant in Models 2 and 3. The sixth control variable, CEO Duality, is inverse and significant in Model 1 (Model 1- β= -5.22; $p < 0.01$).

Robustness Check

The study also performed robustness check to determine if the results would change if the alternative measure of explanatory variables was employed, if year effects were considered, or if lagged variables were introduced to control endogeneity.

First, corporate governance literature is plagued by endogeneity, making results interpretation problematic. Board qualities and firm performance interface is found to be endogenous (Hermalin and Weisbach, 2003). Therefore, the study evaluated all the variables by taking 1-year lagged values as explored by Im and Chung (2017) and conducted supplementary analysis by regressing on business performance (shown in Table 5). Table 4 baseline results remain unchanged. Model 1 and 2 are meaningful at 1% instead of 5% and 10%.

Second, incorporating the year effects, the study considers that year dummies could capture different economic conditions in different years. Hence, this study re-runs the regression analysis by including 17-year dummies, as there are 18 years.

The regression analysis engenders similar results: nominee directors affirmatively influence the performance of Indian SOEs in models 1 and 2 and adversely but insignificantly in model 3, as shown in Table 6.

Table 5. Fixed-effect regression findings with lagged dependent, independent, and control variables

Variables	Model 1	Model 2	Model 3
(Constant)	22.43 (4.59) *	132.85 (3.88)*	-1.24 (-0.66)
ROA_{t-1}	0.67 (16.04) *		
ROE_{t-1}		0.18 (3.41)*	
TBQ_{t-1}			0.23 (3.36)*
PND_{t-1}	0.06 (3.69)*	0.35 (2.82)*	0.01 (0.44)
FS_{t-1}	0.21 (0.30)	17.50 (3.57)*	0.26 (0.87)
FA_{t-1}	-12.71 (-3.33)*	-134.61 (-5.01)*	0.87 (0.60)
LEV_{t-1}	-0.14 (-2.21)**	0.03 (0.07)	-0.01 (-0.26)
SG_{t-1}	-0.45 (-0.48)	0.69 (0.10)	0.03 (0.08)
BS_{t-1}	-0.02 (-0.19)	-0.04 (-0.07)	-0.03 (-0.80)
$CEOD_{t-1}$	-1.93 (-1.98)**	-5.34 (-0.79)	-0.13 (-0.35)
R^2	0.87	0.51	0.23
Adjusted R^2	0.85	0.47	0.17
F statistic	73.17*	11.84*	3.43*
D-W statistic	2.02	2.40	2.02
Number of observations	323	323	323

This table reports fixed effect panel regressions of ROA for model 1, ROE for model 2 and Tobin's Q for model 3 on lagged values of nominee directors, performance variables and various control variables as a robustness check. The details related to all the variables are defined in Table 1 above. D-W: Durbin Watson. T-statistics values are in parentheses. *,** and *** denote significance at the 1, 5, and 10% level, respectively

Source: Author's Self-Compilation

Table 6. Fixed-effect regression findings with year dummies

Variables	Model 1	Model 2	Model 3
(Constant)	-13.52 (-0.94)	-90.11 (-1.11)	-14.21 (-4.05) *
PND	0.05 (2.28) **	0.24 (1.81) ***	-0.00 (-0.07)
FS	6.36 (6.79) *	32.51 (6.12) *	2.68 (11.69) *
FA	-7.84 (-0.86)	-41.68 (-0.80)	2.58 (1.15)
LEV	0.29 (3.31) *	0.71 (1.43)	-0.04 (-2.10) **
SG	2.21 (1.76) ***	-3.37 (-0.47)	0.45 (1.48)
BS	0.29 (2.67)	0.45 (0.72)	-0.01 (-0.50)
CEOD	-5.70 (-4.49)	-7.37 (-1.02)	-0.24 (-0.76)
Year dummies	Yes	Yes	Yes
R^2	0.75	0.49	0.47
Adjusted R^2	0.71	0.42	0.39
F statistic	22.09*	6.93*	6.19*
D-W statistic	0.70	1.67	1.33
Number of observations	342	342	342

This table reports fixed effect panel regressions of ROA for model 1, ROE for model 2 and Tobin's Q for model 3 on nominee directors, performance variables, various control variables and year dummies as a robustness check. The details related to all the variables are defined in Table 1 above. D-W: Durbin Watson. T-statistics values are in parentheses. *,** and *** denote significance at the 1, 5, and 10% level, respectively

Source: Author's Self-Compilation

Third, to validate the findings, the outcomes were compared using an alternate definition of the firm size. Like Kao et al. (2019), the firm size was estimated as the total assets instead of the market cap. Using the alternate definition of firm size yielded similar results to those already obtained, as shown in Table 7. The substitution of this variable in the model 1-3 does not change the influence of the primary explanatory variable. The effect of nominee directors is still affirmative at 5% and 10% significance level in models 1 and 2, respectively, on the performance of Indian SOEs.

Table 7. Fixed-effect regression findings with an alternative measure of firm size

Variables	Model 1	Model 2	Model 3
(Constant)	28.17 (4.62) *	86.20 (2.51)**	-2.43 (-1.64)
PND	0.06 (2.47) **	0.25 (1.90)***	-0.00 (-0.19)
FS	5.99 (7.15) *	30.67 (6.51)*	2.28 (11.22)*
FA	-33.57 (-7.40) *	-149.82 (-5.87)*	-4.63 (-4.21)*
LEV	0.29 (2.46) *	0.44 (0.92)	-0.04 (-2.04)**
SG	2.92 (2.46) **	4.34 (0.65)	0.26 (0.92)
BS	0.27 (2.52)**	0.56 (0.93)	-0.01 (-0.42)
CEOD	-5.22 (-4.08)(	-5.86 (-0.82)	-0.01 (-0.03)
R^2	0.74	0.45	0.41
Adjusted R^2	0.72	0.40	0.37
F statistic	36.43*	10.23*	8.95*
D-W statistic	0.80	1.59	1.38
Number of observations	342	342	342

This table reports fixed effect panel regressions of ROA for model 1, ROE for model 2 and Tobin's Q for model 3 on nominee directors, performance variables, various control variables with alternative definition of firm size as a robustness check. The details related to all the variables are defined in Table 1 above. D-W: Durbin Watson. T- statistics values are in parentheses. *,** and *** denote significance at the 1, 5, and 10% level, respectively

Source: Author's Self-Compilation

It has become evident from the above section that the main results presented in Table 4 remain unaltered for these alternative estimations, regardless of the definition of explanatory variables, the years used in the analyses or the lagged variables. In a few cases of alternative estimates, there is a change in the significance level from 5% or 10% to 1% level for the independent variable, which provides further evidence of the strongness of the results.

Discussion and Implications

The findings offer a breakthrough within the growing literature on the Board member's and SOEs' performance, especially regarding nominee directors. The results reveal that including nominee directors on Indian SOE boards favours their performance.

The findings of the study are in line with Chada and Banerjee (2023) and Jaydev M (2016) and contradict the findings of Panicker et al. (2019), Bhatia and Gulati (2020), Medina-Salgado et al. (2020), and Gupta et al. (2021). The findings also contradict Kiranmai and Mishra (2019), who found no linkage between the nominee directors and Indian SOEs performance The reason why the current findings differ from the previous research could be that they mainly focus on companies and ignored the SOEs. The present research also provides empirical evidence in support of the agency theory. According to agency theorists, state-owned enterprises are plagued by significant agency issues. External to the organization, Nominee directors are crucial in safeguarding the interests of shareholders and state-owned enterprises. It is worth mentioning that the obtained results are robust to alternative firm size variables, endogeneity and year dummies. The rationale behind this discovery is that including nominee directors facilitates seamless information exchange between executive directors, fostering a strong interdependent bond. Nominee directors' affiliations with the government and other board members facilitate their ability to safeguard the welfare of all stakeholders.

CONCLUSION

The paper aims to analyse whether the nominee directors affect the performance of 19 SOEs of India for the period 2001 to 2019. Employing ROA and fixed-effect regression, the outcome of the study indicates that Indian SOEs, on average, have 21% nominee directors in their Board, and they affirmatively impact the SOE's performance. The findings are in agreement with Nachane et al. (2005) and Jayadev M (2016) and inconsistent with Dwivedi (2007) and Dittman et al. (2010). It shows that nominee directors, appointed by the majority shareholders and responsible to the citizens, employees and government, take care of the interest of all and get complete inside information. It is pertinent to acknowledge that the nominee director's fundamental commitment is to the nominator, but only if it doesn't conflict with the company's interests. These directors prioritise company interests over their nominator in conflicts.

The study has practical implications. *First*, the DPE has restricted the total number of nominee directors to two. As depicted from the findings of the study, the government should lift the bar on the appointment of a minimum number of nominee directors that have adequate skills and experience. Being appointed by the government and responsible to the citizens, employees and government, they can take care of the interest of all and get complete inside information. *Second, a*s shown above, nominee directors affirmatively influence SOE's performance. Instead of adding independent and executive directors, Indian SOEs should appoint more nominee directors to improve performance in today's complex business climate. Third, the study's findings could help present and future investors choose the best Board structure and invest in the company, increasing its value. Most shareholders and investors want higher asset returns. Thus, they would increase nominee directors on SOE boards to boost value.

This study is constrained by few limitations. First, while this study determined government nominees on SOEs boards, future studies can check their influence during the presence of leverage in these companies. Second, this study is only limited to well-governed SOEs, i.e., Maharatnas, Navratnas and Miniratnas. Future studies may include other SOEs and private companies.

REFERENCES

Baltagi, B. H. (2008). Forecasting with panel data. *Journal of Forecasting*, *27*(2), 153–173. doi:10.1002/for.1047

Banaji, J. (2004). *Institutional investors and nominee directors. In Corporate Governance, Economic Reforms and Development: The Indian Experience*. Oxford University Press.

Bhatia, M., & Gulati, R. (2020). Does board effectiveness matter for bank performance? Evidence from India. *International Journal of Comparative Management*, *3*(1-2), 9–52. doi:10.1504/IJCM.2020.107335

Booth, J. R., & Deli, D. N. (1999). On executives of financial institutions as outside directors. *Journal of Corporate Finance*, *5*(3), 227–250. doi:10.1016/S0929-1199(99)00004-8

Bubna, A., & Gopalan, R. (2012). Bank Involvement in Firm Management, Panacea or a Pain? *Panacea or a Pain, 1-35.* https://papers.ssrn.com/sol3/papers.cfm?abstract_id=2024801

Dalton, D. R., Daily, C. M., Johnson, J. L., & Ellstrand, A. E. (1999). Number of directors and financial performance: A meta-analysis. *Academy of Management Journal*, *42*(6), 674–686. doi:10.2307/256988

Department of Public Enterprises. (2019). *Public Enterprises Survey, 2018-2019.* https://dpe.gov.in/public-enterprises-survey-2018-19

Dittmann, I., Maug, E., & Schneider, C. (2010). Bankers on the boards of German firms: What they do, what they are worth, and why they are (still) there. *Review of Finance*, *14*(1), 35–71. doi:10.1093/rof/rfp007

Dwivedi, N. (2007). Determinants of Board Effectiveness: Evidence from Large Indian Firms. *Indore Management Journal*, *2*(1), 1–15.

Ghosh, S. (2018). Banker directors and firm performance: Are family firms different? *Future Business Journal*, *4*(1), 1–15. doi:10.1016/j.fbj.2017.11.002

Goel, A. (2021). Board Composition and Performance of Indian Companies: The Moderating Effect of CEO Duality. *SCMS Journal of Indian Management, 18*(4).

Gupta, N., Mahakud, J., Tripathi, P. M., Agarwal, T., & Bakhshi, P. (2021). Do nominee directors influence bank performance. *Corporate Ownership & Control, 19*(1), 121–145. doi:10.22495/cocv19i1art10

Heo, K. (2018). *Effects of corporate governance on the performance of state-owned enterprises*. The World Bank. doi:10.1596/1813-9450-8555

Heo, K. (2018). *Effects of corporate governance on the performance of state-owned enterprises*. The World Bank. doi:10.1596/1813-9450-8555

Hermalin, B., & Weisbach, M. (2003). Board of directors as an endogenously determined institution: A survey of the economic literature. *Economic Policy Review*, (April), 7–26.

Im, J., & Chung, Y. (2017). The effects of insider ownership and board composition on firm performance in the restaurant industry. *The Journal of Hospitality Financial Management*, *25*(1), 4–16. doi:10.1080/10913211.2017.1313604

Jayadev, M. (2016). *Debt, Defaults, and, Corporate Governance*. IIM Banglore.

Jensen, M., & Meckling, W. (1976). Theory of the firm: Managerial behavior, agency costs and ownership structure. *Journal of Financial Economics*, *3*(4), 305–360. doi:10.1016/0304-405X(76)90026-X

Kao, M. F., Hodgkinson, L., & Jaafar, A. (2019). Ownership structure, Board of directors and firm performance: Evidence from Taiwan. *Corporate Governance: The International Journal of Business in Society*, *19*(1), 189–216. doi:10.1108/CG-04-2018-0144

Kaplan, S. N., & Minton, B. A. (1994). Appointments of outsiders to Japanese boards: Determinants and implications for managers. *Journal of Financial Economics*, *36*(2), 225–258. doi:10.1016/0304-405X(94)90025-6

Kaul, A., & Agarwal, R. (2022). Neither here nor there: reconciling nominee directors' dual loyalties under the Indian Companies Act 2013. *Oxford University Commonwealth Law Journal, 22*(2), 205-228. https://www.tandfonline.com/doi/abs/10.1080/14729342.2022.2151793

Kiranmai, J., & Mishra, R. K. (2019). Corporate Governance Practices in Listed State-owned Enterprises in India: An Empirical Research. *Indian Journal of Corporate Governance, 12*(1), 94–121. doi:10.1177/0974686219849760

Kroszner, R. S., & Strahan, P. E. (2001). Bankers on boards: Monitoring, conflicts of interest, and lender liability. *Journal of Financial Economics, 62*(3), 415–452. doi:10.1016/S0304-405X(01)00082-4

Levine, R. (2004). *The corporate governance of banks: A concise discussion of concepts and evidence*. The World Bank. doi:10.1596/1813-9450-3404

Madaan, D. A., Mehta, K., & Sharma, R. (2022). A Revisit to Research on Corporate Governance Using Systematic Literature Review. *ECS Transactions, 107*(1), 4035–4049. doi:10.1149/10701.4035ecst

Mbo, M., & Adjasi, C. (2017). Drivers of organisational performance in state owned enterprises. *International Journal of Productivity and Performance Management, 66*(3), 405–423. Advance online publication. doi:10.1108/IJPPM-11-2015-0177

Mehta, K., & Sharma, R. (2016). SMEs and corporate social responsibility: Indian perception. *SCMS Journal of Indian Management, 13*(3), 58–67.

Mishra, S. (2020). Do Independent Directors Improve Firm Performance? Evidence from India. *Global Business Review*, 1–19. doi:10.1177/0972150920917310

Morck, R., & Nakamura, M. (1999). Banks and corporate control in Japan. *The Journal of Finance, 54*(1), 319–339. doi:10.1111/0022-1082.00106

Nachane, D. M., Ghosh, S., & Ray, P. (2005). Bank nominee directors and corporate performance: Micro-evidence for India. *Economic and Political Weekly*, 1216–1223. https://www.jstor.org/stable/4416370

Peng, M. W., Bruton, G. D., Stan, C. V., & Huang, Y. (2016). Theories of the (state-owned) firm. *Asia Pacific Journal of Management, 33*(2), 293–317. doi:10.100710490-016-9462-3

Rajan, R. G. (1992). 'Insiders and outsiders: The choice between informed and arm' s-length debt'. *The Journal of Finance, 47*(4), 1367–1400. doi:10.1111/j.1540-6261.1992.tb04662.x

Salleh, K., Husaini, M. F., Bidin, A., Harun, N., & Hamid, A. (2021). The Duties and Conflicts of Nominee Directors: The Legal Position in Malaysia. *Psychology and Education*, *58*(2), 1577–1583. doi:10.17762/pae.v58i2.2311

Sharma, R., Mehta, K., & Goel, A. (2022). Non-linear relationship between board size and performance of Indian companies. *The Journal of Management and Governance*, 1–25. doi:10.100710997-022-09651-8

Shawtari, F. A., Mohamad, M. H. S., Rashid, H. M. A., & Moh'd Ayedh, A. (2017). Board characteristics and real performance in Malaysian state-owned enterprises (SOEs). *International Journal of Productivity and Performance Management*, *66*(8), 1064–1086. doi:10.1108/IJPPM-12-2015-0188

Shukla, M. (2017). Losing the tag of 'independent director'-role played by nominee directors in determining firm performance. In *6th International Conference on Trade, Business, Economics and Law* (p. 22). Academic Press.

Srivastava, G., & Kathuria, V. (2020). Impact of corporate governance norms on the performance of Indian utilities. *Energy Policy*, *140*, 111414. doi:10.1016/j.enpol.2020.111414

Thompson, R. M., Alleyne, P., & Charles-Soverall, W. (2019). Exploring governance issues among boards of directors within state-owned enterprises in Barbados. *International Journal of Public Sector Management*, *32*(3), 264–281. Advance online publication. doi:10.1108/IJPSM-04-2018-0099

Chapter 7
Environmental, Social, and Governance (ESG) Integration:
Evidence From an Emerging Economy

Niaz Mohammad
https://orcid.org/0000-0001-9233-2800
American International University-Bangladesh (AIUB), Bangladesh

EXECUTIVE SUMMARY

This chapter is intended to understand how environmental, social, and governance issues are integrated in the annual report of Bangladeshi banking companies from 2020 to 2022. This understanding, in turn, can help investors determine how to integrate ESG analysis into their own investment processes. This study considered the top 30 banks operating in Bangladesh for three years (2020 to 2022). Discourse analysis was used to identify the textual narratives disclosed in this study. Finding of this study showed that many banking organizations are presenting their ESG disclosure in a separate section of annual report and other organizations report such information in the form of sustainability report or corporate social responsibility section. Despite all the regulatory interventions, the level of ESG reporting especially governance is not up to mark in Bangladesh. The main factor for integrating ESG is to face risks and opportunities that can impact the long-term performance and sustainable finance.

DOI: 10.4018/978-1-6684-9867-5.ch007

INTRODUCTION

Environmental, Social and Governance (ESG) is one of the burning issues in recent years. Generally, ESG (Environmental, Social and Governance) reporting is the disclosure of a company's environmental, social, and governance performance to its stakeholders. Stakeholders, especially regulatory agencies, are seeking greater openness and responsibility from businesses as concerns about environmental degradation, social issues, and corporate governance disclosure in Bangladesh. ESG reporting can help to support these efforts by providing a method to monitor and report on a company's sustainability performance, even while the government and civil society organizations are already taking steps to address these problems. ESG reporting can also help businesses become more credible, draw in sustainable investors, and ultimately help them succeed financially in the long run. In order to address sustainable development and green consumerism, global corporate investment and sustainability are attracting more and more attention (Nosratabadi et al., 2019). It has become necessary to disclose environmental, social, and corporate governance on a global scale as sustainability gains importance for economic development and there is concern over the lack of non-financial information in annual reports (Li, Gong, Zhang, & Koh, 2018). Stakeholders have begun to put increasing pressure on businesses in recent years to learn more about the positive and negative effects of their environmental and social policies, as well as how much sustainable development is incorporated into their strategies and business models (Camilleri, 2022; KPMG, 2022). According to (Adams 2017) ESG issues are extremely important in driving corporate reporting and performance. ESG issues like climate change and poverty evaluation [One of sustainability development goals issued by United Nations] motivates everyone to act on including companies (United Nations Development Program 2015). Such issues getting more emphasis at the time of COVID 19 crisis (Wood 2020). In brief, because of the significant changes in the globe, businesses now have to prepare for potential ESG-related challenges as well as satisfy consumer demand for measuring corporate financial performance (Barker & Eccles 2019). Even media pressure plays a vital role in motivating companies for promoting ESG disclosure (Garcia-Sanchez et al. 2014).

In contrast to other developing countries, the performance of Bangladeshi companies for non-financial disclosure is almost voluntary in nature. Due to tremendous economic growth Bangladesh still lacks behind than others. This happens due to lack of demand from stakeholders or insufficient pursuance of existing laws (Ahmed & Rahman, 2014). According to the Environmental Performance Index (EPI), Bangladesh was ranked 162 out of 180 nations in 2018, which is a remarkable indication of how poorly the sustainability and environmental conditions are doing (Bhuyian & Hussain, 2020). However, many businesses intentionally release ESG reports and use transparency as a business strategy to achieve legitimacy as an organization and meet the demands of their many stakeholders (Deegan 2002). Environmental, social, and governance (ESG) considerations are becoming more and more a part of portfolio managers' and analysts' investment analysis. Investors and analysts want additional information on precisely "how" they may "do ESG" and include ESG data into their analysis, as ESG integration is still in its relative start. ESG reporting is still in its early stages in Bangladesh, however the trend is in the right direction. Companies across a range of industries have begun disclosing their ESG performance, and governmental organizations have also made steps to encourage and support ESG reporting. Banks and financial institutions are under pressure to use ESG reporting for decision making (Buallay et al. 2020; Bak & Cheba, 2020). To investigate these questions, the chapter used secondary sources of materials including the latest annual reports of top thirty companies from 2020 to 2022 listed in Dhaka Stock Exchange in Bangladesh and publicly available government policies and action plans. Discourse analysis was used to identify the corporate narratives used in the annual report. To identify such textual analysis, we also used the word list of Dimson et al (2015). Findings of the study discovered that most of the banks and financial institutions present their ESG report separately in the annual report while others present in a disconnected strands as a part of Corporate Social Responsibility initiatives, director's report, chairmen's report, notes and disclosures. The findings have been further associated by the existing literature to understand the present situation and the prospects and challenges of ESG reporting. The study potentially contributes the integration of ESG reporting from Asian country perspectives. Since the main objective of this chapter is to understand the current status of ESG reporting for the banking sectors of Bangladesh, for sustainable business finance it also plays a significant role. Finally, this study has important theoretical contributions and practical implications for regulators, banks and financial institutions for ensuring corporate governance.

Discourse Analysis

Understanding what is meant by "discourse" is essential before talking about discourse analysis. Discourse, in the words of van Dijk (1990, p. 164), is "text in context." As a result, discourse analysis is the examination of writings in light of their surroundings. Howitt and Cramer (2011, p. 360) state that discourse is the way language functions in actual communication events. Discourse analysis is concerned with analyses that go beyond sentence level since it examines speech, text, and conversation. Discourse analysts hold that by emphasizing the communicator's own ideology, language can be used to establish a certain reality (Merkl-Davies and Koller, 2012; Hossain, 2017). Deconstructing this "constructed" reality is the responsibility of a discourse analyst. Discourse analysis can be done in two different methods. It can be done from either a sociological or linguistic perspective (Widdowson, 2007). Corporate narrative research is typically undertaken from a sociological perspective since corporate narratives are created in a socio-economic setting. Furthermore, discourse analysis is typically qualitative in nature. This is done from either an interpretative or a critical standpoint. Critical discourse analysis is conducted from critical perspective (power relation) and analyzes the text from social perspective. Most of the researchers follow an interpretive or a critical perspective. In this chapter, interpretive approach is used for discourse analysis.

Literature Review

The last decade has seen significant developments in the ESG disclosure landscape globally. Investors are becoming cognizant of the fact that competitive financial returns can be generated alongside social and environmental progress, and are beginning to embrace international standards of sustainability. The launch of the Principles of Responsible Investing (PRI) network in 2006 by the United Nations (UN) and more recently the UN Sustainable Development Goals are exemplary milestones in this evolution. Environmental, Social, and Governance (ESG) disclosure is a voluntary, nonfinancial disclosure of information that is growing in importance and gaining significant attention from academic researchers and capital market participants in recent years. The focus has been on encouraging businesses to give additional non-financial information as a result of a recent increase in demand for improved company reporting (Albitar et al., 2020; Arena et al., 2015; Gerged et al., 2021; Lai et al., 2018; Mughal et al., 2020). Due to companies' lack of non-financial disclosure, particularly that related to environmental and social responsibility information, corporate environmental and social responsibility has become an international trend as sustainability has become more important to economic development (Albitar et al., 2020; Chen et al., 2021; Gerged et al., 2021; Li et al., 2020; Liao et al., 2021). In this case ESG integration is material particularly in the form of sustainable business.

ESG stands for environmental, social, and corporate governance factors together. The post-Enron era and the Global Financial Crisis (GFC), which decreased investor confidence (Arjalies, 2010; Galbreath, 2013), have increased the focus on ESG challenges for societal change. By investing in firms with strong ESG track records, investors can play a significant role in protecting their assets and fostering social change. These factors might affect a company's capacity to carry out its business strategy and generate long-term value. There is a shift in emphasis from today's cloudy, philosophical, and aspirational language (sustainability) toward more specific operational and tactical terms (ESG), despite the fact that ESG is often referred to as non-financial or extra-financial. According to Nasdaq's ESG

Reporting Guide 2.0, 2019: 4, ESG reporting in this situation is not only a moral concern but also a financially driven pursuit of best practices and long-term profits that enlightens management. In contrast to environmental disclosure, which does not show a correlation between governance disclosures and analyst prediction accuracy, the ESG disclosure shows one (Bernardi & Stark, 2018). Based on its three basic components, a prior study looked into the quantity and quality of ESG disclosures made by businesses. According to its findings, companies that were subjected to more thorough testing and proper supervision by institutional investors were less likely to engage in ESG greenwashing (Yu et al., 2020). On the other hand Lamanda and Tamásné Vőneki (2023) studied the annual, risk and sustainability reports published by 26 banks in Central European Countries from 2017 to 2021 and found strong association between bank size (total assets) and ESG reporting, and between capital adequacy and ESG reporting.

According to research on ESG compliant companies, they have stronger governance, care more about the environment and sustainable development, have less volatile profitability, and can access capital with cheaper costs (Kumar, 2020). By 2030, businesses should publish their ESG practices, according to the UN (SSE, 2015). Governments must actively encourage companies to engage in ESG disclosures that benefit both their business value chain and their shareholders by providing a variety of tax incentives (Jallai, 2020). According to Sustainability Reporting Guidelines (SRG), Bangladesh Securities and Exchange Commission (BSEC) has mandated that listed companies include ESG reporting in their annual reports, and Bangladesh Bank has published guidelines for Environmental and Social Risk Management (ESRM) and Sustainability Reporting for all banks and financial institutions operating in Bangladesh.

ESG Reporting and Corporate Governance

More than 2000 empirical studies on ESG disclosures and firm success are examined by Friede et al. (2015), and they discovered that 90% of the studies demonstrate a favorable relationship between ESG and corporate performance. Few studies have examined the relationship between a firm's competitive advantage and ESG, despite the fact that ESG improves performance. According to Saurabh (2019), a firm's ability to generate more economic profit than its adversary can be characterized as having a competitive edge. Another study of Lagasio and Cucari (2019) used meta-analysis of 24 empirical studies and found that board independence, board size, and women directorship visibly enhance ESG voluntary disclosure; as well as board ownership and CEO duality do not improve the level of ESG disclosure. The literature on corporate social responsibility (CSR) has demonstrated that the of board composition of directors has an impact on the disclosure of their ESG-related information, which unquestionably benefits the corporate performance of enterprises in respect to shareholders, stakeholders, and society at large. The size of the board, the presence of women and independent members on it, or the absence of the CEO serving as the board chair are some specific factors that aid governing bodies in being more open and disclosing this information to the public. Shareholders are becoming more worried about ESG concerns as a result of the possibility of lawsuit expenses or a loss of reputation for socially irresponsible businesses, which might erode long-term shareholder value (Sultana et al. 2017).

Strong corporate governance can influence decision making regarding company policies related to ESG disclosure practices (Akben-Selcuk, 2019, Albitar et al. 2020, Dam & Scholtens 2013). There was a lack of research on how corporate governance mechanisms affect the CSR narrative tones (Fisher et al. 2019). According to study by Plastun et al. (2020), European nations consistently rank among those with the highest ESG disclosure rates worldwide. Regulations imposed by the government and the stock exchanges of each country are the primary cause of the high-level disclosure that takes place in Europe. Such reporting have not only been implemented in the developed world. Instead, many developing nations, like South Africa, China, and India, have made ESG reporting for listed businesses mandatory.

Prior studies are prevalently country-based and concentrated on specific dimensions of ESG reporting. Primary attention has been devoted to investigating environmental disclosure practices, especially in the United States and other developed countries (Nicolo et al. 2023). Economic, social, and environmental challenges must all be balanced through corporate governance. In order to benefit stakeholders directly and indirectly, corporate governance mechanisms such as the board of directors and the audit committee are set up to oversee and control managers' actions and firm operations that entail community and society engagement. The primary instrument of corporate governance, the board of directors, is in charge of supervising executives and making certain that stakeholders' needs are met. Therefore, the board's organizational structure is essential to the efficiency of its monitoring responsibilities.

Umma et al. (2023) studied the impact of corporate governance on ESG disclosure for 18 banks (Commercial and Islamic) in Bangladesh from 2015 to 2019 and found that there was an increasing trend of ESG disclosures and it has positive relationship with board and firm size. Another study of Sultana et al. (2018), conducted in Bangladesh and their study offers the first empirical proof of how much individual stock market investors are inclined to make ESG investments. They also discussed the existing ESG and sustainability literature by demonstrating that Bangladeshi stock market investors have an equal priority for social and environmental issues. In the context of Bangladesh, research on ESG is relatively low.

The code of corporate governance in Bangladesh places greater focus on social responsibility initiatives by listed companies and the reporting of such activities to the community. The Companies Act of 1994, the Insurance Act of 2015, the Banking Companies Act of 1991, the Income Tax Act 2023 (previously Income Tax Ordinance 1984), the Bangladesh Securities and Exchange Commission Order of 1969, the BSEC Rules of 1987 (revised in 2016 for all limited companies), and numerous other rules established by public sector corporations all play a role in measuring reporting practices in Bangladesh. The introduction of the Corporate Governance Code 2018 which aims to strengthen and advance corporate governance practices in Bangladesh-marked a significant development in the country's capital market. According to Ferdous (2018), good corporate governance is a crucial tool for the growth capital market since it fosters trust among stakeholders and depositors, who are then willing to pay a higher price for a share, boosting a company's potential to attract more investment from stock exchanges. The common issues of ESG are covered in the annual report are laid down below:

Table 1. Common ESG issues and the areas of concern

Environmental	Social	Governance
Biodiversity loss	Diversity and inclusion, race, gender	Transparency, Leadership, accountability
Climate change, reduced carbon emissions	Human rights, supply chain and sources	Board independence, strategic oversights
Renewable energy, green building	Anti-discrimination, bulling, harassment, data privacy	Shareholder activism
Sustainable investment	Native title, cultural heritage	Anti-bribery and corruption
Deforestation	Health and safety practices	Risk mitigation and management
Water usage	Privacy and data security	
Consideration of native title		

(Author's own identification)

METHODOLOGY

The sample size of thirty banks listed from Dhaka Stock Exchange (DSE) are taken into consideration from 2020 to 2022 (Appendix 1). The main sources of information are annual reports of listed companies for three years in Bangladesh. The banking sector ESG disclosure is the key focus of this study. The selection on which banks to affiliate with was driven by recent Bangladesh Bank directives that supported CSR and green reporting. The disclosure of corporate social responsibility (CSR), social and environmental reporting (SER), sustainability reporting (Ullah and Rahman, 2015), and societal and charitable (Dissanayake et al. 2016) activities is at the forefront for banking firms. Additionally, listed businesses typically prioritize completing legislative obligations and providing high-quality reports for various stakeholders. Annual reports of representative banks, reports from the Bangladesh Bank, pertinent publications, periodicals, websites, the Internet, and research papers were also taken into account (Khan et al. 2011). Additionally, all portions of the annual reports (such as the vision statement, mission statement, directors' report, chairman's report, and notes and explanations) were examined in order to verify the validity and credibility of each annual report on social, environmental and governance issues. Discourse analysis was used to identify the key words used in the textual narratives.

ESG reporting practices have significantly increased, particularly among the world's best-performing corporations. The goal of the United Nations Climate Change Conference (also known as COP 21), to attain net-zero carbon emissions by 2021, gave fresh fuel to the ESG reporting debate, notably among financial institutions. That why this study considered banks as a sample. As the aim of this chapter is understand the ESG reporting and disclosure in the banking sectors of Bangladesh, a developing country so it employs a discourse analysis. After discourse analysis, this chapter also followed Dimson et al (2015) wordlist in structuring the data.

Categorization and Integration of Environmental Social and Governance Issues

This study quantitatively demonstrates the ESG content in annual reports in order to determine the ESG activity of an organization. As a result, we develop an ESG word list that can then be applied to various studies on Corporate Social Responsibility (CSR) and Socially Responsible Investments (SRI) investing methods. A method is devised that enables us to make a meaningful list based on the body of textual analysis literature that is already available based on Dimson et al (2015). First of all, this study collected information from the annual report of top 30 banks listed in the DSE from 2020 to 2022 and tried to chalk out whether ESG disclosures are available or not. Then we traced the ESG word list in the annual report and checked the availability of textual narratives used in those reports or not. Finally, by using discourse analysis we analyzed the contents used in ESG integration.

Table 2. Topics, categories, and subcategories of ESG word list

Governance		
Corporate Governance	Business ethics	Sustainability management
Audit and control	Bribery and corruption	Disclosure and reporting
Board structure	Political influence	Stakeholder engagement
Remuneration	Responsible marketing	UNGC compliance
Shareholder's right	Whistle blowing system	Governance of sustainability
Transparency		
Talent		
Environmental		
Ecosystem service	Climate change	Environmental management
Access to land	Biofuels	Environmental standards
Biodiversity management	Climate change strategy	Pollution control
Water	Emission management	Product opportunities
		Waste and recycling
Social		
Public health	Human rights	Labor standards
Access to medicine	Community relations	Diversity
Nutrition	Privacy	Health and safety
Product safety	Security	ILO core conventions
Society	Weak governance zones	Supply chain labor standard
Charity		
Education		

Source: Dimson et al. (2015)

DISCUSSION AND FINDINGS

Due to United Nations Climate Change Conference (COP 21), banks and financial institutions can play a significant role in reaching the zero net carbon emission. Regulators and governments around the world have since adopted a more proactive stance to disclose ESG reporting due to positive impact on cost reduction and optimal investment. We have checked the annual report of banking industries from 2020 to 2022 and found the following narratives by using discourse analysis.

Example 1

We also made rapid strides in further strengthening our **governance**, *particularly in the area of* **risk and sustainability**, *while embedding the principles of* **ESG (environmental, social and governance) into our business model** *for added sustainability and* **stakeholder confidence**. *In 2021, we bolstered our focus on* **business growth, cost optimization, investments in technology, ESG targets adoption, and improving operating efficiency**, *thus representing a* **holistic approach** *to respond to an evolving operating environment and stakeholder needs and expectations. (Brac Bank Annual Report 2021, Authors emphasis)*

In the Brac Bank Ltd they are more focusing on improving their governance issues specifically in risk mitigation and sustainable business. They tried to integrate ESG into their business model in order to meet the demand of stakeholder's need.

Example 2

Formulating strategies, *determining the environmental, social and governance (ESG) factors and overseeing the* **management and monitoring** *of the ESG factors* **that are material to the business**. *(Bank Asia Annual Report 2021, Authors emphasis)*

In the Bank Asia, they tried to focus on the materiality issues so that the top management look after the performance of ESG factors that affect their business performance.

Example 3

City Bank took concomitant steps to **address environmental, social, and governance (ESG) challenges** *in 2022, and this report details the Bank's efforts to uphold these responsibilities. Although both* **short and long-term targets** *have been progressed toward, the Bank acknowledges that there is more work to be done. During the year, the* **ESG framework** *that advances the Bank's improvement* **objectives and targets and identifies potential risks** *was upgraded upon to reflect the evolving realities.* **ESG actions were routinely reported to the management and the Board,** *and it has since been* **prioritized as a topic of discussion at every Board meeting**. *The Bank includes ESG factors into* **its daily operations** *and* **business decisions.** *(City Bank Ltd annual report 2022, Authors emphasis)*

From the perspectives of City bank, they are mainly achieving short and long term targets for addressing ESG challenges and they frequently discussed it in the board meeting. For their regular operation and business decision, they considered ESG factors.

Example 4

The Green Finance and Sustainable Linked Financ*e together comprise the Sustainable Finance. Sustainable financing mainly focuses on taking due account* **of environmental, social and governance consideration** *when* **making investment decisions** *in the financial sectors.* **Government's development plan, its global commitment to sustainability** *and Bangladesh Bank's* **strategic goals** *are the major drivers to formulate the policy. (Dutch Bangla Bank Limited Annual report 2022, Authors emphasis)*

From the Dutch Bangla bank perspective, their sustainable finance, they will consider the ESG performance while taking any investment decision.

Example 5

IFIC Bank Limited has all **unveiled measures to enhance its commitment to ESG** *themes.* **As a highly regulated institution**, *IFIC Bank has long addressed* **governance** *issues. Alongside, the Bank increasingly focused on* **social issues** *in response to the* **policy and guidelines** *of Bangladesh Bank, putting particular* **emphasis on diversity, equity and inclusion**. *(IFIC Bank Annual Report 2021, Authors emphasis)*

IFIC bank not only considered the sustainability issues but also considers the guidance of Bangladesh Bank particularly importance given to diversity, equity and financial inclusion along with corporate governance issues.

Example 6

ONE Bank Limited is committed to contribute **sustainable economy** *by including environmental, social and governance (ESG) considerations in their every* **investment decision and in-house activities.** *ONE Bank Limited cares for* **climate change mitigation and adaptation, preservation of biodiversity, prevention of pollution, promotion of the circular economy, inequality, inclusiveness, investment in human capital** *etc. (One Bank Annual report 2021, Authors emphasis)*

In case of One bank, they also contribute to the sustainable economy and investment in projects with the help of EGS integration. For every business decision and climate change related issues, they strongly care for the sustainable finance.

Example 7

Prime Bank Limited is also putting more emphasis on building **our expertise in environmental, social, and governance** *or 'ESG' areas, across all businesses and is committed to* **reducing the emissions of the projects we finance**. *We are proactively channeling funds to "green" companies. Businesses with* **green credentials, renewable energy, refurbishing plants, and adaptive technologies** *have been prioritized. (Prime Bank Annual report 2021, Authors emphasis)*

Here, Prime bank considered all the green companies that they finance are committed to reduce the carbon emission and adopt new technologies.

Example 8

Our **sustainability strategy** *mirrors our* **business approach** *of* **balancing growth with stability**. *It takes into account the* **influence and impact** *our decisions and actions may have on our* **stakeholders** *and the* **environment**. *It also ensures that we remain* **economically relevant through managing ESG risks and opportunities** *practically and in line with* **market realities. To enable our programs and initiatives** *to take root and to grow, The Premier Bank has ensured* **alignment with the ESG-related laws and regulations** *in Bangladesh. (The Premier Bank Annual report 2020, Authors emphasis)*

From the annual report of the Premier Bank, the stakeholders and businesses are following ESG integration and managing risk and opportunities properly. Abide by all the rules and regulations of Bangladesh bank they are trying to take initiatives to develop from its existing situation.

Example 9

Environmental, Social and Governance (ESG) initiatives are always getting importance in NCCBL. At first step we run **ESCR (Environmental & Social Compliance Rating).** *We always try to* **book top ESCR rated client**. *Under these initiatives we also focused our attention towards* **financing environment friendly projects** *such as through* **compliance of environment certificate, ensuring ETP in required case, energy efficient machinery imports, promoting Bangladesh**

Bank's Green initiatives through refinance program. *(NCC Bank Limited Annual report 2022, Authors emphasis)*

NCC bank mainly prepared score system for identification of top ESCR client. At the time of refinance environment friendly project, they are mainly considering Bangladesh bank's green finance rules and regulation.

Example 10

ESG considerations are becoming increasingly important in modern times, as people are becoming more aware of the **impact on wellbeing and the environment.** *ESG criteria are a set of standards for* **conscientious investors** *to* **evaluate potential investments** *based on their* **sustainability and environmental impacts**. *Shahjalal Islami Bank is committed to creating a better and sustainable world, and as such,* **our vision and strategies are focused on long-term sustainability** *to leave a better world for future generations. We are determined to* **integrate ESG policies** *in building and running our business, and to* **establish our prominence** *as leaders in* **ESG parameters** *in Bangladesh. (Shahajalal Islami Bank Annual report 2022, Authors emphasis)*

Here Shahajalal Islami Bank Ltd considered the ESG parameters for evaluating and monitoring different projects for day-to-day business operation. For better and sustainable world, their mission and vision are in congruence of long-term sustainability.

From the above discussion it is clear that banks are integrating ESG disclosure from their day-to-day operations. But standalone ESG reporting is not available for all banks. Out of thirty banks, only ten banks present their ESG reporting separately in the annual report. Other banks they disclosed such information in the directors' report, chairmen's report, CSR initiatives, notes and disclosures. The level of ESG reporting in Bangladesh has continued to be poor despite all of these regulatory initiatives by the regulatory organizations like Bangladesh Bank. Though most of the banks take initiatives to disclose ESG reporting but also ESG risks and opportunities are taken into consideration. In some cases, sustainable finance and green finance gets priority. In case of ESG word list, most of the banks used governance related words and then environmental and social issues. Moreover, from the annual report, it was found that the EGS reporting has increasingly gained momentum after COVID 19.

CONCLUSION

The chapter examines the environmental, social and governance related disclosure practice in the context of Bangladesh an emerging economy. The data are mainly collected from the annual reports of Banks from 2020 to 2022. The latest annual reports of the thirty banks were analyzed to understand the ESG disclosures in the annual report and archival documents, government publications and websites were reviewed to apprehend the current status of such reporting. The key findings of the study have two-fold. At first the banking sector regularly and consistently presents their ESG disclosure in the annual reports due to Bangladesh Bank rules and regulations. By identifying those factors that affect the corporate performance of banking and non-banking financial institutions. Second, investors can be attracted for foreign direct investment by ensuring governance and safety.

The study has important policy and practice implications. As the policy level, government should identify the gap to ensure more participation from banks and financial institutions to strengthen stakeholders' confidence. Companies would be able to understand the current situation of ESG related disclosures and comprehend the importance of integration of ESG. This would not only help them to be climate sensitive but also enable them to work government, regulators to formulate relative strategies for the achievement of sustainable development goals. Though this study has some limitations since it only considered the banking sectors and time frame is for three years only, so researchers may undertake future research in a different context with an increased sample size. Policymakers can move forward with regulatory requirements to improve sustainable business process. The previous obstacle to ESG integration was the idea that ESG issues weren't important from a financial standpoint and shouldn't be taken into account when making investments. The timing of the investment was another obstacle. ESG risks and possibilities didn't seem relevant in shorter timeframes in the past because many investors had a tendency to consider quite short term. Moreover, lack of information is available on ESG issues in the annual report of Bangladesh. Also, in the absence of external assurance, the authenticity of ESG reporting could be questioned. Since there is no standard format for ESG reporting like financial reporting which is guided by IFRS or IAS so it creates some challenge on management what is required to be reported. Historically, corporations have been accustomed to gathering data for use in financial reporting. However, there have only been a few attempts (and associated investments) to develop and preserve ESG data. This study also contributes to the identification of sustainable business performance by reviewing different indicators of sustainable development goals (SDGs). Businesses and investors will need to manage the ESG impacts to their business or investments alike, while leveraging the sustainability opportunities that abound. Finally, ESG reporting is going to be a significant trend in businesses around the world given the emphasis on net-zero emissions at high-profile events like the COP 2021. And this is high time for Bangladesh to step up and join the regulatory wagon.

REFERENCES

Adams, C. A. (2017). Conceptualising the contemporary corporate value creation process. *Accounting, Auditing & Accountability Journal*, *30*(4), 906–931. doi:10.1108/AAAJ-04-2016-2529

Ahmed, S. U., & Rahman, M. (2014). Incorporating ESG Risk in Bank-Lending in Bangladesh. *International Research Journal of Finance and Economics*, (120), 23–34.

Akben-Selcuk, E. (2019). Corporate social responsibility and financial performance: The moderating role of ownership concentration in Turkey. *Sustainability*, *11*(13), 36–43. doi:10.3390u11133643

Albitar, K., Hussainey, K., Kolade, N., & Gerged, A. (2020). ESG disclosure and firm performance before and after IR: The moderating role of governance mechanisms. *International Journal of Accounting & Information Management*, *28*(3), 429–444. doi:10.1108/IJAIM-09-2019-0108

Arena, C., Bozzolan, S., & Michelon, G. (2015). Environmental reporting: Transparency to stakeholders or stakeholder manipulation? An analysis of disclosure tone and the role of the board of directors. *Corporate Social Responsibility and Environmental Management*, *22*(6), 346–361. doi:10.1002/csr.1350

Arjalies, D. L. (2010). A social movement perspective on finance: How socially responsible investment mattered. *Journal of Business Ethics*, *92*(S1), 57–78. doi:10.100710551-010-0634-7

Barker, R., & Eccles, R. G. (2019). *Should FASB and IASB be responsible for setting standards for nonfinancial information?* Saïd Business School, University of Oxford.

Bernardi, C., & Stark, A. W. (2018). Environmental, social and governance disclosure, integrated reporting, and the accuracy of analyst forecasts. *The British Accounting Review*, *50*(1), 16–31. doi:10.1016/j.bar.2016.10.001

Bhuyian, M., & Hussain, M. (2020, June 06). Bangladesh moves 17 notches up on Environmental Performance Index. *The Business Standard*.

Camilleri, M.A. (2022). Walking the talk about corporate social responsibility communication: an elaboration likelihood model perspective. *Business Ethics, the Environment & Responsibility, 31*(3), 649-661.

Dam, L., & Scholtens, B. (2013). Ownership concentration and CSR policy of European multinational enterprises. *Journal of Business Ethics*, *118*(1), 117–126. doi:10.100710551-012-1574-1

Deegan, C. (2002). Introduction: The legitimising effect of social and environmental disclosures–a theoretical foundation. *Accounting, Auditing & Accountability Journal*, *15*(3), 282–311. doi:10.1108/09513570210435852

Dimson, E., Karakas, O., & Li, X. (2015). Active ownership. *Review of Financial Studies*, *28*(12), 3225–3268. doi:10.1093/rfs/hhv044

Dissanayake, D., Tilt, C., & Xydias-Lobo, M. (2016). Sustainability reporting by publicly listed companies in Sri Lanka. *Journal of Cleaner Production*, *129*, 169–182. doi:10.1016/j.jclepro.2016.04.086

Ferdous, C. S. (2018). Corporate governance in Bangladesh: Evidence of compliance. *International Business Research*, *11*(3), 88–109. doi:10.5539/ibr.v11n3p88

Fisher, R., van Staden, C., & Richards, G. (2019). Watch that tone: An investigation of the use and stylistic consequences of tone in corporate accountability disclosures. *Accounting, Auditing & Accountability Journal*, *33*(1), 77–105. doi:10.1108/AAAJ-10-2016-2745

Friede, G., Busch, T., & Bassen, A. (2015). ESG and financial performance: Aggregated evidence from more than 2,000 empirical studies. *Journal of Sustainable Finance & Investment*, *5*(4), 210–233. doi:10.1080/20430795.2015.1118917

Galbreath, J. (2013). ESG in focus: The Australian evidence. *Journal of Business Ethics*, *118*(3), 529–541. doi:10.100710551-012-1607-9

Garcia-Sanchez, I. M., Cuadrado-Ballesteros, B., & Sepulveda, C. (2014). Does media pressure moderate CSR disclosures by external directors? *Management Decision, London*, *52*(6), 1014–1045. doi:10.1108/MD-09-2013-0446

Gerged, A. M., Albitar, K., & Alhaddad, L. (2021). Corporate environmental disclosure and earnings management—The moderating role of corporate governance structures. *International Journal of Finance & Economics*, *28*(3), 2789–2810. doi:10.1002/ijfe.2564

Graus, S., Rehman, S. U., & García, J. S. (2020). Corporate Social Responsibility and Environmental Performance: The Mediating Role of Environmental Strategy and Green Innovation. *Technological Forecasting and Social Change*, *16*, 120262.

Guerrero-Villegas, J., Pérez-Calero, L., Hurtado-González, J. M., & Giráldez-Puig, P. (2018). Board Attributes and Corporate Social Responsibility Disclosure: A Meta-Analysis. *Sustainability*, *10*(12), 4808. doi:10.3390u10124808

Hossain, D. M. (2017). *Exploring the Main Discourses and Power Relations in The Disclosure on Social Inequality Issues in Corporate Narratives* [Unpublished Doctoral Thesis]. IIUM, Malaysia.

Howitt, D., & Cramer, D. (2011). *Introduction to Research Methods in Psychology (3rdedn.)*. Pearson.

Jallai. (2020). Ethical standards for tax planning by corporations. In *Ethics and Taxation*. Springer.

Khan, H., Azizul Islam, M., Kayeser Fatima, J., & Ahmed, K. (2011). Corporate sustainability reporting of major commercial banks in line with GRI: Bangladesh evidence. *Social Responsibility Journal*, *7*(3), 347–362. doi:10.1108/17471111111154509

KPMG. (2022). https://kpmg.com/xx/en/home/insights/2022/09/survey-of sustainability-reporting-2022/esg.html

Lagasio, V., & Cucari, N. (2019). Corporate governance and environmental social governance disclosure: A meta analytical review. *Corporate Social Responsibility and Environmental Management*, *26*(4), 701–711. doi:10.1002/csr.1716

Lamanda, G., & Tamásné Vőneki, Z. (2023). Is ESG disclosure associated with bank performance? Evidence from the Visegrad Four countries. *Management of Environmental Quality*. Advance online publication. doi:10.1108/MEQ-02-2023-0064

Li, Y., Gong, M., Zhang, X., & Koh, L. (2018). The Impact of Environmental, Social, and Governance Disclosure on Firm Value: The Role of CEO Power. *The British Accounting Review*, *50*(1), 60–75. doi:10.1016/j.bar.2017.09.007

Li, Z., Liao, G., & Albitar, K. (2020). Does corporate environmental responsibility engagement affect firm value? The mediating role of corporate innovation. *Business Strategy and the Environment*, *29*(3), 1045–1055. doi:10.1002/bse.2416

Liao, G., Hou, P., Shen, X., & Albitar, K. (2021). The impact of economic policy uncertainty on stock returns: The role of corporate environmental responsibility engagement. *International Journal of Finance & Economics*, *26*(3), 4386–4392. doi:10.1002/ijfe.2020

Merkl-Davies, D., & Koller, V. (2012). 'Metaphoring' people out of this world: A critical discourse analysis of a chairman's statement of a UK defence firm. *Accounting Forum*, *36*(3), 178–193. doi:10.1016/j.accfor.2012.02.005

Nasdaq. (2019). *ESG reporting guide 2.0, A support resource for companies*. Nasdaq.

Nicolo, G., Zampone, G., Sannino, G., & Tiron-Tudor, A. (2023). Worldwide evidence of corporate governance influence on ESG disclosure in the utilities sector. *Utilities Policy*, *82*, 101549. doi:10.1016/j.jup.2023.101549

Nosratabadi, S., Mosavi, A., Shamshirband, S., Kazimieras Zavadskas, E., Rakotonirainy, A., & Chau, K. W. (2019). Sustainable Business Models: A Review. *Sustainability*, *11*(6), 1663. doi:10.3390u11061663

Plastun, A., Makarenko, I., Khomutenko, L., Osetrova, O., & Shcherbakov, P. (2020). SDGs and ESG disclosure regulation: Is there an impact? Evidence from Top-50 world economies. *Problems and Perspectives in Management*, *18*(2), 231–245. doi:10.21511/ppm.18(2).2020.20

Saurbh, S. (2019). *Economic Value Added for competitive advantage a case of Indian enterprises*. Cambridge Scholar Publishing.

Sultana, S., Zainal, D., & Zulkifli, N. (2017). The influence of environmental, social and governance (ESG) on investment decisions: The Bangladesh perspective. *Pertanika Journal of Social Science & Humanities*, *25*, 155–173.

Sultana, S., Zulkifli, N., & Zainal, D. (2018). Environmental, social and governance (ESG) and investment decision in Bangladesh. *Sustainability*, *10*(6), 1831. doi:10.3390u10061831

Ullah, M. H., & Rahman, M. A. (2015). Corporate social responsibility reporting practices in banking companies in Bangladesh: Impact of regulatory change. *Journal of Financial Reporting and Accounting*, *13*(2), 200–225. doi:10.1108/JFRA-05-2013-0038

Umma, H., Khan, M., Sultana, R., & Acharjee, K. (2023). Impact of corporate governance on ESG and Financial performance: A comparison between Commercial and Islamic Banks. *The Journal of Business*, *8*(1), 1–14.

van Dijk, T. A. (1990). The future of the field: Discourse analysis in the 1990s. *Text*, *10*, 133–156.

Widdowson, H. G. (2007). *Discourse Analysis*. Oxford University Press.

Wood, J. (2020). *Why this moment could be decisive for tackling climate change: Report*. https://www.weforum.org/agenda/2020/07/how-covid-19-could-spark-climate-change-recovery-sustainability/WorldEconomicForum

Ying, M., Tikuye, G. A., & Shan, H. (2021). Impacts of Firm Performance on Corporate Social Responsibility Practices: The Mediation Role of Corporate Governance in Ethiopia Corporate Business. *Sustainability*, *13*(17), 9717. doi:10.3390u13179717

Yu, E.-y., Van Luu, B., & Chen, C. H. (2020). Greenwashing in environmental, social and governance disclosures. *Research in International Business and Finance*, *52*, 101192. doi:10.1016/j.ribaf.2020.101192

APPENDIX

Table 3. List of banks from 2020 to 2022

Serial	Name of the Bank
1	Al-Arafah Islami Bank Ltd
2	AB bank ltd
3	Brac bank ltd
4	Bank Asia ltd
5	City bank ltd
6	Dhaka Bank Ltd
7	Dutch-bangla bank ltd
8	Exim bank ltd
9	Eastern bank ltd
10	First security Islamic bank ltd
11	IFIC bank ltd
12	ICB islami bank ltd
13	Islami bank Bangladesh ltd
14	Jamuna bank ltd
15	Mercantile bank ltd
16	Mutual trust bank ltd
17	NCC bank ltd
18	National bank ltd
19	One bank ltd
20	Premier bank ltd
21	Prime bank ltd
22	Pubali bank ltd
23	Rupali bank ltd
24	Social islami bank ltd
25	Shahjalal islami bank ltd
26	Southeast bank ltd
27	Standard bank ltd
28	Trust bank ltd
29	Uttara bank ltd
30	UCB bank ltd

Chapter 8
Islamic Worldview-Based Corporate Governance Framework in Providing Guidance on Executive Directors' Remuneration in an Islamic Financial Institution

Md Nazim Uddin
Ankara University, Turkey

Ahasanul Haque
International Islamic University, Malaysia

EXECUTIVE SUMMARY

This chapter addresses how corporate governance supports shareholder-director conflicts and company success. Islamic financial institution (IFI) governance and performance have not been studied, yet corporate governance has affected previous financial crises. This examines IFI board size, ownership, CEO duality, and pay committee independent directors. Also studied is how Islamic corporate governance influences executive director pay. Thus, IFIs require an IWBCGF to handle current and future corporate governance issues. Qualitative corporate governance metrics research and qualitative Islamic principle evaluation helped exploratory studies attain these goals. The research shows that corporate governance strongly impacts IFI executive pay. These results show that executive directors require an Islamic-based comprehensive governance framework to navigate corporate governance issues. The study makes literary contributions. It tackles the lack of religious research on Islam and IFI corporate governance. It highlights IFIs' corporate governance and CEO remuneration.

DOI: 10.4018/978-1-6684-9867-5.ch008

INTRODUCTION

These disastrous incidents have eroded shareholders' wealth and questioned CEO remuneration schemes' ethics (Jan et al., 2023). Financial crises often center on CEO pay, raising questions about its influence on business behaviour and its ability to cause financial malfeasance (Kausar Alam et al., 2020). Executive compensation, especially in crises, highlights the need for a robust governance structure to manage Islamic financial institutions' top-tier executives' salaries (IFI). Pay policy inefficiencies and knowledge asymmetry cause economic costs and market failures. Aligning director and shareholder interests is a significant issue. Organisational governance systems strive to reduce this conflict and improve corporate performance (Murphy & Smolarski, 2020). Agency theory emphasises executive salary in motivating top management to prioritise shareholders' interests (Alam et al., 2019).

Directors' pay arrangements that match a company's strategic goals can promote stability and development. Executive compensation in listed companies has surged, but firm performance has lagged, a troubling trend (Bukhari et al., 2013). Islamic financial firms have yet to thoroughly investigate CEO remuneration and corporate governance procedures, especially in developing countries. Executives are seen as "fat cats among bankers," which fuels arguments over their remuneration packages.

The main problem is assessing the complex relationship between corporate governance structures and pay practices in IFIs, where agency conflicts, especially between majority and minority shareholders, grow. Lack of CEO compensation transparency increases knowledge asymmetry and moral hazard (Abd Aziz & Abd Ghadas, 2019). Due to its significant influence on corporate performance, pay has been a study focus. This study explores the complex relationship between corporate governance and executive director pay. This inquiry explores Islam's ideas and ideals beyond the traditional view. Shariah and religious traditions can give directors accountability, trustworthiness, responsibility, and ethics. Directors, custodians of shareholders, stakeholders, and Allah (SWT) can help create a fair and equitable business environment.

This study presents an Islamic worldview-based corporate governance framework (IWBCGF) based on divine teachings. The concept is based on the idea that directors will always find answers to corporate governance issues. This methodology combines modern corporate governance procedures with Islamic teachings to help IFIs negotiate executive director compensation. This study is important for two reasons. First, religion, especially Islam, has not been studied regarding corporate governance, senior directors' pay, and firm performance. Islamic principles applied to company governance and pay can provide insights and actions that differ from IFI norms. Second, this study provides a new viewpoint on how corporate governance structures affect directors' pay and business performance. It offers a new perspective on corporate governance theories in IFIs by examining how Islamic beliefs affect these dynamics.

This research examines the prevalence of corporate governance concerns in IFIs, particularly executive director compensation. Corporate governance failings during financial crises have prompted concerns about the ethical implications of CEO remuneration schemes and financial misconduct. This issue underlines the need for robust IFI governance in regulating executive director salaries and aligning their interests with those of shareholders.

This problem is the core purpose of the research on corporate governance failure, and Islamic corporate governance must be investigated. Islamic ideals can illuminate these governance flaws. Islamic corporate governance methods have the potential to promote director accountability, integrity, and ethics, hence lowering IFI corporate governance failures.

This study aims to offer an Islamic worldview-based corporate governance framework (IWBCGF) that blends Islamic principles with contemporary corporate governance. This technique assists IFIs in managing executive director salaries, resulting in a more equitable and ethical business atmosphere. This research aims to uncover innovative approaches to strengthen corporate governance in IFIs by investigating the relationship between corporate governance, CEO salary, and Islamic principles.

The chapter explores Islamic finance's complex ethical compensation landscape. The following sections explore the proposed IWBCGF and Islamic principles to demonstrate the transformational potential of a comprehensive governance framework for executive directors' pay in IFIs. There are four parts to the chapter. The study will examine agency theory, CG mechanism, and executive compensation literature. The final piece explains why IFIs should follow Islamic principles in business and religion and use them to establish corporate governance frameworks. After the conclusion this document will conclude.Top of Form

LITERATURE REVIEWS

Prior Studies on Corporate Governance and Executive Remuneration

Corporate governance and its effects on performance have been extensively studied (Ghayad, 2008; Noordin & Kassim, 2019). Executive compensation drives an organisation's incentive structure and is crucial to corporate governance (Sadek et al., 2018). Corporate governance procedures and CEO remuneration have drawn the attention of studyers and practitioners. Scholars have linked corporate governance elements, including board size, independence, meeting frequency, and control, to CEO pay and firm success (Ghayad, 2008; Htay, 2012). Corporate governance has increasingly been shown to affect top director remuneration. Executive compensation is an essential internal governance tool that helps shareholders and owners resolve disagreements (Mollah & Zaman, 2015).

The significance of agency theory in corporate governance compensation discussion continues (Muneeza & Hassan, 2014; Sencal & Asutay, 2021). Due to its prominence in business, its consequences and possible links to corporate governance are investigated. This study examines how corporate governance characteristics affect Malaysian Islamic Banking and Finance Institutions' (IBFI) executive pay. Multiple initiatives have been made to improve corporate governance to increase openness and accountability. Executive contracts, pay, board arrangements, and monitoring committees have been studied (Kok & Shahgholian, 2023).

Corporate governance's influence on CEO pay has been criticised, especially following the 2008 financial crisis. Business compensation schemes influenced managers' risk-taking throughout this crisis (Mamatzakis et al., 2023). The financial crisis showed a favourable association between exorbitant pay and risk-taking. The ethical framework of Islamic banking organisations complicates CEO compensation. A comprehensive Islamic governance structure is needed in this situation (Bhatti & Bhatti, 2009; Jan et al., 2021). This study presents a governance system that aligns Islamic finance objectives with CEO salaries to guarantee ethical compensation in Islamic financial firms. It explores corporate governance and executive pay literature to provide the groundwork for an ethical compensation paradigm for Islamic finance.

A study on corporate governance and executive pay shows that governance procedures shape compensation systems. The intricate link between corporate governance characteristics, agency theory, and executive salary is shown (Harun et al., 2020; Swandaru & Muneeza, 2022). After the 2008 financial crisis, ethical and responsible compensation became more important. Islamic finance requires a unique governance system due to ethical concerns. This essay will discuss building an ethical compensation system for Islamic financial institutions, addressing this specialised field's particular problems and potential.

Conventional and Islamic Corporate Governance Systems

The evaluation begins with standard corporate governance characteristics. Western corporate governance paradigms, such as the shareholder-centric US and European approaches, dominate these systems(Kok & Shahgholian, 2023). Traditional governance systems put the interests of shareholders and profit maximization first. Market conditions, norms, and laws guide their accountability and transparency.

According to the study, traditional corporate governance methods have flaws. Concerns include agency difficulties, moral hazards, and executive director compensation (Uddin et al., 2022). Analysts say normal CEO pay is usually extravagant and unrelated to corporate profitability, presenting ethical and fairness concerns. Unlike conventional techniques, Islamic corporate governance systems are founded on Shariah and Islamic standards. The research examines Islamic governance ideas such as "Mudarabah" (profit-sharing) and "Musharakah" (partnership), which stress risk-sharing and ethics. Islamic governance places a premium on shareholder wealth and resource sharing(Razak et al., 2020).

The survey of literature contrasts traditional and Islamic corporate governance methods. It emphasizes that Islamic rule is founded on economic, moral, and ethical principles. Islamic administration differs from traditional techniques regarding ethics, accountability to Allah (SWT), and the larger good (Uddin et al., 2020). The research model for bridging conventional and Islamic corporate governance is described in the summary. The strategy seems to integrate contemporary governance concepts with Islamic values to impact IFI executive director remuneration (Hamdan et al., 2021). The study aims to resolve ethical difficulties with executive compensation structures aligned with Islamic teachings. This literature analysis highlights the need to distinguish between conventional and Islamic corporate governance systems. It sets the stage for further investigation of the proposed Islamic worldview-based corporate governance structure and its capacity to steer IFI executive director remuneration.

Remuneration

Executive compensation has become a hot topic in business, especially in public companies. This emphasis on executive pay has drawn attention from studies, regulators, industry practitioners, and the public. Due to worldwide market competitiveness, especially among public businesses, it is becoming more prevalent. The phrase "remuneration" includes employee salary, bonuses, and allowances. This study defines remuneration as top-tier management pay (Shamsudheen & Rosly, 2021).

Alam (2022) defines corporate pay as wealth provided to firm managers. This resource allocation determines the cost-benefit dynamics of performance, determining the executive director's salary and its influence on the firm's economic results. Executive pay methods are dual-purpose. They resolve agency issues caused by the separation of control and ownership and realign the board of directors and shareholders' vested interests (Almutairi & Quttainah, 2020). The Malaysian Code on Corporate Governance (MCCG), 2012, recommends linking directors' remuneration packages to the company's business strategy and long-term goals.

Executive remuneration includes cash, stock, option awards, and bonuses. These aspects may be combined to create pay contracts incentivising managers to serve shareholders (Mutamimah & Saputri, 2023). The study suggests that cash-based components, including wages, fees, and bonuses, are essential to compensation systems (Mnif & Tahari, 2021).

Cash-based pay is crucial to performance. Shareholders prefer cash compensation because it is directly related to wealth. Thus, this analysis will stress CEO compensation's overall income. The relationship between total remuneration and business performance is well-established (Rashid et al., 2023). Salary components are a portion of pay and an incentive tool to urge directors toward optimum business performance, boosting their social standing (Alam et al., 2021).

Bonuses can encourage management success by rewarding results based on shareholder-relevant criteria. Strategic incentives motivate directors to work more, improve company performance, and help the business succeed (Pahlevi, 2023). Companies provide 73% to 85% incentives to incentivise leaders to improve their contributions (Algabry et al., 2020). Directors concentrate on business success because share-based remuneration fits their anticipation of increasing dividends, making them shareholders (Muneeza & Hassan, 2014).

The complex relationship between corporate governance and business success affects CEO pay (Sadek et al., 2018). Effective controls are needed to restrict executive discretion and exorbitant pay (Aribi & Gao, 2010). Therefore, pay committee makeup is crucial to making wise executive compensation choices. Independent directors on these committees may offer checks and balances and motivate directors to serve shareholders' interests via financial incentives. As shareholders' agents, directors safeguard stakeholder assets. This agency's function includes service, legal requirements, and daily tasks. Director participation in corporate wealth is appropriate. Compensation must be balanced to recruit and retain qualified directors for the firm's growth.

Executive remuneration is a crucial internal governance instrument that resolves shareholder-manager agency disputes (Choudhury & Alam, 2013; Mollah & Zaman, 2015). This makes it essential in difficult-to-monitor situations. Thus, executive compensation is the best contracting method for agency difficulties. Scholars, regulators, and practitioners worldwide have extensively discussed executive salaries under various good governance rules. Transparency requires a clear link between pay package design and business performance.

This literature analysis establishes a complete governance framework for executive directors' salaries to investigate ethical compensation in Islamic finance. It highlights the complex aspects that affect pay choices, directors' incentives, and the need for strong governance structures in aligning stakeholders' interests.

THE ISLAMIC WORLDVIEW

The ethical alignment of financial processes has garnered attention in Islamic finance. This ethical congruence is significant in executive director compensation. This literature analysis examines how Islamic financial organisations integrate ethics into their executive director compensation governance system. The Islamic worldview, which underpins human and corporate behaviour, is the focus (Shamsudheen et al., 2023).

The Islamic worldview underpins all elements of life, including finance and commerce (Jallali & Zoghlami, 2022). Based on *Tawhid*, the Islamic worldview stresses God's unity and oneness, molding believers' realities. This view sees life as a path to *falah*, everlasting happiness in the hereafter (Pahlevi, 2023). This viewpoint emphasises corporate ethics, linking economic goals with morality.

The *Shari'ah*, the divine rule that governs ethics, is integral to Islam. Aziz (2019) links the Islamic worldview, *Shari'ah* principles, and ethics. The *Shari'ah* guides transactions, contracts, and engagements from an ethical perspective (Hailu & Tekdoğan, 2023; Olorede et al., 2022). This shows how the Islamic worldview shapes Islamic financial institution governance. Islamic worldview, Shari'ah values, and ethics are crucial to corporate governance (CG). The concepts of Islamic accountability provide openness, justice, and social responsibility in CG interactions. Executive directors' pay structure combines ethics and financial feasibility, drawing from Islamic literature and AAOIFI norms.

THE ISLAMIC PERSPECTIVE ON CORPORATE GOVERNANCE

Zahid & Khan (2019) stresses that Muslim directors are prompted by *falah* to follow *Shari'ah* rules in their professional roles. This includes economic decision-making, commercial transactions, and corporate administration. As noted (Alam & Thakur, 2022), *falah's* capacity to influence directors' views and attitudes might help promote good corporate governance.

The study emphasises the interplay between *falah* as a spiritual incentive and accountability as the essential foundation of business governance. When incorporated into a complete framework, these two variables can synergistically promote ethical decision-making, transparency, and accountability in Islamic finance (Jan et al., 2023; Uddin et al., 2020). The approach intends to improve Islamic financial institution governance by connecting directors' motives with Islamic ethical standards to bridge the gap between financial success and spiritual purity.

Islamic values, *falah*-driven incentives, and efficient corporate governance among Muslim directors are interconnected (Enguix, 2021; Anissa, 2018; Uddin et al., 2023). It shows how spiritual ideals and responsibility awareness can shape an ethical pay system for Islamic finance executive directors. The chapter anticipates balancing financial success and morality via a comprehensive governance framework, advancing Islamic financial institutions and corporate governance ethics.

Islamic Finance Corporate Governance Framework for Executive Directors' Remuneration

The research foundation is based on Islamic financial ideas. These ideals include justice, equality, social responsibility, and the ban of gharar, riba, and maysir (gambling). Importantly, financial transactions and Islamic financial institutions are governed by Islamic finance principles (IFIs). The framework is distinguished by its incorporation of Islamic values and practices into company governance. It recognizes moral and ethical components of corporate governance in addition to economic considerations. The framework strives to create a company culture that promotes Islamic financing by infusing Islamic ideas into governance.

Figure 1. Islamic finance corporate governance framework

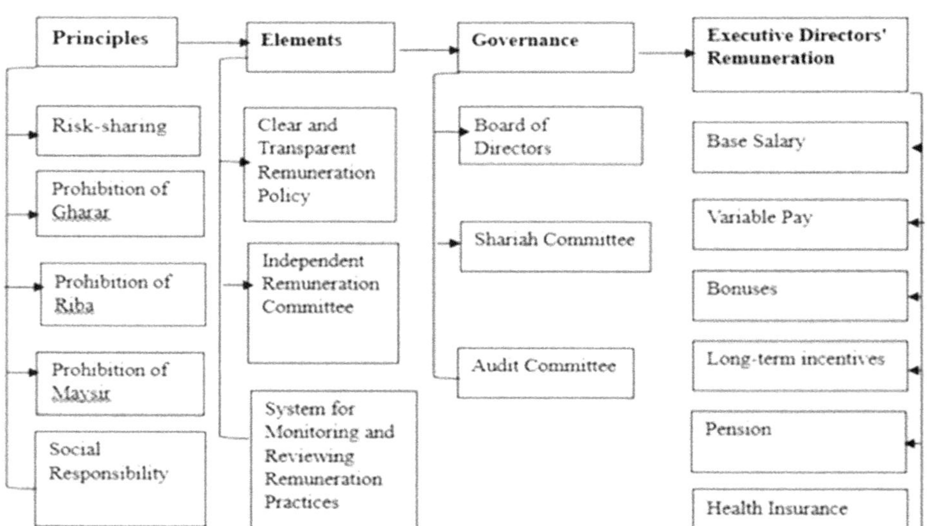

The framework encourages stakeholder risk sharing, an important Islamic finance principle. It emphasizes that executive director salaries should be aligned with risk-sharing to avoid excessive risk-taking that might harm the company or its stakeholders. This strategy reduces executive salary agency concerns. In executive compensation agreements, gharar and riba are prohibited. In pay agreements for transparency and fairness, Gharar—excessive uncertainty and ambiguity—is eliminated. Riba, or usurious conduct, is replaced with ethical pay without interest-based incentives.

Furthermore, the framework emphasizes social responsibility, a fundamental tenet of Islamic finance. It calls on IFIs to analyze the social impact of executive director compensation. This involves promoting income equity and ensuring that IFI wealth benefits shareholders and society. The Islamic Finance Corporate Governance paradigm proposed in this article deviates significantly from traditional corporate governance methodologies. Its governance structure encourages justice, ethics, risk-sharing, and social responsibility. By controlling executive director remuneration, the framework supports Islamic finance and solves corporate governance challenges in IFIs. It offers a fresh perspective on how Islamic principles may influence financial sector governance.Top of Form

PRINCIPLES UNDERLYING ISLAMIC FINANCE

Risk-Sharing

Financial transactions in Islamic finance emphasise risk-sharing, which distributes risk and reward fairly. Sharing responsibility prevents excessive risk-taking (Ahmad & Ishak, 2021). Risk-sharing proposes that executive directors can be paid based on the company's success, not individual profits. This reduces moral hazard by aligning directors' interests with shareholders and stakeholders.

The risk-sharing concept in Islamic finance provides a new approach to executive director compensation. This approach encourages directors to be compensated for their contributions to the company's success rather than benefits by stressing shared accountability (Mazlan et al., 2023). Thus, it aligns directors' interests with shareholders and stakeholders, encouraging ethical decision-making. Incorporating this notion into corporate governance frameworks might change CEO remuneration, motivating directors to behave in the organisation's long-term best interests.

Prohibition of *Gharar*

Islamic finance is based on *gharar* prohibition, which promotes openness, justice, and ethics. *Gharar*—unpredictability—occurs in contracts owing to unclear language or speculative aspects. Islamic finance considers *gharar* harmful to both parties and risks disagreements or exploitation (Amrani & Najab, 2023; Uddin et al., 2020). This concept affects executive director pay since it must follow *gharar* prohibition.

Gharar requires a clear pay strategy for executive directors to avoid uncertainty (Qudah et al., 2023). Ambiguity in pay terms can cause conflicts of interest and compromise the compensation system. Transparent pay policies eliminate uncertainty and disagreements between directors, shareholders, and stakeholders.

The requirement to remove speculative components in executive directors' pay packages emphasises the ban on gharar (Hailu & Tekdoğan, 2023). These speculative components can be tied to variable remuneration like bonuses and incentives, which depend on unknown results. These variable components are related to quantifiable performance objectives and explicitly defined standards to reduce misunderstanding and disagreements.

Gharar restriction focuses on executive directors' pay ethics and fairness (Aziz, 2019). According to Islamic teachings, directors should get fair pay for their contributions to the company's success. Islamic finance seeks a reasonable and equitable financial environment.

Finally, the ban on gharar in Islamic finance affects executive director pay. A transparent pay strategy promotes fairness, ethics, and conflict prevention by reducing uncertainty. Organisations may enhance openness, fairness, and ethical financial behaviour by arranging executive directors' remuneration according to this idea.

Prohibition of *Riba*

The ban on usury, or *riba*, underpins Islamic banking. This principle prohibits executive directors from receiving interest or unfair gain. According to *riba's* restriction, financial agreements between corporations and executive directors must exclude interest-bearing components (Ayaz et al., 2018; Haque et al., 2022). Interest-driven techniques encourage exploitation at the cost of shared wealth generation, which is incompatible with Islamic financial ethics. The ban on *riba* assures executive directors' compensation is fair, equitable, and accountable, in line with Islamic finance. By respecting this ideal, companies promote ethical governance and financial integrity that align with Islamic finance.

Prohibition of *Maysir*

Islamic finance principles provide a solid framework for organising executive directors' compensation, ensuring ethics and fairness (Naysary et al., 2020; Razak et al., 2020). One principle prohibits *maysir*, which is gambling and chance. Executive director salary in Islamic finance should not depend on unpredictable results. This concept states that compensation should not depend on chance or uncertainty. Instead, compensation should be closely tied to firm success and social well-being. Eliminating *maysir* emphasises the necessity of responsible and effective company governance by prohibiting chance-based pay. This method promotes responsibility, ethics, and long-term wealth development, which aligns with Islamic financing. Integrating *maysir* prohibition into senior directors' compensation emphasises Islamic financial values of justice, transparency, and shared wealth.

Social Responsibility

Islamic finance is based on ethics and social welfare (Rashid et al., 2023). Social responsibility is a crucial concept (Mutamimah & Saputri, 2023). Islamic finance prioritises social good above financial gain. This idea directly affects Islamic finance executive director compensation. Executive directors' compensation should include social welfare as well as financial incentives.

To reflect this idea, executive directors' compensation should promote contributions beyond company performance. This might be done via charitable and community development approaches (Alam, 2022; Uddin et al., 2020). Organisations can promote ethics and purpose by connecting pay with social responsibility. This strategy follows Islamic financial principles and promotes the organisation's social improvement mission. Integrating social responsibility into executive directors' compensation within the Islamic finance framework displays a comprehensive vision of accomplishment that blends financial success with community well-being.

ELEMENTS OF THE FRAMEWORK

The framework's components govern executive directors' Islamic finance-compliant pay (Jallali & Zoghlami, 2022). A transparent pay strategy that outlines compensation standards promotes responsibility, and prevents disputes supports the prohibition of ambiguity (*gharar*). The independent pay committee, comprised of outside specialists, ensures fair compensation based on corporate performance and Islamic principles. A watchful system for monitoring and analysing processes ensures continuing accountability, allowing frequent evaluations and modifications to meet corporate goals and growing ethical standards. These factors promote openness, fairness, and ethics in executive salary governance, enshrining Islamic financial principles.

Clear and Transparent Remuneration Policy

In Islamic finance-driven corporate governance, executive directors' pay depends on a clear and transparent remuneration strategy (Algabry et al., 2020; Uddin et al., 2020). This fundamental concept stresses the necessity for a well-defined policy that outlines the principles, criteria, and procedures for assessing directors' compensation. The framework intends to help executive directors, shareholders, and stakeholders comprehend the pay system by following this approach. The policy's clarity promotes openness, trust, and accountability (Jan et al., 2021; Uddin et al., 2022). A clear explanation of the pay policy's complexities reduces conflicts of interest and increases equality. This focus on open pay policies emphasises the framework's commitment to ethical standards and equal reward distribution, creating an Islamic finance-compliant business environment.

Independent Remuneration Committee

An Independent Remuneration Committee (IRC) is essential for good company governance. The IRC, composed of experienced non-operational staff, evaluates and proposes various compensation plans (Sencal & Asutay, 2021). This method reduces conflicts of interest and ensures executive remuneration follows Islamic funding principles.

IRCs are popular in corporate governance because they can reduce conflicts of interest. Since its members are knowledgeable and objective, the committee acts independently of the company's daily operations (Choudhury & Alam, 2013; Muneeza & Hassan, 2014). This separation ensures independent appraisals of executive pay packages, preventing internal agendas from influencing these choices.

The IRC carefully evaluates compensation offers. Committee members evaluate compensation measures against organisational objectives using their sector expertise (Htay, 2012; Mollah & Zaman, 2015; Uddin et al., 2022). This method improves transparency and legitimacy since multiple viewpoints influence executive compensation choices.

The main advantage of IRCs is aligning CEO remuneration with Islamic funding (Aribi & Gao, 2010). IRCs reduce risk-taking, wealth growth, and wealth distribution inequities by ensuring pay arrangements follow Islamic ethics. These committees properly analyse remuneration packages, avoiding interest-based and speculative activity, in line with Islamic finance.

An Independent Remuneration Committee is essential to good company governance (Sadek et al., 2018). Through its unbiased composition and careful review methods, the IRC reduces conflicts of interest and increases executive remuneration transparency. IRC's involvement in aligning remuneration practices with Islamic finance principles emphasises its importance in fostering ethical and socially responsible financial practices in companies.

System for Monitoring and Reviewing Remuneration Practices

An effective salary monitoring, and review mechanism is essential to the Islamic finance-based corporate governance framework for senior directors' compensation (Alam et al., 2019). This method is crucial to maintaining Islamic finance principles and aims while adapting to economic and social changes.

Implementing a strong system requires frequent and comprehensive payment policy and practice reviews (Aziz & Ghadas, 2019; Hossain et al., 2022). This continuing procedure maintains executive directors' salaries in line with Islamic financial principles, including risk-sharing and prohibition of *gharar, riba, and maysir*. This process promotes ethics and prevents Islamic aberrations.

Additionally, proactive compensation monitoring helps firms to quickly adjust to changing economic and social circumstances. This method keeps senior directors' remuneration current, fair, and accountable when economic, social, and cultural circumstances evolve.

GOVERNANCE STRUCTURE

Effective executive director remuneration governance is crucial in Islamic finance. These brief covers governance elements that connect compensation with Islamic ideals. The board of directors' controls compensation. The board actively ensures that pay plans match firm success and promote fairness and equality (Alam et al., 2019; Bukhari et al., 2013; Ghayad, 2008; Kok & Shahgholian, 2023). The Shariah committee, unique to Islamic finance, improves governance. It evaluates and validates pay practices to guarantee Islamic conformity and avoid non-compliance. However, the audit committee oversees financial concerns, including executive directors' salaries, to ensure accountability and transparency. The audit committee strengthens the Islamic financial system and stakeholder confidence via thorough investigation and transparency. The board of directors, *shariah*, and audit committees provide a strong structure that aligns executive directors' pay with Islamic beliefs, promotes ethics, and protects financial practices.

Board of Directors

The board of directors is tasked with the responsibility of playing a crucial role in the control of the pay of executive directors (Rashid et al., 2023). The board needs to be actively engaged in creating and refining the pay policy. This will ensure the policy remains aligned with the organisation's performance criteria and ethical values (Pahlevi, 2023). This engagement protects against adopting compensation methods that might potentially put the Islamic financial framework's integrity at risk. The board guarantees that the principles of risk-sharing, prohibition of gharar, *riba*, and *maysir*, as well as the focus on social responsibility, are adequately preserved by actively engaging in the decision-making process around the remuneration of executive directors. As a result, the vigilance of the board helps to create a fair and transparent pay system that not only conforms to the principles of Islamic finance but also encourages ethical behaviour and the production of sustainable value.

Shariah Committee

The Shariah committee is crucial for maintaining Islamic financial practices in Islamic finance (Mutamimah & Saputri, 2023). This committee's incorporation into the corporate governance framework for executive directors' compensation helps assess and approve remuneration plans' compatibility with Islamic principles. The Shariah committee's main job is to monitor and evaluate financial transactions for Islamic compliance (Mazlan et al., 2023). This committee ensures that executive directors' pay structures and practices comply with risk-sharing, *gharar* (uncertainty), *riba* (usury), and *maysir* (gambling or chance). The committee's participation reduces the danger of adding payment aspects that violate these standards, protecting the Islamic financial system.

The *shariah* committee helps create an ethical executive director's pay scheme via its thorough review. By consulting Islamic jurisprudence experts, the committee ensures that pay policies are linked with Islamic ideals and promote fair distribution, social responsibility, and society's well-being. The *Shariah* committee's active involvement strengthens company governance and ensures executive directors' compensation follows Islamic financial ethics.

Audit Committee

Effectively increasing the control of financial matters, especially concerning the compensation of executive directors, the audit committee is an essential component of the corporate governance structure based on Islamic finance (Mazlan et al., 2023; Qudah et al., 2023). This committee plays an important part in ensuring that the disclosures and presentations of compensation practices within financial statements are accurate and transparent in how they are carried out (Bussin et al., 2023; Pahlevi, 2023). The structure of Islamic finance is based on the values of accountability and openness, and its function is ideally in line with those ideals. The audit committee plays a critical role in protecting the integrity of the pay structure and ensuring that it stays in conformity with the concepts of Islamic finance by analysing the remuneration methods and their subsequent documentation. The audit committee is a sentinel of financial practices, substantiating the commitment to ethical behaviour and solid financial governance. This strengthens the framework that aligns executive directors' compensation with Islamic finance principles.

COMPONENTS OF EXECUTIVE DIRECTORS' REMUNERATION

Islamic finance executive director pay requires careful consideration of equality, transparency, and social responsibility (Mutamimah & Saputri, 2023; Shamsudheen et al., 2023). This scholarly overview discusses an Islamic finance-based corporate governance framework for senior directors' pay and its key elements.

Risk-sharing, *gharar* (uncertainty), *riba* (usury), *maysir* (gambling), and social responsibility underlie the paradigm. These guidelines match executive directors' pay with Islamic financial ethics. The framework comprises a transparent and open pay policy and an independent remuneration committee that impartially evaluates and recommends executive director salaries.

The Shariah, audit, and board of directors comprise the governance structure. These groups supervise Islamic finance remuneration practices to ensure compliance and ethics. The basic income of executive directors incorporates their duties, variable pay based on business success, and perks, including bonuses, long-term incentives, pensions, and health insurance (Kok & Shahgholian, 2023; Mamatzakis et al., 2023).

This framework combines Islamic financing with executive director salaries to provide a fair, transparent, and socially responsible compensation system. It protects against risk and exploitation, improves social welfare, and aligns directors, shareholders, and stakeholders.

Base Salary

Base pay is the foundation of executive director compensation. This core component is essential in Islamic banking (Alam & Thakur, 2022; Anissa, 2018). Base salaries provide justice, accountability, and performance-driven incentives in this environment, aligning with Islamic beliefs.

Islamic finance believes executive directors' base salaries should reflect their duties, performance, and business success (Adam et al., 2018; Mergaliyev et al., 2021). This guarantees senior directors' salary is closely related to their value creation. Linking the basic income to these essential elements prevents unfair enrichment and speculation, which are against Islamic financing.

The alignment of base wage with Islamic beliefs promotes ethics and social responsibility (Mazlan et al., 2023). This strategy focuses on the company's financial performance and social impact. Thus, the base compensation represents individual achievement and a commitment to the welfare of stakeholders and communities where the firm works. In Islamic finance, the basic wage goes beyond money. It combines justice, accountability, and social duty to provide an Islamic executive director remuneration model that promotes organisational development and prosperity.

Variable Pay

The Islamic finance-based corporate governance structure for senior directors includes variable compensation, bonuses, and long-term incentives (Amrani & Najab, 2023; Jan et al., 2021). This remuneration component is closely related to firm success and aligned with risk-sharing and ethics. Variable compensation promotes risk-sharing, a key Islamic financial philosophy (Naysary et al., 2020). Bonuses should promote ethical conduct and sustained value creation via quantifiable benchmarks. This method reduces moral dangers and promotes executive director responsibility.

Linking variable compensation to firm performance combines financial benefits with business success. This symbiotic connection shows executive directors' dedication to the company's success, matching their interests with shareholders and stakeholders. The variable compensation structure promotes ethical and responsible business activity in Islamic finance by following these principles.

Pension and Health Insurance

An Islamic finance-based corporate governance structure for senior directors' compensation emphasises pension and health insurance (Alam et al., 2021). Fairness and social responsibility, important to Islamic finance, govern these factors (Pahlevi, 2023). The framework aligns executive directors' rewards with Islamic finance's equality and community welfare ideals.

Executive directors' pensions and health insurance should reflect long-term well-being (Rashid et al., 2023). Companies demonstrate justice by providing directors with pension funds and adequate health care, acknowledging their long-term service. These advantages contribute to directors' financial stability and quality of life, essential to Islamic finance's social duty.

Pension and health insurance are integrated into the pay system, combining Islamic financial principles with modern company methods. This combination honours equality and social welfare while attracting and retaining top executives. Thus, corporations follow Islamic ideals by including pension and health insurance in senior directors' pay while promoting director and societal well-being.

CONCLUSION

In summary, a corporate governance system based on Islamic finance for senior directors' compensation encourages risk-sharing, *gharar, riba, maysir* prohibition, and social responsibility. This framework comprises an open pay policy, an impartial committee, and a monitoring and review system. The board of directors provides Islamic governance, the audit committee, and the *Shariah*. Executive directors' compensation can be crafted to uphold Islamic financial principles, encourage integrity, and serve society by considering these considerations.

This chapter discusses ethical pay in Islamic finance and outlines a comprehensive governance mechanism for executive director compensation. The chapter has shown how maintaining Islamic finance and ensuring long-term economic and social well-being depends on ethical financial practices. Due to the complexity and challenges of contemporary business, executive director compensation in Islamic financial institutions must evolve. The complete governance structure that is being proposed takes into consideration Islamic principles, corporate responsibility, and economic feasibility. The framework is based on Sharia's fairness, justice, and accountability ideals. These principles protect executive pay against excessive or unfair rewards, promoting financial success and ethical conscience.

This chapter's focus on openness and stakeholder participation is crucial. The framework promotes inclusiveness among shareholders, workers, and social concerns. This method increases CEO remuneration transparency and fosters stakeholder accountability for the institution's ethical and financial well-being.

The piece also stresses adaptation and situational awareness. The governance framework recognises cultural and contextual differences amongst Islamic financial organisations while providing a systematic approach. This adaptability keeps the framework current and successful across organisational contexts, improving its practicality.

The essay has focused on balancing ethics and finance. The framework's focus on ethical reward aligns with Islamic finance and might boost the sector's competitiveness. Islamic financial organisations can build stakeholder confidence, attract ethical investors, and improve the financial ecosystem by adopting ethical pay.

Limitations and Future Study

Ethical compensation in Islamic finance has led to a strong governance system for senior directors' pay. This concept shows that ethical principles and financial success can coexist, reflecting Islamic finance's ethics. As the financial world faces ethical difficulties and demands more responsibility, this framework provides a current and resonant answer that can guide Islamic financial institutions toward a more fair, equitable, and ethical future. By adopting this complete governance approach, executive directors, shareholders, and society can create an environment where ethical pay drives long-term performance.

Ethical compensation in Islamic finance via a complete governance structure is a significant step toward ethical financial operations. Cultural differences and practical issues hamper the study. Future studies should empirically validate the framework, compare studies, engage stakeholders, analyse long-term repercussions, and examine regulatory implications. By addressing these issues, studies can improve Islamic financial institutions' ethical compensation policies and mitigate this study's weaknesses.

REFERENCES

Abd Aziz, H., & Abd Ghadas, Z. A. (2019). the Propose Governance Framework for Shariah Corporation. *International Journal of Law, Government and Communication*, 84–90. doi:10.35631/ijlgc.415009

Adam, S. B., Al-Aidaros, A. M. H., & Ishak, S. B. (2018). The moderating effect of Islamic work ethics on the relationship between corporate governance and performance of Islamic financial institutions in Nigeria: A proposed framework. *Journal of Social Sciences Research, 2018*(Special Issue 6), 1041–1048. doi:10.32861/jssr.spi6.1041.1048

Ahmad, A., & Ishak, M. S. I. (2021). Shari'ah Governance of Islamic Non-Banking Financial Institutions in Malaysia: A Conceptual Review. *The Journal of Management Theory and Practice*, *2*(1), 70–77. doi:10.37231/jmtp.2021.2.1.91

Alam, M., & Thakur, O. A. (2022). Why does Bangladesh require a centralized shariah governance framework for Islamic banks? *Journal of Nusantara Studies*, *7*(1), 24–42. doi:10.24200/jonus.vol7iss1pp24-42

Alam, M. K. (2022). A proposed centralized Shariah governance framework for Islamic banks in Bangladesh. *Journal of Islamic Accounting and Business Research*, *13*(2), 364–389. doi:10.1108/JIABR-03-2021-0106

Alam, M. K., Ab Rahman, S., Mustafa, H., Shah, S. M., & Hossain, M. S. (2019). Shariah governance framework of islamic banks in bangladesh: Practices, problems and recommendations. *Asian Economic and Financial Review*, *9*(1), 118–132. doi:10.18488/journal.aefr.2019.91.118.132

Alam, M. K., Rahman, M. M., Islam, F. T., Adedeji, B. S., Mannan, M. A., & Sahabuddin, M. (2021). The practices of Shariah governance systems of Islamic banks in Bangladesh. *Pacific Accounting Review*, *33*(4), 505–524. doi:10.1108/PAR-10-2020-0195

Alam Choudhury, M., & Nurul Alam, M. (2013). Corporate governance in Islamic perspective. *International Journal of Islamic and Middle Eastern Finance and Management*, *6*(3), 180–199. doi:10.1108/IMEFM-10-2012-0101

Algabry, L., Alhabshi, S. M., Soualhi, Y., & Alaeddin, O. (2020). Conceptual framework of internal Sharīʿah audit effectiveness factors in Islamic banks. *ISRA International Journal of Islamic Finance*, *12*(2), 171–193. doi:10.1108/IJIF-09-2018-0097

Almutairi, A. R., & Quttainah, M. A. (2020). Foreign directors and corporate governance in Islamic banks. *Journal of Islamic Accounting and Business Research*, *11*(3), 765–791. doi:10.1108/JIABR-07-2017-0104

Amrani, O., & Najab, A. (2023). The Impact of Multi-Layer Corporate Governance on Banks' Performance under the GFC and the COVID-19: A Cross-Country Panel Analysis Approach. *Journal of Risk and Financial Management*, *16*(1), 15. Advance online publication. doi:10.3390/jrfm16010015

Anissa, N. D. (2018). Toward A Comprehensive Sharia Governance Framework for Islamic Finance: A Contribution to the Debate. *International Journal of Management Sciences and Business Research*, *7*(11), 14–26. http://www.ijmsbr.com

Aribi, Z. A., & Gao, S. (2010). Corporate social responsibility disclosure: A comparison between Islamic and conventional financial institutions. *Journal of Financial Reporting and Accounting*, *8*(2), 72–91. doi:10.1108/19852511011088352

Ayaz Assistant Professor, M., Shakeel Shah Assistant Professor, H., & Bin Yusuf, J. (2018). Islamic Banking and Finance Review Legal and Corporate Governance Framework for Islamic Banks in Pakistan. *Islamic Banking and Finance Review*, *5*(01), 24–37. doi:10.32350/ibfr.2018.05.02

Bhatti, M., & Bhatti, I. (2009). Development in legal Issues of Corporate Governance in Islamic Finance. *Journal of Economic and Administrative Sciences*, *25*(1), 67–91. doi:10.1108/10264116200900004

Bukhari, K. S., Awan, H. M., & Ahmed, F. (2013). An evaluation of corporate governance practices of Islamic banks versus Islamic bank windows of conventional banks: A case of Pakistan. *Management Research Review*, *36*(4), 400–416. doi:10.1108/01409171311315003

Bussin, M., Wöcke, A., & Deysel, B. (2023). The impact of remuneration governance on chief executive officer overpayment. *Suid-Afrikaanse Tydskrif vir Ekonomiese en Bestuurswetenskappe*, *26*(1). Advance online publication. doi:10.4102ajems.v26i1.4860

Enguix, L. P. (2021). The new EU remuneration policy as good but not desired corporate governance mechanism and the role of CSR disclosing. *Sustainability (Switzerland)*, *13*(10). Advance online publication. doi:10.3390u13105476

Ghayad, R. (2008). Corporate governance and the global performance of Islamic banks. *Humanomics*, *24*(3), 207–216. doi:10.1108/08288660810899368

Hailu, S. M., & Tekdoğan, Ö. F. (2023). Ensuring The Compliance of Islamic Finance Applications with Shariah Principles in Ethiopia: The Way Forward. *Hitit İlahiyat Dergisi*. doi:10.14395/hid.1247875

Hamdan, H., Razak, D. A., Huridi, H., & Uddin, N. (2021). Factors contributing to financial literacy among MSMEs in Klang Valley. *Turkish Online Journal of Qualitative Inquiry*, *12*(6), 9223–9232. https://www.researchgate.net/publication/353646187

Harun, M. S., Hussainey, K., Mohd Kharuddin, K. A., & Al Farooque, O. (2020). CSR Disclosure, Corporate Governance and Firm Value: A study on GCC Islamic Banks. *International Journal of Accounting and Information Management*, *28*(4), 607–638. doi:10.1108/IJAIM-08-2019-0103

Htay, S. N. N. (2012). Towards Islamic worldview based corporate governance framework. *Corporate Governances Practices in Malaysia*, 17–36. http://irep.iium.edu.my/29629/

Jallali, S., & Zoghlami, F. (2022). Does risk governance mediate the impact of governance and risk management on banks' performance? Evidence from a selected sample of Islamic banks. *Journal of Financial Regulation and Compliance*, *30*(4), 439–464. doi:10.1108/JFRC-04-2021-0037

Jan, A., Rahman, H. U., Zahid, M., Salameh, A. A., Khan, P. A., Al-Faryan, M. A. S., Che Aziz, R. B., & Ali, H. E. (2023). Islamic corporate sustainability practices index aligned with SDGs towards better financial performance: Evidence from the Malaysian and Indonesian Islamic banking industry. *Journal of Cleaner Production*, *405*, 136860. Advance online publication. doi:10.1016/j.jclepro.2023.136860

Jan, A. A., Lai, F. W., Draz, M. U., Tahir, M., Ali, S. E. A., Zahid, M., & Shad, M. K. (2021). Integrating sustainability practices into islamic corporate governance for sustainable firm performance: From the lens of agency and stakeholder theories. *Quality & Quantity*. Advance online publication. doi:10.100711135-021-01261-0

Jan, A. A., Lai, F. W., & Tahir, M. (2021). Developing an Islamic Corporate Governance framework to examine sustainability performance in Islamic Banks and Financial Institutions. *Journal of Cleaner Production*, *315*, 128099. Advance online publication. doi:10.1016/j.jclepro.2021.128099

Kausar Alam, M., Ab Rahman, S., Ahad Thakur, O., Abdul Bashir, M., Hosen, S., Alam, M. K., Ab Rahman, S., Thakur, O., Bashir, M. A., & Hosen, S. (2020). The Reasons Behind the Absence of a Comprehensive Shariah Governance Framework of Islamic Banks in Bangladesh. International Journal of Economics and Business Administration, 8(1).

Kok, S. K., & Shahgholian, A. (2023). The impact of proximity within elite corporate networks on the Shariah governance-firm performance nexus: Evidence from the global Shariah elite. *Emerging Markets Review*, *54*, 100998. Advance online publication. doi:10.1016/j.ememar.2023.100998

Mamatzakis, E., Alexakis, C., Al Yahyaee, K., Pappas, V., Mobarek, A., & Mollah, S. (2023). Does corporate governance affect the performance and stability of Islamic banks? *Corporate Governance (Bingley)*, *23*(4), 888–919. doi:10.1108/CG-05-2022-0217

Mazlan, P. N. B. M., Hersh, N. F., Masron, T. A., & Malim, N. A. K. (2023). Islamic finance and governance indicators: Empirical evidence from Islamic finance-permitting countries. *International Journal of Disclosure and Governance*. Advance online publication. doi:10.105741310-023-00177-5

Mergaliyev, A., Asutay, M., Avdukic, A., & Karbhari, Y. (2021). Higher Ethical Objective (Maqasid al-Shari'ah) Augmented Framework for Islamic Banks: Assessing Ethical Performance and Exploring Its Determinants. *Journal of Business Ethics*, *170*(4), 797–834. doi:10.100710551-019-04331-4

Mnif, Y., & Tahari, M. (2021). The effect of Islamic banks' specific corporate governance mechanisms on compliance with AAOIFI governance standards. *Journal of Islamic Accounting and Business Research*, *12*(1), 21–43. doi:10.1108/JIABR-11-2018-0188

Mollah, S., & Zaman, M. (2015). Shari'ah supervision, corporate governance and performance: Conventional vs. Islamic banks. *Journal of Banking & Finance*, *58*, 418–435. doi:10.1016/j.jbankfin.2015.04.030

Muneeza, A., & Hassan, R. (2014). Shari'ah corporate governance: The need for a special governance code. *Corporate Governance (Bingley)*, *14*(1), 120–129. doi:10.1108/CG-02-2011-0015

Murphy, M. J., & Smolarski, J. M. (2020). Religion and CSR: An Islamic "Political" Model of Corporate Governance. *Business & Society*, *59*(5), 823–854. doi:10.1177/0007650317749222

Mutamimah, M., & Saputri, P. L. (2023). Corporate governance and financing risk in Islamic banks in Indonesia. *Journal of Islamic Accounting and Business Research*, *14*(3), 436–450. doi:10.1108/JIABR-09-2021-0268

Naysary, B., Salleh, M. C. M., & Abdullah, N. I. (2020). A comprehensive appraisal of Sharī'ah governance practices in Malaysian Islamic banks. *ISRA International Journal of Islamic Finance*, *12*(3), 381–400. doi:10.1108/IJIF-09-2018-0104

Noordin, N. H., & Kassim, S. (2019). Does Shariah committee composition influence Shariah governance disclosure?: Evidence from Malaysian Islamic banks. *Journal of Islamic Accounting and Business Research*, *10*(2), 158–184. doi:10.1108/JIABR-04-2016-0047

Olorede, T., Abogun, S., & Olowookere, J. (2022). Executive Compensation, Corporate Governance and Financial Reporting Quality: Evidence from listed firms in Nigeria. *Istanbul Management Journal*, *0*(93), 1–19. doi:10.26650/imj.2022.93.001

Pahlevi, R. W. (2023). Mapping of Islamic corporate governance research: a bibliometric analysis. In Journal of Islamic Accounting and Business Research (Vol. 14, Issue 4, pp. 538–553). Emerald Publishing. doi:10.1108/JIABR-12-2021-0314

Qudah, H., Malahim, S., Airout, R., Alomari, M., Hamour, A. A., & Alqudah, M. (2023). Islamic Finance in the Era of Financial Technology: A Bibliometric Review of Future Trends. *International Journal of Financial Studies*, *11*(2), 76. doi:10.3390/ijfs11020076

Rashid, A., Akmal, M., & Shah, S. M. A. R. (2023). Corporate governance and risk management in Islamic and convectional financial institutions: Explaining the role of institutional quality. *Journal of Islamic Accounting and Business Research*. Advance online publication. doi:10.1108/JIABR-12-2021-0317

Razak, D. A., Hamdan, H., & Uddin, M. N. (2020). The Effect of The Demographic Factors of Micro-Entrepreneur on Financial Literacy: Case of Amanah Ikthiar Malaysia (AIM). *International Journal of Business, Economics and Law*, *21*(3), 47–56. https://www.researchgate.net/publication/343404101

Rosli Abdul Aziz, A. A.-R. (2019). Best Practices for Internal Shariah Governance Framework: Lessons from Malaysian Islamic Banks. *Asian Journal of Accounting and Governance*, *12*(1), 1–14. doi:10.17576/AJAG-2019-12-15

Sadek, D. M., Rahim, K. A., & Abas, Z. (2018). Islamic Corporate Governance In Islamic Financial Institutions. *International Journal of Academic Research in Business and Social Sciences*, *8*(4). Advance online publication. doi:10.6007/IJARBSS/v8-i4/3993

Sencal, H., & Asutay, M. (2021). Ethical disclosure in the Shari'ah annual reports of Islamic banks: Discourse on Shari'ah governance, quantitative empirics and qualitative analysis. *Corporate Governance (Bingley)*, *21*(1), 175–211. doi:10.1108/CG-01-2020-0037

Shamsudheen, S. V., & Rosly, S. A. (2021). Measuring ethical judgement on ethical choice in an ethical system: A confirmatory study on Islamic banks in UAE. *International Journal of Islamic and Middle Eastern Finance and Management*, *14*(2), 301–316. doi:10.1108/IMEFM-03-2018-0112

Shamsudheen, S. V., Rosly, S. A., & Muneeza, A. (2023). Assessing ethical praxis of ethical (Islamic) financial institutions: a survey of empirical discoveries. *International Journal of Law and Management*. doi:10.1108/IJLMA-11-2022-0256

Swandaru, R., & Muneeza, A. (2022). Can fraud in Islamic financial institutions be prevented using high standards of shariah governance? *International Journal of Law and Management*, *64*(6), 469–485. doi:10.1108/IJLMA-07-2022-0162

Uddin, Md. N., Hamdan, H., Saad, N. B., Haque, A., Kassim, S., Embi, N. A. C., & Agarwal, K. (2022). The Governance Structure of Microfinance Institutions: A Comparison of Models of Sustainability and their Implication on Outreach. *Asian Journal of Economics. Business and Accounting*, *22*(19), 104–123. doi:10.9734/ajeba/2022/v22i1930662

Uddin, M. N., Hamdan, H., Che Embi, N. A., Kassim, S., & Saad, N. B. M. (2020). Governance Structure of Microfinance Institutions: A Comparison of Models and Its Implication on Social Impact and Poverty Reduction. *Journal of Ibn Haldun Studies*, *5*(1), 95–118. doi:10.36657/ihcd.2020.68

Zahid, S. N., & Khan, I. (2019). Islamic Corporate Governance: The Significance and Functioning of Shari'ah Supervisory Board in Islamic Banking. *Turkish Journal of Islamic Economics*, *6*(1), 87–108. doi:10.26414/A048

ENDNOTE

1 Corresponding author: Post-Doctoral Research fellow, Department of of Business Administration, Ankara University, Turkey, and International Islamic University Malaysia, Email: nuddin@ankara.edu.tr

APPENDIX

1. What are Islamic Financial Institutions' (IFIs) ' key challenges in corporate governance, and why must they be addressed?
2. How can corporate governance systems align director and shareholder interests in IFIs?
3. What are the consequences of CEO compensation schemes for IFI behavior and financial misconduct?
4. How do Islamic concepts and beliefs affect director responsibility, trustworthiness, and ethics in corporate governance?
5. How does the Islamic worldview-based corporate governance framework (IWBCGF) address corporate governance problems in Islamic financial institutions?
6. How can the IWBCGF manage executive director compensation by merging corporate governance practices with Islamic teachings?
7. How will the proposed IWBCGF affect executive director compensation at IFIs while promoting risk-sharing and social responsibility?
8. What role does ethical financial practice play in Islamic financial institutions' long-term economic and social well-being?
9. How might the governance mechanism presented in this chapter enhance IFI openness and stakeholder engagement?
10. What are the potential benefits of adopting ethical pay practices, and how can IFIs balance ethics and money when compensating executive directors?

Chapter 9
Financial Misreporting and Corporate Governance Lapses:
A Deep Dive Into the 1MDB Scandal in Malaysia

Mohamad Zreik
https://orcid.org/0000-0002-6812-6529
Independent Researcher, Lebanon

EXECUTIVE SUMMARY

This chapter investigates the 1Malaysia Development Berhad (1MDB) controversy by analyzing the system of financial misreporting that allowed for the large misuse of funds and the roles and duties that were overlooked. Cultural, sociological, and political contexts that exacerbated the problem are examined. This chapter elucidates the effects of the scandal on the Malaysian economy, the reactions of various stakeholders, and the lessons it offers for corporate governance. Finally, corrective measures like new regulations and institutional shifts are discussed to drive home the point that strong corporate governance is essential to the success of businesses and the economy as a whole.

1. INTRODUCTION

In recent years, the corporate world has been rife with examples of financial fraud, embezzlement, and unethical behaviors, which have eroded public trust in institutions. The 1Malaysia Development Berhad (1MDB) scandal stands out as a glaring manifestation of this trend. It not only captured global headlines but also

DOI: 10.4018/978-1-6684-9867-5.ch009

shed light on the complexities of financial mismanagement within state-owned entities, while simultaneously offering a poignant lesson on the importance of effective corporate governance.

The 1Malaysia Development Berhad (1MDB) scandal, including a sophisticated web of corruption and embezzlement involving billions of dollars, is one of the most prominent financial frauds in history (Marzuki et al., 2020). 1MDB was a state-owned development corporation established in 2009 by then-Prime Minister Najib Razak. Its stated mission was to advance initiatives that would boost Malaysia's economy. However, the fund became a vehicle for widespread theft and monetary corruption (Abadi, 2022).

The 1MDB affair, at its core, was a case of gross financial mismanagement, poor corporate governance, and outright corruption within a Malaysian state-owned investment company. Billions of dollars meant for economic development were siphoned off, leading to a political upheaval, international investigations, and serious ramifications for global financial entities (Zreik, Marzuki, & Iqbal, 2023). This vast and intricate network of deceit not only had direct financial implications but also posed fundamental questions about the integrity and accountability of those at the helm of large corporations, especially when they are tied closely to political establishments.

Around 2015, reports began appearing indicating that roughly $4.5 billion had been siphoned off the fund (Dettman, 2020). Misappropriated funds were utilized for everything from investing in personal art and real estate to producing the Hollywood film "The Wolf of Wall Street" (Teichmann & Falker, 2021). The trail of money led to other nations and included prominent politicians, businesses, and public figures, prompting a global probe.

Financial embezzlement was only one aspect of the controversy; it also revealed widespread corruption, a lack of accountability, and flaws in the Malaysian regulatory system. It was a devastating breach of public confidence that served as a clear example of what can happen when corporate governance checks and balances fail. The 1MDB scandal severely impacted Malaysia's economy and sent shockwaves through the global investment community.

The Malaysian public was the main target of the scandal, which exploited the public's trust and stole from the country. In 2018, Prime Minister Najib Razak's administration fell because of the scandal, which sparked widespread protests, legal lawsuits, and substantial political upheaval (Neo, 2021).

The 1MDB crisis is significant because of the ripple effects it has had on corporate governance, financial regulation, and public faith in government. It serves as an example of how widespread corruption and a lack of accountability can lead to massive financial embezzlement and serves as a case study for the catastrophic collapse of checks and balances in a corporate governance structure. Insightful information can be gained by corporations, investors, and regulators by better comprehending these dynamics.

The interconnections among the spheres of government, society, and business can also be investigated. It highlights how society values and norms can affect corporate governance standards and how political influence can worsen corporate malfeasance. More nuanced and efficient policies and practices in governance may result from a thorough examination of these factors, which would benefit both Malaysia and the rest of the world.

As an added bonus, investigating the 1MDB issue allows us to evaluate the performance of global financial supervision and regulation systems. This case raises serious concerns about the efficacy of current cross-border regulatory cooperation and enforcement because the money trail of the scandal spans numerous countries and involves key global financial institutions.

This chapter aims to dissect the establishment, operations, and downfall of 1MDB, offering a comprehensive analysis of how the scandal unfolded, the roles played by various stakeholders, and the systemic and institutional flaws that enabled such large-scale malfeasance. By studying the 1MDB affair in detail, it will be easier to understand the multifaceted factors that contributed to its occurrence, from internal corporate structures to external political influences.

From a societal and economic standpoint, this research is essential. The scandal had a major effect on Malaysia's economy and government spending. It caused a drain on public coffers, a fall in investor confidence, and a hit to Malaysia's creditworthiness (Case, 2017). This research is crucial for policymakers, economists, and social scientists due to the economic implications and social and political turmoil brought on by the scandal. To better protect the economy from shocks in the future and restore public confidence, it is important to have a firm grasp of these factors.

Despite the extensive media coverage and initial investigations surrounding the 1MDB scandal, there exists a gap in academic literature that systematically and holistically analyzes the underlying mechanisms, enablers, and ramifications of the scandal. This study aims to bridge this gap by offering a comprehensive exploration, not just of the events as they transpired, but of the deeper institutional, cultural, and political dynamics that played a pivotal role in shaping the scandal. By doing so, we contribute a nuanced perspective that goes beyond sensational headlines, anchoring the 1MDB narrative within the broader discourse on corporate governance, financial ethics, and state-business relations. This analysis is of paramount interest and relevance in today's globalized world, as the scandal's tentacles reached across continents, affecting financial institutions and political arenas worldwide. Understanding such a complex web of interactions and implications is crucial for scholars, policymakers, and corporate leaders who are grappling with the challenges of ensuring transparency, accountability, and ethical practices in a highly interconnected financial landscape.

The scale of the 1MDB scandal and its reverberating effects on global finance make it a significant case for exploration. By understanding the gaps and vulnerabilities in the corporate governance of 1MDB, it will be possible derive lessons that are applicable to other corporations and institutions worldwide, thereby potentially preventing similar occurrences in the future. The 1MDB scandal offers a unique lens through which researchers can examine the intricate relationship between political power and business interests, especially within state-owned entities. In an era where public trust in institutions is waning, understanding such scandals and addressing the underlying issues becomes crucial for restoring faith in corporate and governmental bodies. In light of the aforementioned aspects, this chapter will delve deep into the intricacies of the 1MDB scandal, seeking to present a holistic view of its origins, the web of deceit it wove across the globe, and the aftermath that led to significant institutional and regulatory changes.

2. THE ESTABLISHMENT OF 1MDB AND ITS BUSINESS OPERATIONS

2.1. Historical Background

In 2009, Najib Razak, then the prime minister of Malaysia, formed 1Malaysia Development Berhad (1MDB) (Nor, Firdaus, & Kaur, 2020). Terengganu Investment Authority (TIA) was established as a sovereign wealth fund to promote economic growth in Terengganu. Disagreements between Najib and the Terengganu Sultan over the fund's control and governance led to its renaming and transformation into a national body (Gin, 2017).

The origins of 1Malaysia Development Berhad (1MDB) can be traced back to the Terengganu Investment Authority (TIA), which was established in 2009 as a sovereign wealth fund aimed at ensuring sustainable long-term economic development for the state of Terengganu. TIA's primary funding came from the oil royalties that the state received (Gin, 2017). However, the vision for TIA soon expanded beyond Terengganu's borders. A pivotal moment in the transition came when the Malaysian federal government, under then-Prime Minister Najib Razak, saw the potential of transforming TIA into a larger entity that could drive strategic investments for Malaysia. Consequently, in a move to nationalize the fund, it was renamed 1Malaysia Development Berhad, or 1MDB, later in 2009 (Nor, Firdaus, & Kaur, 2020). While the objectives of 1MDB remained somewhat similar to those of TIA – mainly to drive strategic investment into the country – the scope expanded significantly, and its undertakings became more diverse, complex, and unfortunately, controversial. Throughout this transition, the relationship between TIA and 1MDB remained intricately tied, not only in terms of origins but also in the underlying dynamics of governance and decision-making.

The Malaysian government marketed 1MDB as a strategic development firm it owned in its entirety. Its goal was to attract FDI and strengthen international partnerships so that Malaysia could grow economically in a sustainable way. With the goal of transforming Malaysia's economy into a high-income one by the year 2020, the fund was also tasked with financing infrastructure and other development projects, such as those in the energy industry, real estate, tourism, and agribusiness (Mills et al., 2020).

The partnership between Najib Razak and the state of Terengganu was rooted in strategic economic and political considerations. Terengganu, being one of Malaysia's oil-rich states, received significant revenues from oil royalties (Hope & Wright, 2018). Najib Razak, recognizing the potential for leveraging these funds for broader national development objectives, saw an opportunity to create a sovereign wealth fund that could invest in high-impact projects across Malaysia. By partnering with Terengganu, the federal government could tap into these resources, ensuring a steady influx of capital for its ventures. Moreover, the establishment of the Terengganu Investment Authority (TIA) would also foster closer ties between the federal government and the state, potentially solidifying political alliances (Gin, 2017). The broader vision was to transform Malaysia's economic landscape, positioning it as a major player in the global economy. In a sense, the partnership was a win-win; while Terengganu got a platform to invest its royalties efficiently and ensure long-term state development, the federal government, under Najib Razak, was able to drive strategic investments that would benefit the entire nation (Zreik, 2023).

The fund's original capital was RM 1 million (about $240,000), with ostensible guarantees for borrowings provided by the government of Malaysia (Jusoh, Abd Razak, & Mazlan, 2017). Due to its status as a sovereign wealth fund, 1MDB was able to access cheap funding from investors around the world. The fund expanded swiftly, racking up debts that would total roughly $12 billion by the time they were paid off (Jones, 2020). The fund had a bold plan and a lot of money, but its business dealings were soon engulfed in scandal, culminating to one of the worst financial scandals ever.

The 1Malaysia Development Berhad (1MDB) did indeed originate from the Terengganu Investment Authority (TIA). The TIA was established in 2009 as a sovereign wealth fund for the state of Terengganu to invest the state's oil royalties in stable and long-term income sources. However, within months of its inception, the scope of TIA expanded beyond the boundaries of Terengganu. In a move to nationalize the fund's goals and objectives, the federal government of Malaysia, under the leadership of then-Prime Minister Najib Razak, acquired a stake in TIA (Saravanamuttu & Mohamad, 2020). This transition was not just in name but also in purpose. The fund was rebranded as 1Malaysia Development Berhad (1MDB) later that year, shifting its focus from regional to national development projects. As 1MDB, the entity aimed to drive strategic initiatives for a long-term economic development of Malaysia through global partnerships and foreign direct investments (Gomez et al., 2017).

2.2. Initial Business Operations and Objectives

In its early years, 1MDB undertook a number of initiatives with the goal of boosting Malaysia's economy and international profile. Its principal fields of business were energy, real estate, and investments, and their overarching objective was to make Malaysia a high-income economy by the year 2020.

The energy industry was home to one of its earliest and most successful forays into commerce. With the goal of guaranteeing Malaysia's long-term energy security, 1MDB bought independent power providers to form a cooperative called 1MDB Energy (Lim, Li, & Ji, 2022). The fund took on enormous debt to finance these purchases, arguing that doing so was essential to achieving its goal of becoming a major player in the energy sector.

1MDB's real estate endeavors included some notable construction projects. The Tun Razak Exchange was planned as a new commercial and financial center for Kuala Lumpur (Case, 2017). Bandar Malaysia was another proposed transportation hub, with connections to both Singapore and Kuala Lumpur (Al Shaher & Zreik,, 2022).

The fund also actively pursued strategic alliances with international organizations in an effort to entice FDI. For instance, 1MDB partnered with private Saudi Arabian firms like as PetroSaudi International and with a firm connected to Abu Dhabi's sovereign wealth fund, Aabar Investments PJS (Smith, 2022). While first framed as programs to attract investment and expertise, these partnerships have become at the center of allegations of financial theft and controversy surrounding 1MDB.

As 1MDB grew, so did its borrowings, but the company had nothing to show for its efforts in the way of income or completed projects. Financial analysts and investigators first saw problems with the fund due to its secretive dealings, massive borrowing, and lack of noticeable tangible results, all of which contributed to its eventual demise and the exposure of the 1MDB crisis.

3. THE LAPSES IN CORPORATE GOVERNANCE AND FINANCIAL MISREPORTING

3.1. Role of the Board and Management Failures

In the intricate web of the 1MDB scandal, the role of banks came under sharp scrutiny. Some of the world's leading banks were linked to the flow of funds related to 1MDB, and their involvement raised pertinent questions about the efficacy of corporate governance in financial institutions. While certain banks displayed weak corporate governance, failing to uphold adequate due diligence or turning a blind eye to suspicious transactions, others took proactive measures by flagging and reporting dubious activities (Waring, 2016). The discrepancy in behavior underscores the broader issue in the banking sector: the tension between aggressive pursuit of profits and adherence to stringent ethical standards and regulatory requirements (Ferrell & Fraedrich, 2021). Consequently, the 1MDB episode serves as a stern reminder of the vital importance of robust corporate governance mechanisms in banking, not just to protect their own reputation but also to safeguard the larger financial ecosystem from systemic risks. The 1MDB crisis exposed systemic problems with management and oversight at the highest levels of the company (Hess, 2021). The board of directors, who are responsible for monitoring the decisions made by management, appeared to have failed in their duty.

The board's make-up was an issue in and of itself. Former Prime Minister Najib Razak served as the chairman of 1MDB and presided over its advisory board. Because of this lack of checks and balances, the management team was able to act with impunity, and a conflict of interest developed (Welsh, 2022). There were no major questions or concerns from the board despite the increasing levels of indebtedness and the lack of transparency surrounding several transactions. There was a noticeable lack of skepticism over the high speed of borrowings and the feasibility of investment projects, which led to key investment choices involving enormous sums of money being taken without thorough due diligence.

Banks played a pivotal role in the unfolding of the 1MDB saga. As gatekeepers of the global financial system, banks are entrusted with the responsibility to ensure that funds flow through legitimate channels and are not used for illicit purposes. However, during the 1MDB scandal, several prominent financial institutions facilitated the movement of billions of dollars, either through lack of proper due diligence or potential complicity (Teichmann & Falker, 2021). These transactions, which spanned across multiple countries and involved complex financial instruments, provided an environment for the misappropriation of funds. The banks' involvement not only highlights the shortcomings in their internal compliance mechanisms but also emphasizes the critical need for stronger international cooperation in monitoring and regulating cross-border financial flows (Brun et al., 2021). The 1MDB case serves as a testament to the enormous responsibility banks bear in upholding the integrity of the global financial system and the repercussions when they fall short.

Swiss banks undeniably played a significant part in the 1MDB saga. Switzerland, known for its banking secrecy, became a focal point when several billions of the 1MDB funds were found to have been channeled through Swiss financial institutions. The Swiss Financial Market Supervisory Authority (FINMA) found lapses in anti-money laundering controls in several banks, indicating that they had failed to adequately scrutinize the source of the funds and the backgrounds of their clients involved with 1MDB (Teichmann & Falker, 2021). Some banks were found to have processed transactions linked to suspicious and, at times, clearly illegal activities related to the misappropriation of these funds. The revelations resulted in punitive measures against some Swiss banks, underscoring the significance of robust corporate governance and stringent financial checks even in reputed banking jurisdictions (Lee, 2016). The role of Swiss banks in the 1MDB scandal serves as a stark reminder of the potential vulnerabilities within the global banking system and the need for relentless vigilance.

The board's oversight of 1MDB's financial accounts was consistently late, and auditors qualified their reports multiple times. However, the board did not act to rectify the situation. The company's repeated changes in auditing firms over time should have raised red flags about the possibility of fraud.

To prevent financial mismanagement, the board also did not establish sufficient internal controls. Despite the fund's ambitious investment plan, it failed to set up processes for discovering, assessing, and managing risks. Thus, enormous sums of money were secretly removed (Case, 2017).

3.2. Flaws in the Internal and External Audit Systems

Internal and external audit systems, which should have functioned as crucial mechanisms of checks and balances to detect and prevent fraudulent acts, were shown to have serious flaws, as evidenced by the 1MDB crisis.

When evaluating the efficacy of a company's risk management and internal controls, an internal audit is an indispensable resource. The internal auditing process seems to have been seriously broken in the 1MDB affair. Internal auditors failed to detect massive money embezzlement despite the company's complicated and high-risk activities (Levi, 2020). This was a serious breach of internal control, whether as a result of carelessness, a lack of resources, or pressure from beyond.

There were major breakdowns in the external audit mechanism as well. 1MDB changed auditing firms many times during its operations (Ali, 2016). In principle, these auditors were supposed to serve as a third party to verify the accuracy of the company's financial statements. However, there were substantial questions regarding the administration of 1MDB's finances because its financial statements were regularly late and qualified. But the auditors didn't do anything to fix the problems they found.

It was also claimed that 1MDB's management knowingly omitted or misrepresented important information from the auditors (Hashim et al., 2020). Despite these obstacles, the auditors still failed to adequately confront management or raise their concerns, which resulted in a lengthy delay in the fraud's discovery.

3.3. Deficiencies in Regulatory Oversight

The 1MDB affair exposed major flaws in Malaysia's regulatory monitoring. The Securities Commission, Central Bank, and Companies Commission play critical roles in protecting the public interest, ensuring that financial regulations are followed, and preserving the stability of financial markets (Hamilton-Hart, 2018). These organizations appear to have failed to live up to their obligations in the case of 1MDB.

Because of its unusual structure as a state-owned corporation, 1MDB had inadequate checks and balances, which was one of the key problems. 1MDB avoided rigorous regulatory scrutiny for years despite incurring substantial debt and partaking in high-risk economic operations. Its audited financial statements were repeatedly late and riddled with errors, but regulators took little discernible action to remedy the situation (Dettman & Gomez, 2020).

It appears that regulators also failed in their responsibility to oversee 1MDB-related financial institution activity. The investigation into the theft of 1MDB funds uncovered the complicity of multiple Malaysian and international banks. A lack of regulatory control in the banking sector may have allowed these anomalies to go undetected for years.

There was also evidence of possible political involvement in the regulatory process that was revealed by this case (Jones, 2020). Political interference can weaken regulatory independence and effectiveness, as evidenced by reports that regulators' attempts to investigate the fund were hindered.

3.4. Network of Financial Misreporting

Many people and organizations across a number of countries were implicated in the 1MDB affair, which entailed widespread financial misreporting and money laundering. At issue was the theft of billions of dollars intended for 1MDB but instead taken by individuals.

Several primary strategies were used to conceal the true state of the company's finances. Overpayment for goods and services was one technique used. For instance,

1MDB allegedly used far more than necessary to acquire power plants, with the extra funds going into personal accounts (Case, 2017).

The use of made-up entities was another tactic. For instance, Aabar Investments PJS, a genuine Abu Dhabi investment firm, appeared to have ties to a company that received a large chunk of 1MDB funding. However, this British Virgin Islands corporation was really a front set up to divert money (Abu-Hussin et al., 2021).

Money was also transferred fraudulently under the pretense of "business" operations. Most notably, 1MDB formed a partnership with the private Saudi Arabian firm PetroSaudi International. However, according to the allegations, the money wasn't actually used for the advertised company purposes (Hope & Wright, 2018).

These illegally obtained funds were laundered through an intricate web of financial transactions involving multiple banks and businesses in several different countries. This system was meant to make it hard to discover where money came from and where it went.

A lack of effective control from both within the corporation and from external regulatory agencies allowed for the massive financial misreporting that led to the 1MDB disaster. This incident highlights the need for strict internal controls, clear dealings, and strict regulatory scrutiny to prevent large-scale financial fraud.

4. THE SOCIOCULTURAL AND POLITICAL CONTEXT

4.1. Influence of Malaysian Culture and Society on Corporate Governance

The 1MDB crisis was heavily influenced by the social and cultural norms and values prevalent in Malaysia, which in turn affected the way in which corporations were governed. The high-power distance index in Malaysian society reflects the widespread acceptance of inequality and hierarchy (Mohamad & Saad, 2016). This cultural norm could explain why no one questioned or challenged the leadership at 1MDB, including the then-Prime Minister Najib Razak.

Furthermore, Malaysian society places a premium on loyalty and respect for authority, which may have contributed to 1MDB's culture of compliance by silencing criticism and preventing critical inquiry (Muzaffar, 2022). Since of this, widespread money embezzlement was possible since anomalies and suspicious activity were allowed to continue unchecked.

The way the 1MDB scandal was handled may have been affected by cultural norms like "saving face" or upholding one's honor and respectability. It's possible that frank discussions regarding the worrying indications in 1MDB's operations were stifled out of fear of public shame or of embarrassing superiors.

The cultural elements mentioned above do not justify the fraud and corruption that occurred. They are merely background information that helps shed light on potential causes of the incident. This knowledge is essential for developing culturally sensitive and effective interventions and reforms that account for these nuances.

4.2. The Role of Politics in the 1MDB Scandal

Politics played a crucial part in the development of the 1MDB affair. Former Malaysian Prime Minister Najib Razak formed 1MDB and sat on its advisory board, making him a focal point of the scandal. Being a political leader and the head of a significant investment fund at the same time created an environment of impunity and lax scrutiny (Siddiquee & Zafarullah, 2022).

A major problem arose when people began to worry that regulatory agencies weren't truly independent from political influence. Authorities were allegedly impeded in their efforts to investigate the fund's transactions despite mounting evidence of financial misconduct. This indicated a high level of political meddling, which harmed the efficacy and trust of these regulatory bodies.

Efforts were taken to stifle coverage of the scandal by the media, which was also under political control. There was an atmosphere of fear and self-censorship as media outlets faced legal and financial constraints for reporting on the topic. Due to restrictions on journalistic freedom, the controversy was not made public until much later (George & Venkiteswaran, 2019).

The case also demonstrated the potential financial benefits of improperly using political connections. The misuse of 1MDB funds involved a wide network of Malaysian and international government figures and their associates (Jones, 2020).

5. THE IMPACT OF THE SCANDAL

5.1. Effect on Malaysia's Economy

The 1MDB scandal had serious short-term and long-term effects on Malaysia's economy. One of the most noticeable effects was the rapid depreciation of the Malaysian ringgit as news of the scandal spread (Umezaki, 2019). This was because capital left the economy as investors lost faith in its future. Inflation and the cost of living rose for Malaysians as a result of the weakening currency, which made imported goods more expensive (Chung et al., 2022).

The sovereign credit rating of Malaysia was also threatened. Some credit rating agencies threatened to reduce Malaysia's rating on worries about the country's fiscal management as a result of the 1MDB scandal. Borrowing costs for governments and businesses could have gone up as a result, stifling economic expansion (Menon, 2017).

Foreign direct investment in Malaysia fell as a result of the controversy. Foreign investors were wary of investing in Malaysia because of the scandal surrounding 1MDB, which exposed a lack of transparency and accountability in the country's governance and regulatory practices. Economic growth plans that counted on substantial FDI were impeded as a result (Gomez et al., 2017).

The 1MDB crisis may have lasting repercussions because it revealed systemic flaws in Malaysia's economic administration (Dettman & Gomez, 2020). The controversy demonstrated the need for more openness and responsibility in government financial management, better control of state-run businesses, and more checks and balances. These are huge problems that need fixing if Malaysia wants to attract investors again and keep its economy growing.

The aftershocks of the 1MDB scandal reverberated well beyond just the political and financial sectors; they also permeated the broader Malaysian economy. Initial revelations around the misappropriation of funds raised concerns in international markets about Malaysia's financial accountability and governance, leading to weakened investor confidence. This decline in confidence had a domino effect on exports, as Malaysia faced reduced demand from wary international partners. The uncertainty surrounding the scandal also led some foreign investors to withhold or withdraw investments, further exacerbating unemployment rates as businesses scaled back operations or shut down altogether. Concurrently, Malaysia's GDP growth faced deceleration, with the scandal impacting both foreign direct investment and domestic business sentiments. While it's challenging to quantify the exact economic toll of the 1MDB scandal, it's undeniable that its fallout had a tangible adverse effect on key economic indicators, reflecting the profound interconnection between political integrity, financial governance, and economic prosperity.

5.2. Implications for Malaysia's Corporate Governance System

The corporate governance structure in Malaysia was severely affected by the 1MDB scandal. The scandal revealed systemic flaws in the country's government, including as insufficient checks and balances, a culture of impunity, and a lack of effective oversight and accountability procedures.

The urgent need for structural changes to improve corporate governance is a major implication. One way to do this is by giving boards of directors more responsibility and giving them the tools they need to oversee management and hold them accountable. The internal and external audit functions must be bolstered to guarantee they can detect and handle anomalies efficiently and quickly.

The crisis also demonstrated the importance of strengthening regulatory frameworks and safeguarding regulatory agencies' autonomy. In order to ensure that financial regulations are followed, regulatory authorities require the authority and autonomy to do so successfully. To do their jobs well and without bias, they need to be able to operate independently from any political pressure.

The controversy also highlighted the importance of promoting a culture of honesty and responsibility in the business world. As part of this mission, we must encourage open communication, honesty, and ethical behavior at all levels of a company. It also entails making sure that people of any status or connections who participate in unethical or fraudulent activities face consequences.

5.3. Stakeholders' Reactions

Different groups' responses to the 1MDB affair reflected their individual priorities and concerns. The issue was a serious betrayal of confidence for the company's stockholders and investors. There was astonishment and fury when word of the cash theft spread. Both domestic and foreign investors panicked, contributing to a steep drop in stock prices and a devaluation of the Malaysian ringgit. Investors' confidence in a market where such widespread deception could persist for so long was called into doubt (Jones, 2020).

The response from authorities charged with regulating this was equally crucial. The political gravity of the situation caused initial hesitation, but escalating public pressure and evidence of misconduct eventually forced them to act. There were probes conducted, and eventually those responsible for the incident faced legal consequences. A need for regulatory adjustments to prevent a repeat of such a catastrophe was recognized in its wake.

Over time, the government's reaction morphed. There was an initial effort to downplay the problem and stifle inquiries. However, opinions changed as the controversy became a focal point of the 2018 midterm elections. For the first time in Malaysia's history, the election resulted in a change of government, and the new administration has promised to investigate the issue and bring those guilty to justice. This resulted in the trial and conviction of Najib Razak, a former prime minister of Malaysia (Gomez, Cheong, & Wong, 2021).

The general populace reacted with outrage and disappointment. Public trust in institutions plummeted as a result of the incident, which was perceived as an extreme example of corruption and poor management. It also became a catchphrase for those demanding government and business reforms that would increase openness, accountability, and efficiency. Angry voters in the 2018 midterms were a clear indication of the influence of public opinion in shaping policy.

6. THE AFTERMATH AND REMEDIAL ACTIONS

6.1. Regulatory Amendments

Significant regulatory reforms were undertaken after the 1MDB affair to address the obvious corporate governance flaws that had been exposed. The government, seeing the need for change, implemented a number of new policies to improve corporate monitoring, accountability, and transparency.

Laws regulating corporations were tightened by recent reforms. The Companies Act, for instance, was revised to increase directors' accountability and responsibility (Jamil, Mohd Ghazali, & Puat Nelson, 2021). Companies now have a harder time trying to hide their true financial condition because to stricter financial reporting standards.

More authority was granted to regulators to monitor and investigate business operations. In order to better detect and handle financial irregularities, the Malaysian government has granted expanded investigation powers to the Securities Commission, the Central Bank, and the Companies Commission of Malaysia (Md Nasir & Hashim, 2021). In tandem with this, efforts were made to further insulate these entities from political meddling by increasing their independence.

More openness was sought in business dealings, particularly those involving state-owned companies. To achieve this goal, regulations were put in place mandating more detailed disclosures for deals involving public funds (Dettman & Gomez, 2020). The goal was to establish a mechanism by which public monies would be managed with the same diligence as private ones.

However, these changes to the regulations are merely a piece of the puzzle. Their success will hinge on how well they are implemented and how much they are complimented by shifts in the attitude and actions of the business as a whole. Nonetheless, they are a necessary first step in ensuring that another 1MDB-style crisis will never happen again.

6.2. Legal Repercussions

The 1MDB scandal's legal implications were far-reaching and significant, highlighting the gravity of the crimes committed. They had an impact not just on those directly implicated in the scandal but also on financial institutions, auditors, and others with tangential ties to it.

Former Prime Minister Najib Razak was the target of several of the lawsuits. In July of 2020, he became the first person to be convicted of a felony relating to the 1MDB affair. The charges against him included abuse of power, money laundering, and criminal breach of trust. After being found guilty, he received a 12-year prison term and hefty fines (Jones, 2022).

In addition to Najib, several other prominent Malaysian and international politicians and businesspeople were sued over the affair. Executives at 1MDB, government officials who ignored the financial misdeeds, and international financiers who aided in the laundering of illicit funds all fit into this category (Levi, 2022).

Global financial institutions implicated in the scam were also hit with heavy fines and suffered irreparable damage to their reputations. For instance, Goldman Sachs settled with the Malaysian government for $3.9 billion for underwriting and organizing three bond offerings that brought in $6.5 billion for 1MDB (Pitre & Claiborne, 2021).

Legal ramifications were also felt by 1MDB's auditors. Deloitte, the firm that audited 1MDB's financial accounts in 2013 and 2014, has settled with the Malaysian government for $80 million (Smith, 2022).

These court cases demonstrated the need of good corporate governance and the gravity of financial crimes. They stressed that no one is immune to legal consequences for financial wrongdoing, not even the most powerful. This had far-reaching effects on how businesses and financial institutions everywhere viewed and dealt with the dangers of poor corporate governance and sloppy bookkeeping.

6.3. Institutional Changes

Large-scale institutional adjustments were implemented in the wake of the 1MDB affair to improve corporate governance and forestall a recurrence of the scandal. The board of directors and management team at 1MDB, along with those of other state-owned firms, were recently replaced (Chen, 2022). To achieve this goal, new members were recruited who possessed the expertise and moral fiber to guide these institutions toward higher standards of governance and accountability.

Organizational internal auditing has also been strengthened, which is a significant institutional development. Internal auditors' roles were strengthened to make sure they could successfully identify and mitigate financial risks, as their importance was recognized. They were given additional leeway and funding to undertake in-depth audits and were given the authority to directly submit their findings to the board of directors.

Reforms were enacted to make state-owned businesses more open and answerable to the public. For this reason, they implemented stricter financial reporting standards and established procedures for regulator and public oversight of their operations on a regular basis (Md Nasir & Hashim, 2021).

Efforts were also made to enhance company culture. Specifically, this meant pushing for an environment where honesty and decency are highly valued and promptly punished. To that end, the company instituted measures including ethics training for workers, whistleblowing rules to safeguard individuals who disclose misconduct, and performance criteria that take into account both financial success and adherence to moral principles.

The 1MDB affair exposed systemic issues, and this concerted effort to solve them included institutional changes, regulatory modifications, and legal ramifications. They highlight the significance of having the proper people, procedures, and culture in place to enforce rules and regulations.

7 LESSONS FROM THE 1MDB SCANDAL

7.1. The Importance of Transparency and Accountability

The 1MDB controversy has demonstrated the vital need of openness and responsibility in business administration. Lack of transparency and accountability at numerous levels inside the company and the wider corporate governance framework enabled the substantial cover-up and financial misreporting at the heart of the incident.

The foundation of good corporate governance is transparency, or the timely and complete disclosure of relevant information. Shareholders, investors, regulators, and the general public can all benefit from having this information at their disposal. The 1MDB affair showed how damaging it can be when authorities conceal information. 1MDB's fake financial statements deceived investors for years, allowing the criminals behind them to get away with their crimes (Hashim et al., 2020).

Another important takeaway from the 1MDB controversy is the importance of accountability, or taking personal and institutional responsibility for one's actions. The board of directors, upper management, auditors, and regulatory bodies all failed miserably in their responsibilities throughout the 1MDB affair (Brown & Peterson, 2022). Because of these failures, money was stolen for a long time without anyone noticing.

There has been a determined push to increase corporate responsibility and transparency in Malaysia since the scandal broke. Reforms to increase the independence and oversight capacities of regulatory agencies, as well as institutional improvements to boost internal controls and the function of auditors, are all examples.

The true test, however, will come in the form of seeing these changes put into action. The 1MDB affair shows how disastrous it can be to disregard accountability and openness in business, highlighting the importance of always being on guard to protect these cornerstones of good corporate governance.

7.2. The Role of Strong Corporate Governance

The 1MDB affair is a harsh reminder of the need of good corporate governance in protecting businesses and economies. When in place, a solid corporate governance framework ensures that businesses prioritize the welfare of their stakeholders, follow the law, and do the right thing ethically.

Transparency in financial reporting, strict internal controls, and the presence of a capable board of directors are all hallmarks of good corporate governance (Zreik, Iqbal, & Rahman, 2022). But in the 1MDB affair, there were many governance flaws that allowed for huge amounts of money to be stolen. In this way, the dangers associated with the ineffective operation of any part of the governance system are made clear.

Strategic guidance, management responsibility, and shareholder interests can only be effectively protected with a strong board of directors. The board's lax oversight and control of executive activity played a significant role in facilitating the fraud at 1MDB (Velayutham & Hasan, 2021).

An organization's financial health can only be verified and abnormalities can be uncovered with the help of both internal and external audit operations (Jans & Eulerich, 2022). The 1MDB affair showed what can happen when auditors don't do their jobs properly.

In addition, a robust set of internal controls aids in the prevention of fraud and monetary mismanagement. Massive financial theft at 1MDB was undiscovered for years due to a failure to implement adequate internal controls.

To give investors an accurate view of a company's financial health, transparent financial reporting is essential. The damage that may be done when transparency is compromised is demonstrated by the misleading financial reporting at 1MDB.

The 1MDB affair serves as a stark warning about the need for strict corporate oversight. The reforms implemented in Malaysia in the wake of the crisis are encouraging, but they also highlight the importance of remaining vigilant and dedicated to keeping and improving corporate governance standards.

7.3. Recommendations for Future Prevention

The 1MDB affair shows how serious the consequences may be when good corporate governance is ignored. Several suggestions are made to avoid a repeat of this unfortunate situation.

To begin, there must be an initiative to increase openness throughout an organization at all levels. This requires not only a commitment to transparent financial reporting practices, but also the cultivation of a company culture that prizes such practices. Businesses have an obligation to make sure that their financial dealings are transparent and easily understood by those who have a stake in them. They should also foster an open environment where employees feel safe coming forward with concerns.

Second, corporate accountability, particularly at the top levels, needs to be bolstered. When directors and executives fail to respect the highest standards of corporate governance, they should be held accountable for their actions and decisions. This action sends a strong message to would-be offenders that misconduct will not be overlooked.

Third, we need to give auditors more power. Auditors, both internal and external, need more leeway and funding to do their jobs properly. They need to be protected against anything that could hinder their capacity to conduct thorough audits of a company's finances.

In a fourth point, regulatory agencies need to be given authority and protection from political meddling. They should be given the authority to investigate and take action on possible corporate governance violations without fear of retaliation. This means that authorities can keep a close eye on businesses and intervene swiftly when necessary.

Finally, businesses should spend money on training and education to foster a culture of ethics. Companies can protect themselves from corporate governance failures by encouraging and rewarding ethical behavior among their personnel.

The risk of corporate governance problems will still be there, but it will be much smaller if these suggestions are implemented. The 1MDB affair is a sobering reminder of the value of strong corporate governance and the necessity of preserving and improving these standards.

8. CONCLUSION

One of the most extreme incidents of corporate governance failure and financial misreporting in recent history, the 1MDB controversy in Malaysia has been thoroughly studied in this chapter. The chapter has highlighted the different components and conditions that contributed to the crisis and the following ramifications for corporate governance in Malaysia and worldwide by a careful analysis of the establishment, operation, and eventual downfall of 1MDB.

Laxity on the part of the board of directors, ineffective internal and external audit controls, and insufficient regulatory monitoring are just some of the corporate governance failings that have been brought to light by this research. It has also shed light on the complex system of false accounting that enabled the theft of such vast sums of money. Culture, society, and politics have been singled out as major contributors to an environment where wrongdoing like this can flourish.

This chapter has shown how the controversy affected many different parties, including shareholders, investors, regulators, and the government of Malaysia, and how their responses varied. In response, many legislative changes, legal implications, and institutional shifts were implemented to improve corporate governance and forestall future occurrences of the same.

This in-depth analysis of the 1MDB controversy is informative and should be used in subsequent studies. More research on the relationships among culture, society, and corporate governance is warranted, the chapter argues. Given its centrality to the 1MDB affair, the impact of politics on corporate governance is another area worthy of scrutiny.

This chapter highlights the necessity for strong corporate governance frameworks that place an emphasis on openness, accountability, and a culture of ethics, all of which have policy consequences. The steps Malaysia has taken to rectify the situation are admirable, but they are only the beginning. Constant vigilance is required as attempts are made to keep and improve these benchmarks.

The 1MDB scandal is a stark warning that weakened corporate controls can have far-reaching effects, damaging not only specific businesses but entire economies. It highlights the significance of ensuring that the highest standards of corporate governance are maintained by all parties involved, including the board, the auditors, the regulators, and the shareholders. Strong corporate governance is essential to the long-term success of businesses and the economy, and the lessons learned from the 1MDB affair can serve as a guide for future studies and policies. By doing so, they help promote an atmosphere of honesty and openness in the workplace that is essential to avoiding future scandals.

REFERENCES

Abadi, A. M. (2022). Kleptocracy and Foreign Loan Decision-Making Process: Insights from Malaysia's Deals and Renegotiations with China. *Journal of Current Southeast Asian Affairs*, *41*(1), 135–158. doi:10.1177/18681034211058470

Abu-Hussin, M. F., Idris, A., Yaakop, M. R. M., & Salleh, M. A. (2021). Essential Factors Influencing Malaysia's Relations with the United Arab Emirates. *Contemporary Review of the Middle East*, *8*(4), 477–495. doi:10.1177/23477989211031785

Al Shaher, S., & Zreik, M. (2022). Reflections on the China-Malaysia Economic Partnership. *The Journal of Asian Finance, Economics and Business*, *9*(3), 229–234.

Ali, A. M. (2016). 1MDB: The Audit Firms" Questions. *Journal of Public Administration and Governance*, *6*(1), 73–86. doi:10.5296/jpag.v6i1.9057

Brown, G., & Peterson, R. S. (2022). *Disaster in the Boardroom*. Springer Books. doi:10.1007/978-3-030-91658-9

Brun, J. P., Sotiropoulou, A., Gray, L., & Scott, C. (2021). *Asset recovery handbook: a guide for practitioners*. World Bank Publications.

Case, W. (2017). Stress testing leadership in Malaysia: The 1MDB scandal and Najib Tun Razak. *The Pacific Review*, *30*(5), 633–654. doi:10.1080/09512748.2017.1282538

Chen, V. (2022). Corporate Law and Political Economy in a Kleptocracy. *The American Journal of Comparative Law*, *70*(3), 480–509. doi:10.1093/ajcl/avac041

Chung, Y. L., Tan, H. C. P., How, C. X., & Tan, C. E. (2022). *The impact of corruption on innovation activities: The case of Malaysia* [Doctoral dissertation]. UTAR.

Dettman, S. (2020). Authoritarian innovations and democratic reform in the "New Malaysia". *Democratization*, *27*(6), 1037–1052. doi:10.1080/13510347.2019.1705791

Dettman, S., & Gomez, E. T. (2020). Political financing reform: Politics, policies and patronage in Malaysia. *Journal of Contemporary Asia*, *50*(1), 36–55. doi:10.1080/00472336.2019.1571218

Ferrell, O. C., & Fraedrich, J. (2021). *Business ethics: Ethical decision making and cases*. Cengage Learning.

George, C., & Venkiteswaran, G. (2019). *Media and power in Southeast Asia*. Cambridge University Press. doi:10.1017/9781108665643

Gin, O. K. (2017). *Historical dictionary of Malaysia*. Rowman & Littlefield.

Gomez, E. T., Cheong, K. C., & Wong, C. Y. (2021). Regime changes, state-business ties and remaining in the middle-income trap: The case of Malaysia. *Journal of Contemporary Asia*, *51*(5), 782–802. doi:10.1080/00472336.2021.1933138

Gomez, E. T., Padmanabhan, T., Kamaruddin, N., Bhalla, S., & Fisal, F. (2017). *Minister of Finance Incorporated: Ownership and control of corporate Malaysia*. Springer.

Hamilton-Hart, N. (2018). *Asian states, Asian bankers: central banking in Southeast Asia*. Cornell University Press. doi:10.7591/9781501721731

Hashim, H. A., Salleh, Z., Shuhaimi, I., & Ismail, N. A. N. (2020). The risk of financial fraud: A management perspective. *Journal of Financial Crime*, *27*(4), 1143–1159. doi:10.1108/JFC-04-2020-0062

Hess, D. (2021). The management and oversight of human rights due diligence. *American Business Law Journal*, *58*(4), 751–798. doi:10.1111/ablj.12197

Hope, B., & Wright, T. (2018). Billion dollar whale: The man who fooled Wall Street, Hollywood, and the world. Hachette UK.

Jamil, A., Mohd Ghazali, N. A., & Puat Nelson, S. (2021). The influence of corporate governance structure on sustainability reporting in Malaysia. *Social Responsibility Journal*, *17*(8), 1251–1278. doi:10.1108/SRJ-08-2020-0310

Jans, M., & Eulerich, M. (2022). Process mining for financial auditing. In *Process Mining Handbook* (pp. 445–467). Springer International Publishing. doi:10.1007/978-3-031-08848-3_15

Jones, D. S. (2020). 1MDB corruption scandal in Malaysia: A study of failings in control and accountability. *Public Administration and Policy*, *23*(1), 59–72. doi:10.1108/PAP-11-2019-0032

Jones, D. S. (2022). Challenges in combating corruption in Malaysia: Issues of leadership, culture and money politics. *Public Administration and Policy*, *25*(2), 136–149. doi:10.1108/PAP-01-2022-0002

Jusoh, S., Abd Razak, M. F., & Mazlan, M. A. (2017). Malaysia and Investor-State Dispute Settlement: Learning from Experience. *The Journal of World Investment & Trade*, *18*(5-6), 890–917. doi:10.1163/22119000-12340065

Lee, C. M. (2016). *Fault lines in a rising Asia*. Brookings Institution Press.

Levi, M. (2020). Evaluating the control of money laundering and its underlying offences: The search for meaningful data. *Asian Journal of Criminology*, *15*(4), 301–320. doi:10.100711417-020-09319-y PMID:32837603

Levi, M. (2022). Lawyers as money laundering enablers? An evolving and contentious relationship. *Global Crime*, *23*(2), 126–147. doi:10.1080/17440572.2022.2089122

Lim, G., Li, C., & Ji, X. (2022). Chinese financial statecraft in Southeast Asia: An analysis of China's infrastructure provision in Malaysia. *The Pacific Review*, *35*(4), 647–675. doi:10.1080/09512748.2020.1868556

Marzuki, M. M., Majid, W. Z. N. A., Azis, N. K., Rosman, R., & Abdulatiff, N. K. H. (2020). Fraud risk management model: A content analysis approach. *The Journal of Asian Finance, Economics and Business*, *7*(10), 717–728.

Md Nasir, N. A., & Hashim, H. A. (2021). Corporate governance performance and financial statement fraud: Evidence from Malaysia. *Journal of Financial Crime*, *28*(3), 797–809. doi:10.1108/JFC-09-2020-0182

Menon, J. (2017). Government-linked Companies: Impact on the Malaysian Economy. *Policy Ideas*, *45*, 1–26.

Mills, G., Obasanjo, O., van der Merwe, E., & Desalegn, H. (2020). *The Asian Aspiration: Why and How Africa Should Emulate Asia—and What It Should Avoid*. Oxford University Press.

Mohamad, R., & Saad, N. M. (2016). Power distance culture and the construction of the followership identity. *Asia Pacific Journal of Advanced Business and Social Studies*, *2*(1), 149–160.

Muzaffar, C. (2022). *Protector: An Analysis of the Concept and Practice of Loyalty in Leader-Led Relationships Within Malay Society*. Strategic Information and Research Development Centre.

Neo, R. (2021). The failed construction of fake news as a security threat in Malaysia. *Contemporary Politics*, *27*(3), 316–335. doi:10.1080/13569775.2021.1884397

Nor, N. H. M., Firdaus, A., & Kaur, S. (2020). Rise of the 5th estate: How online public discourse on Najib Razak's 1MDB scandal foreshadowed Pakatan Harapan's win in the 14th general election. *Jurnal Komunikasi: Malaysian Journal of Communication*, *36*(2), 179–195.

Pitre, R., & Claiborne, C. (2021). Corporate ethical training: An answer to white-collar crimes. *The Journal of Values Based Leadership*, *14*(2), 11. doi:10.22543/0733.142.1362

Saravanamuttu, J., & Mohamad, M. (2020). The monetisation of consent and its limits: Explaining political dominance and decline in Malaysia. *Journal of Contemporary Asia*, *50*(1), 56–73. doi:10.1080/00472336.2019.1569710

Siddiquee, N. A., & Zafarullah, H. (2022). Absolute power, absolute venality: The politics of corruption and anti-corruption in Malaysia. *Public Integrity*, *24*(1), 1–17. doi:10.1080/10999922.2020.1830541

Smith, D. (2022). *Fraud and Corruption: Cases and Materials*. Springer Nature. doi:10.1007/978-3-031-10063-5

Teichmann, F. M. J., & Falker, M. C. (2021). The 1MDB case and the Swiss banking sector. *Journal of Money Laundering Control*, *24*(2), 278–290. doi:10.1108/JMLC-04-2020-0037

Umezaki, S. (2019). The Malaysian economy after the global financial crisis: International capital flows, exchange rates, and policy responses. *Public Policy Review*, *15*(1), 69–98.

Velayutham, S., & Hasan, R. (2021). Sovereign wealth funds and corporate social responsibility: A comparison of Norway's Government Pension Fund Global and Abu Dhabi Fund for Development. *Public Administration and Policy*, *24*(2), 139–151. doi:10.1108/PAP-08-2020-0037

Waring, A. (2016). *Corporate risk and governance: an end to mismanagement, tunnel vision and quackery*. Routledge. doi:10.4324/9781315574318

Welsh, B. (2022). *The End of Umno? Essays on Malaysia's Former Dominant Party*. Strategic Information and Research Development Centre.

Zreik, M. (2023). Governance in Post-COVID-19 China: Challenges, Responses, and Opportunities. In Multidisciplinary Approaches to Organizational Governance During Health Crises (pp. 214-235). IGI Global.

Zreik, M., Iqbal, B. A., & Rahman, M. N. (2022). Outward FDI: determinants and flows in emerging economies: evidence from China. *China and WTO Review*, *8*(2), 385–402. doi:10.14330/cwr.2022.8.2.07

Zreik, M., Marzuki, S. Z., & Iqbal, B. A. (2023). Deepening Financial Inclusion through Digitization: A Case Study of Microfinance in China. *ASEAN Entrepreneurship Journal*, *9*(2), 9–21.

KEY TERMS AND DEFINITIONS

1Malaysia Development Berhad (1MDB): A strategic development company wholly owned by the Government of Malaysia, established to drive long-term economic development. It later became embroiled in a multi-billion-dollar financial scandal involving misuse of funds.

Corporate Governance: The system of rules, practices, and processes by which a company is directed and controlled. It essentially involves balancing the interests of a company's many stakeholders.

Exports: Goods and services produced in one country and sold to another. A significant component of a nation's economy, influencing its trade balance and currency strength.

Financial Misreporting: The intentional act of presenting distorted financial statements, often to present a more favorable view of a company's financial position than what is accurate.

Foreign Direct Investment (FDI): An investment made by a firm or individual in one country into business interests located in another country. It often takes the form of establishing businesses operations or acquiring assets in the foreign country.

Gross Domestic Product (GDP): The total value of goods produced and services provided in a country during one year, often used as an indicator of a country's economic performance.

Institutional Changes: Alterations or reforms in the structure, policies, or practices of key establishments or organizations in a society, often aimed at improving efficiency, transparency, or accountability.

Legal Repercussions: Consequences arising from the legal system, typically as a result of unlawful actions. This can include things like lawsuits, fines, imprisonment, and other judicial penalties.

Regulatory Amendments: Changes or additions to the set of rules, standards, or laws that govern a particular activity or sector. These are often made in response to identified gaps or deficiencies in existing regulations.

Terengganu Investment Authority (TIA): An investment fund created by the state of Terengganu in Malaysia. It was the precursor to 1MDB and was initially established to manage the state's oil royalty payments.

Chapter 10
Cheque Truncation Mechanism Using Blockchain

Venkat Reddy Kumbam
Vignana Bharathi Institute of Technology, India

K. Kalaivani
https://orcid.org/0000-0002-5527-7010
Vignana Bharathi Institute of Technology, India

M. Balakrishna
Vignana Bharathi Institute of Technology, India

EXECUTIVE SUMMARY

Cheque truncation system (CTS) is an image-based cheque-clearing framework. The semi-manual process has certain limitations and takes up to three working days to clear an inter-bank national cheque. Faced with the limitations of this system, cheque users and commercial banks need an efficient and secure system which can clear a cheque within less than 24 hours along with providing integrity and confidentiality to the system. All banks intending towards participating in this framework must connect towards the proposed blockchain-based system. A comprehensive framework among four primary phases—(1) paper check clearing process, (2) digital check issuing and clearing process, (3) check fraud detection process, and (4) check transaction security procedure—was presented as a solution.

DOI: 10.4018/978-1-6684-9867-5.ch010

LITERATURE SURVEY

The 2008 global financial crisis imposed rigorous and rigid banking norms and regulations worldwide in an effort to stop and deflect a crisis of this nature from occurring ever again. Nguyen makes an effort to highlight the part played by blockchain technology in the creation of a financial system that is much more focused on the needs of the client and transparent. As an industry, Barclays is the first to use blockchain technology in its operations. Moreover, Santander began utilising blockchain technology for in-the-moment trade operations. The first blockchain application for the insurance industry is called InsurChain. Starbase also started utilising crypto-tokens (Singh et al., 2018) for various types of crowd fundraising. in their study, Guo and Lang explain how blockchain technology combines various other current computer technologies, including distributed data storage and peer-to-peer networking.

INTRODUCTION

Technology development has significantly changed every sector, including the financial, industrial, educational, and administrative ones. The banking industry has developed rapidly and kept up with these technological changes. The banking industry underwent a significant transition in the late 1980s or early 1990s. Electronic clearing system (ECS) and card-based payment systems were launched during this decade, allowing for the electronic movement of funds between bank accounts. Real Time Gross Clearance (RTGS) and NEFT (National Electronic Funds Transfer) were also incorporated into the banking sector in later decades. Due to the high volume of transactions for these products, the financial institutions have implemented the cheque truncation system (CTS).

Cheques (PaissaBazaar, 2023) are electronically transferred to the drawer's bank (scanned images of the cheques). The time it takes to clear checks is shortened by this method. In their discussion of numerous methods of forgery in digital cheques, mention replacing a duplicate signature of any individual and altering the precision of the cheque amount using digital image processing techniques (Ghandali and Moghaddam, 2009). To detect any check fraud, Rajender and Pal (2014) suggest a digital watermarking-based technique. The e-cheque framework's architecture is suggested by Anderson (1998). An electronic cheque system based on mutual drawer and payee authentication is proposed by Chang et al. Researchers are becoming more interested in blockchain-based major e-governance applications like the blockchain-based property transaction system.

The blockchain stores every transaction as a chain of interconnected blocks. The immutable characteristic of the blockchain is attributed to each block's unique header, which is computed cryptographically and commits to the header of the previous block.

Figure 1 shows how cheque will be created and how it broadcast in all nodes, how it validates and how block will be added to blockchain.

To ensure the validity of the data being incorporated into the blocks, a transaction must be approved by the network's active members before it is committed to the ledger. The distributed ledger consensus procedures (Singh et al., 2021) play a key role in deciding which database state is chosen to be valid and true at this point. The new transaction is only added to the block and connected to an existing transaction once consensus has been reached.

Cheques are one of the reports that banks utilise most regularly and where duplication occurs most frequently. The most common non-cash payment method, valued 96.8 billion USD in 2018 (Anderson, 1998), is checks. To clear a check, a lot of time and work are required. The current check clearing process is semi-manual (Abd-ElZaher, 2014).

Figure 1.

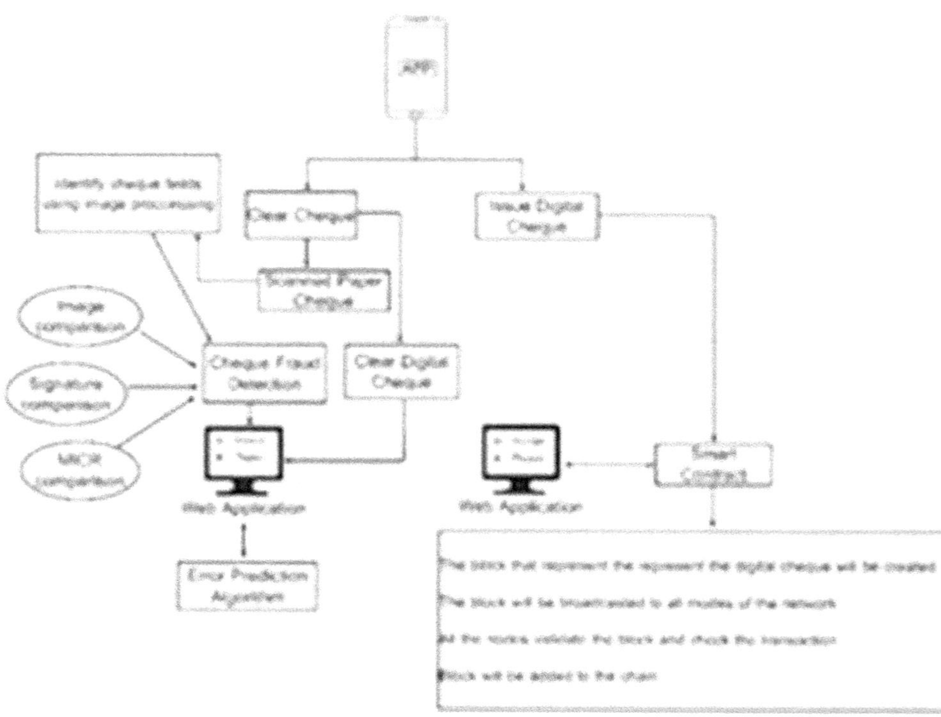

The Cheque Imaging & Truncation (CIT) System, which was put into use on May 11, 2006, increased system efficiency by reducing the amount of time required for clearing and settlement checks. Since the CIT system was adopted towards T+1, where T is the day the clearing house receives the check for clearing and 1 represents one business day following T, the time it takes for a check to clear has decreased. The complete process typically takes two to three business days. because of Commercial banks and check users need a speedy, secure check clearing system that clears checks more quickly due to the lengthy traditional check clearing process. Due to technology advancements that have made check fraud more difficult to detect, it is now a widespread occurrence. Currently, bank employees usually spot fraudulent checks by looking at their qualities. In addition, a lot of commercial banks use hardware tools like scanners and software development kits (SDK). These procedures take too much time and are ineffective, therefore no commercial bank could possibly set them up.

The cheque system, which is presented to the bank as a tangible instrument, has superseded traditional cash payment methods with the introduction of information technology. The cheque clearance procedure on the other hand, entails a manual handshake between the presenter and the clearing bank with settlement taking place through a third-party clearing house (Kabra et al., 2020). The actual instrument is lost since the relevant banks must physically transfer the check. In order to enable inter-bank payment settlements using a scanned copy of the manual check given to the clearing houses, CTS was established (Chang et al., 2009).

Traditional CTS systems employ MICR technology, which concentrates on the features of watermarks, ultraviolet (UV) rays, pantographic pictures, and many tiny features on the scanned copy of the check. However, the functionality of the conventional CTS is restricted to checking the check's grayscale image, which makes all of the aforementioned aspects less visible. As a result, anomalies in the beneficiary name and amount, feature duplication using picture editing software, the use of invisible ink, and damaged photographs may result in security violations and the creation of a fake check. Bypassing the clearing house's image authentication processing system, this fraudulent check causes the bank to pay the malicious user in error (Ghandali and Moghaddam, 2009). Bank databases are dispersed, with servers using fault-tolerance methods including mirroring, redundant arrays of cheap discs (RAID) layers, and system checkpoints, aside from the restrictions described above.

The conventional check clearing process is depicted in Figure 1 and includes the following steps:

- The user delivers the check to the presenting bank, the check is transmitted to a central bank for validation, it is then sent on to the issuing bank for further processing, the issuing bank can then approve or reject the transaction, and lastly, the check is cleared.

- An alert is delivered to the user.
- There is a chance of a security attack at every stage where there are two parties, known as Points of Contact (PoC).
- Transactions with inconsistent states may result in security problems, which a bad user could utilise to launch nefarious security attacks (*Support innovative projects with star,* 2019).
- The most exposed PoC is the one where the majority of security assaults occur.

Hence, a distributed ledger system that is immutable and consistent can resolve the needs for data storage. Additionally, because databases are dispersed, they can be altered by interested parties and even compromised by an enemy. Therefore, among participating users, a sense of interoperability and trust is necessary. Blockchain can therefore be integrated into the banking system to support the present clearing framework restrictions. Blockchain integration can improve user transparency and the effectiveness of banking processes (Tschorsch and Scheuermann, 2016). A check can take up to three working days to clear manually (Chang et al., 2009) and there are additional challenges. Due to security restrictions, a secure check-clearing system that provides confidentiality and integrity to the system and clears checks in less than 24 hours is required.

OBJECTIVE OF THE PROJECT

The major goal of "Online Digital Cheque Clearing Using Blockchain" is to deliver confidentiality, integrity, and the ability to clear checks at any time.

Existing Systems

Traditional CITS, which focus on watermarks, brilliant (UV) beams, pantographic images, and other microscopic components on filtered duplicate for human check, have a limited effectiveness. These CITS make use of optical character recognition (OCR) and appealing ink character recognition (MICR) technologies. In this way, errors in the name and sum, copying of highlights using picture-editing software, using invisible ink, and damaged images may result in security violations and ultimately lead to the manufacture of a fake paper check. This fake check can slip through the house's picture verification processing process, which would result in the bank paying the wrong person. Drawee Business Bank discovers and discloses a greater portion of true cheats.

Less frequently, the gathering business bank, where the checks are stored, discovers and reports these frauds. As often as possible, manual identifiable proof is used to identify these incorrect checks. In actuality, manually differentiating evidence is the least effective method of preventing extortion. Staff members should be able to identify phoney checks based on visual characteristics, such as security features. Also, if the paper check is damaged, OCR will be unable to read it. As a result, it needs to be physically cleansed by someone. Seen as a whole, robotized technique will fall short. Also, the existing CITS-based paper check clearance process needs at least one working day and maybe up to three working days to complete. Also, the client must spend time and money travelling to the bank to store a cheque.

DISADVANTAGES OF EXISTING SYSTEM

1. Taking up time & money
2. Automation procedure won't work
3. Security breaches

PROPOSED SYSTEM

To provide their clients speedier check clearing, all banks that are interested in participating must join to the proposed blockchain-based system, which is the foundation of the proposed system. Solutions were provided in the form of a comprehensive framework divided into four main stages: procedures for clearing paper checks, issuing and clearing digital checks (Tschorsch and Scheuermann, 2016)., identifying check fraud, and securing check transactions. The three key technologies for system implementation were Ethereum, Python, and the Flutter framework. The suggested solution is very scalable because of Ethereum's improved integrity. The concept encourages a check clearing procedure that is substantially quicker, easier, and more secure for both the customer and the bank.

Advantages of Proposed System

1. Increased security

Figure 2. Represent online digital cheque clearance and verification system

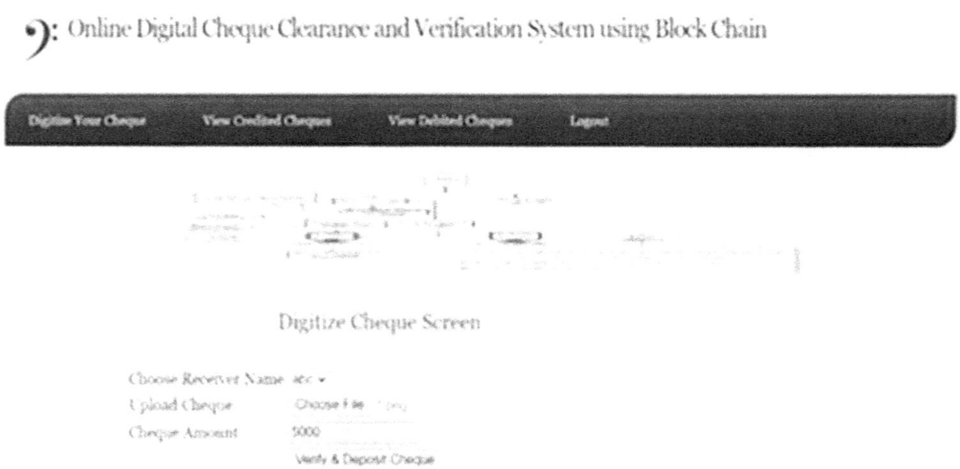

SHA ALGORITHM

Hashing is the process of scrubbing raw data until it can no longer be reproduced in its original form. It takes a chunk of data and runs it through a function that manipulates the plaintext numerically. The hash function produces a result or digest that is known as a hash value.

The hash function is in charge of transforming the plaintext into the appropriate hash digest. Since they are intended to be irreversible, your digest should not, under any circumstances, provide you access to the original plaintext. No matter how many times they are used, hash functions always produce the same result when the input is left untouched.

Hashing is mostly used for two purposes:

- Password Hashes: Prior to being kept on the server, user passwords are often converted into a hash value by the majority of website servers. For validation, it makes a comparison between the hash value recalculated after login and the one saved in the database.
- Integrity Verification: It also provided the file's hash as a bundle when uploading the file to a website. It can recalculate the hash and compare it when a user downloads it to ensure data integrity.

Secure Hash Algorithm (Schwartz et al., 2014), or SHA, is a hashing algorithm that is used to hash data and certificate files.

Each piece of data generates a distinct hash that can never be duplicated by any other piece of data.

Because it is based on the hash that is produced from the data, the final digital signature is also unique.

Secure Hashing Algorithm is referred to as SHA.Data and certificates are hashed using the modified version of MD5 known as SHA.

Using bitwise operations, modular additions, and compression techniques, a hashing algorithm reduces the input data into a smaller, unintelligible format.

Because of how SHA operates, if even one character in the message changes, a different hash will be produced.

As an illustration, hashing two similar, but Because of how SHA operates, if even one character in the message changes, a different hash will be produced.

As an illustration, consider hashing the messages Heaven and Heaven Is Different, which are similar but distinct.

But there is only a little difference between a capital and a small letter.

Digital Signatures Using SHA

Digital signatures are used in transactions to ensure their integrity. To create a signature, the data used in the transaction is first hashed with the SHA-256 algorithm and then encrypted using the sender's private key.

After that, the miner checks this signature to confirm the transaction.

METHODOLOGY

The complete system is implemented in four stages: I the paper check clearing process and error prediction algorithm; (ii) the paper check fraud detection process; (iii) the digital check issuing and clearing process utilising block chain; and (iv) the procedure for protecting cheque transactions.

The methodology and approaches utilised for the four stages are explained separately in sections B, C, D, and E since different approaches were employed for constructing the full system and to better understand the system flow.

Proposed Network Architecture for e-Cheque System

The suggested system's network architecture consists of entities like several participating banks and their replicated web servers, miner nodes for each of these web servers, cloud data centers, and certain professional miners who might also be employed because they have cutting-edge hardware resources.

Figure 3. How transactions will be done with time stamps

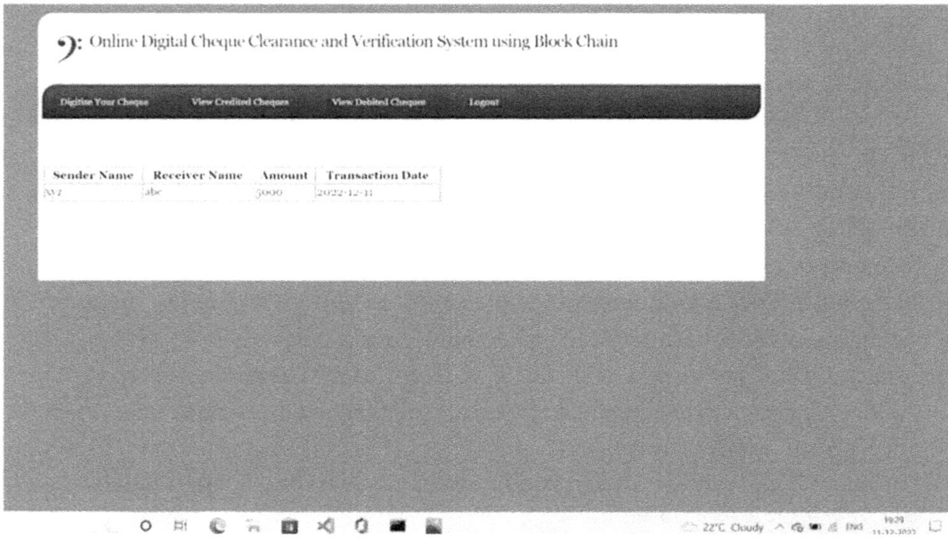

Each bank offers a gateway via which customers can generate and deposit electronic checks.

The teller machine retrieves data from the bank's and the cloud data center's miners.

REQUIREMENTS

Hardware Requirements

The bare minimum hardware needs vary greatly depending on the software an Enthought Python, Canopy, or VS Code user is working on.

Programs that need to swiftly do a large number of calculations or activities will need a faster CPU, but applications that need to store big arrays or objects in memory would need more RAM.

Windows or Linux operating systems;
An Intel i3 processor;
4 GB of RAM;
250 GB hard drive are required.

CONCLUSION

The project's results include a block chain-based method for issuing and passing checks. It will assist in enhancing and accelerating the automated process as well as the features of the check. Also, when used in conjunction with paper checks, digital checks will save costs. The blockchain-based smart contact used in this study component will strengthen the security of the check truncation mechanism. Also, by replacing paper checks with digital ones, paper waste and labour costs will be reduced.

FUTURE ENHANCEMENT

The traditional CITS, which focuses on the characteristics of watermarks and ultraviolet light (UV) rays and uses magnetic ink character recognition (MICR) and optical character recognition (OCR) technologies, has changed thanks to the blockchain, which provides users with integrity and confidentiality. provide clients with quicker cheque clearance. This strategy advocates for both the consumer and the bank by streamlining and accelerating the passing of checks while enhancing security.

Persian signatures are different from other signature types in that people typically do not use text in them and instead draw a shape as their signature, so there won't be any kind of frauds in the digitisation of the cheques. It also includes the digital signature, not the users, but the user can find the system more protective with the help of the Persian signatures.

Cheques are more secure since they are used so frequently in the financial industry. So, anyone with an interest in blockchain may choose to pursue a profession in this area in the future.

REFERENCES

Abd-ElZaher, M. A. E. (2014). Different types of inks having certain medicolegal importance: Deciphering the faded and physically erased handwriting. *Egyptian Journal of Forensic Sciences*, *4*(2), 39–44. doi:10.1016/j.ejfs.2013.09.002

Anderson, M. (1998). The electronic check architecture. Financial Services Technology Consortium, 123.

Chang, C. C., Chang, S. C., & Lee, J. S. (2009). An on-line electronic check system with mutual authentication. *Computers & Electrical Engineering*, *35*(5), 757–763. doi:10.1016/j.compeleceng.2009.02.007

Ghandali, S., & Moghaddam, M. E. (2009). Off-Line Persian Signature Identification and Verification Based on Image Registration and Fusion. *Journal of Multimedia*, *4*(3). Advance online publication. doi:10.4304/jmm.4.3.137-144

Kabra, N., Bhattacharya, P., Tanwar, S., & Tyagi, S. (2020). MudraChain: Blockchain-based framework for automated cheque clearance in financial institutions. *Future Generation Computer Systems*, *102*, 574–587. doi:10.1016/j.future.2019.08.035

PaisaBazaar. (2023). *What is a Cheque – Types, Features, Chequebook, Advantages*. Retrieved from https://www.paisabazaar.com/banking/what-is-cheque/

Rajender, M., & Pal, R. (2014, January). Detection of manipulated cheque images in cheque truncation system using mismatch in pixels. In *2014 2nd International Conference on Business and Information Management (ICBIM)* (pp. 30-35). IEEE. 10.1109/ICBIM.2014.6970928

Schwartz, D., Youngs, N., & Britto, A. (2014). The ripple protocol consensus algorithm. *Ripple Labs Inc White Paper, 5*(8), 151.

Singh, K., Singh, N., & Kushwaha, D. S. (2018, September). An interoperable and secure e-wallet architecture based on digital ledger technology using blockchain. In *2018 international conference on computing, power and communication technologies (GUCON)* (pp. 165-169). IEEE.

Singh, N., Kumar, T., & Vardhan, M. (2021). Blockchain-based e-cheque clearing framework with trust based consensus mechanism. *Cluster Computing*, *24*(2), 851–865. doi:10.100710586-020-03163-6

Support innovative projects with star. (2019). *Starbase*. Retrieved from https://starbase.co/contracts

Tschorsch, F., & Scheuermann, B. (2016). Bitcoin and beyond: A technical survey on decentralized digital currencies. *IEEE Communications Surveys and Tutorials*, *18*(3), 2084–2123. doi:10.1109/COMST.2016.2535718

Chapter 11
Audit Committee and Dividend Policy of Financial Firms in Malaysia

Rashedul Hasan
https://orcid.org/0000-0003-0130-0665
Coventry University, UK

Muhammad Ashfaq
IU International University of Applied Sciences, Germany

EXECUTIVE SUMMARY

The corporate governance structure encompasses a set of guidelines meticulously crafted to ensure that a firm operates in a manner that diligently safeguards the interests of all stakeholders. In this study, the authors examine the role of audit committee in the dividend policy of Malaysian financial firms. They collect data from a sample comprising 40 financial institutions, spanning a 13-year period from 2010 to 2022. The empirical findings gleaned from this study unequivocally affirm a statistically significant relationship between the existence of audit committee and the formulation of dividend policies within these financial institutions. Notably, audit committees have been revealed to exert a robust and statistically significant influence on dividend policy within these financial institutions. The implications of these findings extend beyond the confines of academia; they hold substantial relevance for regulatory bodies, financial institutions themselves, and their shareholders in the Malaysian context.

DOI: 10.4018/978-1-6684-9867-5.ch011

1. INTRODUCTION

The structure of corporate governance represents a set of established guidelines utilised by firms to assess the sustainability of their performance and the profitability of their business operations (Securities Commission Malaysia, 2011; Tan, 2015). It ensures that firms conduct their operations in a legal and advantageous manner whilst safeguarding the interests of all stakeholders (Tan, 2015). Within the financial landscape, the governance structure assumes a pivotal role in mitigating the deleterious effects of financial crises (Securities Commission Malaysia, 2011). A robust governance structure establishes a firm foundation that reduces risk exposure and facilitates sustainable growth (Securities Commission Malaysia, 2011).

Moreover, sound governance practices enhance operational transparency, affording shareholders insight into the quality of management and the rationale behind each board decision (Ponnu, 2008; Alzeaideen & Al-Rawash, 2014; Tan, 2015). The Securities Commission Malaysia staunchly advocates for a culture of robust corporate governance, as these structures are rigorously enforced across the global financial landscape (Securities Commission Malaysia, 2017).

In the Malaysian corporate sector, the emphasis on corporate governance practices leans more towards internal governance mechanisms, as opposed to external ones (Zulkafli et al., 2003; Tan, 2015). External governance mechanisms, such as market forces, corporate controls, and legal and regulatory systems, fall beyond the purview of the firm's control (Zulkafli et al., 2003). Internal governance mechanisms encompass the board of directors and equity ownership (Zulkafli et al., 2003). The signaling theory underscores the existence of information asymmetry between firms and shareholders due to the limited disclosure of information to shareholders (Iqbal, 2013; Hassan et al., 2003). This theory accentuates the critical role of cultivating and nurturing a trust-based relationship between shareholders and firms (Iqbal, 2013; Ponnu, 2008; Securities Commission Malaysia, 2011). High-performing firms are expected to accompany their success with an increased distribution of dividends to shareholders (Iqbal, 2013), as dividend payments are intrinsically tied to stock prices, reflective of a firm's performance (Mehdi et al., 2017; Iqbal, 2013). A misalignment between dividends and stock prices could erode trust between directors and shareholders (Iqbal, 2013; Mehdi et al., 2017), fostering skepticism among shareholders regarding company performance (Iqbal, 2013).

Furthermore, a robust governance structure can engender an improved dividend policy framework (Iqbal, 2013; Mehdi et al., 2017) by aligning the interests of directors and shareholders, thereby safeguarding shareholder wealth (Iqbal, 2013). The primary aim of this study is to assess the effectiveness of the governance structure and its impact on dividend policy within licensed local financial institutions in Malaysia. We aim to complement the prior findings of Buertey et al. (2023) that a positive relationship exists between audit committee and dividend policy. The outcomes of this study will be of substantial benefit to shareholders, offering them insights into the optimal board structure for financial institutions in the Malaysian context.

2. LITERATURE REVIEW AND HYPOTHESIS DEVELOPMENT

The corporate governance structure represents a set of established guidelines employed by firms to assess the sustainability of their performance and the profitability of their business operations (Securities Commission Malaysia, 2011; Tan, 2015). It ensures that firms conduct their operations in a legal and advantageous manner while safeguarding the interests of all stakeholders (Tan, 2015). Within the financial landscape, the governance structure assumes a pivotal role in mitigating the deleterious effects of financial crises (Securities Commission Malaysia, 2011). A robust governance structure establishes a firm foundation that reduces risk exposure and facilitates sustainable growth (Securities Commission Malaysia, 2011).

Furthermore, sound governance practices enhance operational transparency, affording shareholders insight into the quality of management and the rationale behind each board decision (Ponnu, 2008; Alzeaideen & Al-Rawash, 2014; Tan, 2015). The Securities Commission Malaysia staunchly advocates for a culture of robust corporate governance, as these structures are rigorously enforced across the global financial landscape (Securities Commission Malaysia, 2017).

Internal governance mechanisms encompass the board of directors and equity ownership (Zulkafli et al., 2003). The governance landscape in Malaysia grapples with weakened management incentives in guiding the board of directors, a phenomenon attributable to shrinking management ownership and widely dispersed shareholder ownership (Zulkafli et al., 2003; Tan, 2015). In such circumstances, boards tend to be ineffectual in executing their duties and fall short in safeguarding shareholder rights (Zulkafli et al., 2003; Tan, 2015).

An independent director is defined as an individual who possesses independence from any business or other relationships that might impede their capacity to exercise unbiased judgment. They are expected to function independently of management, thereby enabling them to make impartial judgments that serve the best interests of the company (Securities Commission Malaysia, 2017; Securities Commission Malaysia, 2011). The concept of board independence holds significant importance as the absence of an independent director on the board can potentially compromise the board's ability to make objective and impartial decisions, potentially prioritizing other interests over those of the company (Securities Commission Malaysia, 2017). Hence, the presence of an independent director on the board plays a pivotal role in averting conflicts of interest.

Previous research into board independence has produced mixed results, with some studies demonstrating a significant negative relationship between board independence and both dividend payout ratios and dividend policies (Mehdi et al., 2017; Iqbal, 2013). Conversely, others have reported an insignificant relationship between board independence and these same dividend-related metrics (Tahir et al., 2014). Additionally, certain studies have uncovered a significant positive relationship between board independence and both dividend payout ratios and dividend policies (Shahid et al., 2016; Cha et al., 2015; Uwalomwa et al., 2015; Batool & Javid, 2014). Notably, Kurawa and Ishaku (2014) found an insignificant negative relationship between board independence and dividend policies. Consequently, we posit the following hypothesis:

Past studies have indicated that board diversity can enhance the monitoring function of directors, fostering a climate of increased independence, creativity, and the introduction of fresh perspectives within the company (Byoun et al., 2016). This diversity-driven benefit can lead to improved strategic decision-making and overall performance (Byoun et al., 2016). Furthermore, companies with diverse boards tend to distribute higher dividends because the diversity within the board elevates the potential for agency problems related to free cash flow (Byoun et al., 2016). Consequently, companies employ dividends as a tool to mitigate these agency problems (Byoun et al., 2016).

The importance of gender diversity within the board cannot be overstated, as male and female directors often bring distinct perspectives (Securities Commission Malaysia, 2017). Empirical evidence suggests that a diverse board is more effective and efficient compared to a non-diverse one (Securities Commission Malaysia, 2017). This enhancement leads to more robust decision-making, as gender diversity facilitates constructive debates that allow for the exploration of the same ideas from different angles (Securities Commission Malaysia, 2017).

The influence of female directors on company performance has attracted increasing attention from researchers. Thi (2017) reports a positive impact of female directors on company performance. Furthermore, evidence suggests differences between male and female directors concerning dividend policy (Thi, 2017). The importance of a higher proportion of female directors has been widely advocated for public listed companies (Dimovski et al., 2016). Dimovski et al. (2016) found that a diverse board is more adept at improving performance by virtue of its broader perspectives (Lückerath-Rovers, 2013).

Past studies have consistently reported a significant positive relationship between female directors and both dividend payout ratios and dividend policies (Chen et al., 2017; Al-Rahahleh, 2017; Pucheta-Martinez & Bel-oms, 2016; Wellalage & Locke, 2013; Lückerath-Rovers, 2013; Byoun et al., 2016). Elmagrhi et al. (2017), however, reported a significant negative relationship between female directors and dividend policies. Thus, we propose the following hypothesis:

The audit committee is a group of experts, comprising both internal and external individuals, upon which a company relies to ensure that the board makes decisions that align with the company's best interests (Al-Dhamari & Ismail, 2013). The internal audit committee is primarily responsible for monitoring the risks that the company faces, with a view to preventing these risks from impeding the company's objectives (Securities Commission Malaysia, 2017). Additionally, the internal audit committee assumes responsibility for overseeing the company's internal controls, including the governance structure and the financial reporting process (Securities Commission Malaysia, 2017). They also provide advice to the company for improvements and offer an independent opinion on the risks facing the company (Securities Commission Malaysia, 2017).

An effective internal audit committee plays a pivotal role in enhancing transparency and fostering impartial judgment in the processing of financial reports, thereby rendering financial statements a reliable source of information for both the company and its shareholders (Securities Commission Malaysia, 2017; Al-Dhamari & Ismail, 2013). Furthermore, the external audit committee is tasked with reviewing financial statements and scrutinizing the company's financial position to ensure that it is presented to the public, including shareholders, in an accurate and truthful manner (Securities Commission Malaysia, 2017). The existence of an audit committee is regarded as a fundamental instrument in implementing good corporate governance (Muhtar et al., 2014). Therefore, we formulate the following hypothesis:

H_1: The audit committee has a positive influence on dividend payout.

3. RESEARCH METHODS

The scope of this study encompasses all licensed financial institutions listed on Bursa Malaysia. The focus of this research on financial institutions is driven by the inherent disparities in regulatory frameworks and final account structures between the financial and non-financial sectors, rendering meaningful comparisons between the two sectors challenging (Gray, 2013; Ponnu, 2008). To maintain clarity and consistency, foreign financial institutions operating in Malaysia and other local financial institutions lacking sufficient data are excluded from this study.

Consequently, the final dataset for this study comprises 460 observations, encompassing 40 locally licensed financial institutions in Malaysia, spanning thirteen years from 2010 to 2022. This dataset represents an unbalanced panel dataset. The financial data for these institutions are sourced from Refinitiv database. For a comprehensive overview of the selected firms, Table 1 provides a summary. The sample encompasses various types of financial institutions, including commercial banks, Islamic banks, investment banks, insurance companies, and insurance firms. To facilitate the reader's understanding, Table 2 furnishes definitions for all variables employed in the subsequent analysis.

In this study, a regression model has been formulated to explore the relationships between audit committee and dividend pay-out. The model is articulated as follows:

$$Dividend_{it} = \beta_0 + \beta_1 AC_{it} + \beta_2 Control_{it} + \varepsilon_{it} \quad (1)$$

Table 1. The summary of the selected firm in this study

Type of Institution	Number of Firms
Commercial Bank	11
Closed-end funds	1
Consumer lending	4
Diversified investment Services	1
Financial and commodity market operators	2
Investment banks and fund operators	12
Insurance	9
Grand Total	**40**

Where $Dividend_{it}$ is the dependent variable of this study that defines as the cash dividend paid by the firm i in the period of t which is from 2016 to 2017. AC denotes audit committee characteristics. $Control_{it}$ denotes ascontrol variables which included the firm size, leverage and tire 1 capital ratio. The firm size is measured by the natural logarithm of total assets. The leverage is measured by the total liabilities divided by the total equity. The tier 1 capital ratio represents the percentage of tier 1 capital of the risk-weighted assets.

4. RESULTS AND DISCUSSION

Table 3 provides a statistical summary of each variable. Cash dividend has an average value of 16.992 and a standard deviation of 1.896, indicating a dispersion of cash dividends around the mean. The minimum and maximum values observed were 12.657 and 21.514, respectively. Audit Board Committee, Audit Committee

Table 2. Variables explanation

Variable		Explanation
Abbreviation	**Full**	
Dependent Variables		
Dividend	Cash dividend paid	Natural logarithm of cash dividend paid.
Independent Variables		
AC	Audit board committee	Dummy variable, 1 if the firm has an audit committee, 0 otherwise
AC_IND	Audit committee independence	% of independent board members on the audit committee.
AC_MIND	Audit committee management expertise	Dummy variable, 1 if the firm reports that audit committee members are non-executives, 0 otherwise
AC_EXP	Audit committee expertise	Dummy variable, 1 if the firm has at least 3 members and 1 with financial expertise, 0 otherwise
AC_NONEX	Audit committee non-executives	% of non-executive members on the audit committee
Control Variables		
Size	Firm Size	The natural logarithm of the total asset.
Leverage	Leverage	Total liabilities are divided by the total equity.
Tire 1	Tire 1 capital ratio	A ratio of tier 1 capital as a percentage of risk-weighted capital

Independence, Audit Committee Management Independence, Audit Committee Expertise and Audit Committee Non-Executive Members are dummy variables, each with 520 observations except for the latter two which have 506 and 509 observations respectively. The means of these variables range from 0.237 to 0.258, suggesting that a quarter or less of the committees possess the respective attributes of the audit committee. The average size of firms is 22.888 with a standard deviation of about 2.098, indicating variability in firm size. Leverage is centred around -0.046 (mean). Finally, the Tier 1 Capital Ratio has an average ratio of approximately 0.038 with a standard deviation of about 0.068, indicating variability in this ratio among firms.

Table 4 provides regression results examining the impact of audit committee on dividend payout. The coefficients represent the change in the dividend payout for a one-unit change in the respective independent variable. In all five models, we use the same controls: size, leverage, and tier 1 capital. In model 1, we report audit Committee is significant and positively associated with dividend payout, with a coefficient of 2.546. In models (2) through (5), different aspects of the audit committee are considered. 'Audit Committee Independence' in model (2), 'Audit Committee Management Independent' in model (3), 'Audit Committee Expertise'

Table 3. The result of descriptive statistics analysis

Variable	Obs	Mean	Std. Dev.	Min	Max
Cash dividend	329	16.992	1.896	12.657	21.514
Audit board committee	520	0.258	0.438	0.000	1.000
Audit committee independence	520	0.240	0.414	0.000	1.000
Audit committee management independent	506	0.237	0.426	0.000	1.000
Audit committee expertise	509	0.242	0.429	0.000	1.000
Audit committee non-executive members	520	0.254	0.432	0.000	1.000
Firm size	226	22.888	2.098	18.196	26.081
Leverage	520	0.046	1.051	0.007	4.710
Tire 1 capital ratio	520	0.038	0.068	0.000	0.417

in model (4), and 'Audit Committee Non-Executive Members' in model (5) are all significant and positively associated with dividend payout, with coefficients ranging from approximately 2.52 to 2.59. Hence, H_1 is accepted.

This finding aligns with prior research and provides further affirmation that companies with a lower proportion of independent directors on their boards tend to adopt high dividend payout policies (Iqbal 2013; Al-Dhamari & Ismail 2013; Mehdi et al. 2017; Elmagrhi et al. 2017). This suggests that independent directors may encounter limitations in their effectiveness on the board due to the absence of specific authority vested in them (Iqbal 2013; Securities Commission Malaysia 2011).

In contrast, the audit committee demonstrates a significant positive relationship with dividend policy, implying that an increase in the number of audit committee members on the board correlates with higher dividend distributions to ordinary shareholders. Consequently, Hypothesis 4 is corroborated. These findings accord with the expectations set forth in Hypothesis 4, indicating that firms with a larger proportion of audit committee members exhibit a greater inclination towards dividend payments. This inclination is attributed to the fact that a larger audit committee contributes to enhanced managerial oversight, thereby mitigating agency issues. It achieves this by dissuading managers from investing in projects with negative net present value and encouraging the distribution of surplus cash when no positive net present value projects are available (Elmagrhi et al. 2017).

The regression model employed in this study holds statistical significance, boasting an adjusted R-squared value of 17 per cent. However, the variables representing board size and female directors display an insignificant relationship with dividend policy. Consequently, Hypotheses 1 and 3 are rejected. The observed negative correlation between board size and dividend policy contradicts the outcomes of previous studies, which have consistently shown a positive and significant relationship (Mehdi et

Table 4. The result of the regression analysis

	Dividend Payout				
	(1)	(2)	(3)	(4)	(5)
Audit Committee	2.546***				
	(15.42)				
Size	0.484***	0.498***	0.497***	0.483***	0.482***
	(8.56)	(8.57)	(7.85)	(8.42)	(5.21)
Leverage	0.178**	0.143*	0.182**	0.178**	0.170**
	(3.04)	(2.39)	(3.02)	(3.01)	(2.90)
Tier 1 capital	4.730***	4.826***	4.896***	4.669***	4.645***
	(4.44)	(4.38)	(4.44)	(4.31)	(4.33)
Audit committee independence		2.589***			
		(14.46)			
Audit committee management independent			2.518***		
			(14.7)		
Audit committee expertise				2.574***	
				(15.17)	
Audit committee non-executive members					2.575***
					(15.34)
Intercept	15.73***	15.78***	15.73***	15.73***	15.74***
	(168.9)	(166.17)	(168.25)	(167.28)	(168.86)
Observations	329	329	316	318	329

al. 2017; Subramaniam & Devi 2011; Iqbal 2013; Elmagrhi et al. 2017). These studies contend that a larger board excels in monitoring functions, thanks to its diversified pool of directors with varied skills (Mehdi et al. 2017; Subramaniam & Devi 2011; Iqbal 2013; Elmagrhi et al. 2017). Nevertheless, this result finds support in other previous studies where board size negatively and significantly impacted a firm's earning predictability (Al-Dhamari & Ismail 2013). These studies argue that a smaller board proves more effective due to enhanced coordination, swifter decision-making processes, and a reduced likelihood of free-rider problems (Al-Dhamari & Ismail 2013).

While evidence underscores the benefits of board gender diversity in terms of improved managerial oversight and enhanced company performance, the limited presence of female directors can potentially exert a negative influence on the board's dynamics (Elmagrhi et al. 2017). This suggests that female directors may face constraints in exerting effective authority on the board, as their inclusion in firms is often driven by the desire to establish a positive image through good governance practices, rather than active involvement in decision-making processes. The control variables exhibit a positive but insignificant relationship with dividend per share, encompassing variables such as leverage, return on assets, return on equity, and firm size.

5. DISCUSSION AND CONCLUSION

The primary focus of this study lies in identifying the relationship between dividend policy and governance structures, more specifically the existence and characteristics of the audit committee. The study's findings furnish evidence that the presence of an audit committee exerts a strong and significant influence on dividend policy within financial institutions in Malaysia. These findings propose that financial institutions in Malaysia should consider expanding the proportion of audit committee members on their boards while concurrently increasing the proportion of independent directors. This strategic adjustment aims to enhance the effectiveness of dividend distribution in Malaysia.

In the context of Malaysia, female directors currently wield limited influence over dividend decisions. This is primarily due to the restricted representation of female directors on the audit committee of Malaysian financial institutions. Consequently, female directors face significant challenges in playing a substantial role in shaping dividend policy decisions. Overall, this study underscores the dearth of the role the audit committee plays in shaping the dividend policy of financial institutions operating in Malaysia. Moreover, this study also addresses the research question concerning the role the audit committee plays between external auditors and the top management.

REFERENCES

Al-Dhamari, R. A., & Ismail, K. N. I. K. (2013). Governance structure, ownership structure and earnings predictability: Malaysian evidence. *Asian Academy of Management Journal of Accounting and Finance*, *9*(1), 1–23.

Al-Rahahleh, A. S. (2017). Corporate Governance Quality, Board Gender Diversity and Corporate Dividend Policy: Evidence from Jordan. *Australasian Accounting, Business and Finance Journal*, *11*(2), 86–104.

Alzeaideen, K. A., & Al-Rawash, S. Z. (2014). The Effect of Ownership Structure on Share Price Volatility of Listed Companies in Amman Stock Exchange. *Research Journal of Finance and Accounting*, *5*(6), 192–201.

Batool, Z., & Javid, A. Y. (2014). *Dividend Policy and Role of Corporate Governance in Manufacturing Sector of Pakistan*. Academic Press.

Byoun, S., Chang, K. & Kim, Y.S. (2016). Does Corporate Board Diversity Affect Corporate Payout Policy? *Journal of Financial Studies*, *45*(1), 48–101.

Cha, P.C. (2015). *The Effect of Corporate Governance on Dividend Policy: Trading/Services Sector in Malaysia*. Universiti Tunku Abdul Rahman.

Chen, J., Leung, W. S., & Goergen, M. (2017). The impact of board gender composition on dividend payouts. *Journal of Corporate Finance*, *43*, 86–105. doi:10.1016/j.jcorpfin.2017.01.001

Dimovski, B., Lombardi, L., Ratcliffe, C., & Cooper, B. J. (2016). Australian Real Estate Management and Development companies and women directors. *Property Management*, *34*(1), 18–28. doi:10.1108/PM-12-2014-0052

Elmagrhi, M. H. (2017). Corporate governance and dividend payout policy in the UK listed SMEs: The effects of corporate board characteristics. *International Journal of Accounting and Information Management*, *25*(4), 459–483. doi:10.1108/IJAIM-02-2017-0020

Gray, W. (2013). *Why Exclude Financial Firms from Quantitative Studies*. Alpha Architect.

Hassan, M. K., Farhat, J., & Al-zu'bi, B. (2003). Dividend signalling hypothesis and short term. *Islamic Economic Studies*, *11*(1), 1–30.

Ikunda, C., Muiru, M., & Kamau, S. M. (2016). The Impact of Corporate Governance on Dividend Payout of Manufacturing Firms Listed at the Nairobi Securities Exchange. *Journal of Finance and Accounting*, *4*(5), 254–261. doi:10.11648/j.jfa.20160405.12

Iqbal, S. (2013). The impact of corporate governance on the dividend decision of firms : Evidence from Pakistan. *African Journal of Business Management*, *7*(11), 811–817.

Jahanzeb, A. (2016). Impact of Corporate Governance and Firm-Level Control Variables on Dividend Policy of Service Trade Sector of Malaysia. *Journal of Economic and Social Development*, *3*(2), 102–111.

Kurawa, J. M., & Ishaku, A. (2014). The Effect Of Corporate Governance On Dividend Policy Of Listed Banks In Nigeria : A Panel Data Analysis. *The Journal of Finance*, *2*(8), 1–12.

Lückerath-Rovers, M. (2013). Women on boards and firm performance. *The Journal of Management and Governance*, *17*(2), 491–509. doi:10.100710997-011-9186-1

Mansourinia, E. (2013). The Effect of Board Size, Board Independence and CEO Duality on Dividend Policy of Companies: Evidence from Tehran Stock Exchange. *International Journal of Economy. Management and Social Sciences*, *2*(6), 237–241.

Mehdi, M., Sahut, J.-M., & Teulon, F. (2017). Do corporate governance and ownership structure impact dividend policy in emerging market during the financial crisis? *Journal of Applied Accounting Research*, *18*(3), 274–297. doi:10.1108/JAAR-07-2014-0079

Muhtar. (2014). Effect Of The Audit Committee, Capital Structure, Managerial Ownership Structure, Management Of Profit And Dividend Policy Value Company Group Public In Indonesia Stock Exchange. *Journal of Research in Business and Management*, *2*(11), 40–49.

Ponnu, C. H. (2008). Corporate Governance Structures and the Performance of Malaysian Public Listed Companies. *International Review of Business Research Papers*, *4*(2), 217–230.

Pucheta-Martinez, M. C., & Bel-oms, I. (2016). The Board of Directors and Dividend Policy: The Effect of Gender Diversity. *Industrial and Corporate Change*, *25*(3), 523–547. doi:10.1093/icc/dtv040

Reinsurance Group of American. (2014). *RGA Global Reinsurance Company, Ltd., Labuan Branch Malaysian Life Reinsurance Group Berhad (MLRe)*. RGA.

Sani, A. A., & Musa, A. M. (2017). Corporate Board Attributes and Dividend Payout Policy of Listed Deposit Money Banks in Nigeria. *International Journal of Research in IT, Management and Engineering*, *7*(1), 7–13.

Securities Commission Malaysia. (2017). *Malaysian Code on Corporate Governance, Securities Commission Malaysia, 2011. Malaysian Corporate Governance Blueprint 2011*. Author.

Shahid, M.S., Rizwan, M., & Bucha, M.H. (2016). Ownership Structure, Board Size, Board Composition and Dividend Policy : New Evidence From Two Emerging Markets. *Journal of Business Studies*, *12*(2), 25–36.

Subramaniam, R., & Devi, S. S. (2011). Corporate Governance and Dividend Policy in Malaysia. *2010 International Conference on Business and Economics*, 200–207.

Tahir, S. H. (2016). Effect of Corporate Governance Index on Dividend Policy: An Investigation of Textile Industry of Pakistan. *Journal of Economic and Social Development*, *3*(1), 139–146.

Tahir, S. H., Aslam, M. A., & Akhtar, M. A. (2014). the Impact of Board Characteristics and Ownership Structure on Corporate Dividend Policy in Canada. *The International Journal's Research Journal of Economics and Business Studies*, *3*(6), 18–24.

Tan, W. C. (2015). *Corporate Governance Structure and Performance of Malaysian Listed Companies*. Universiti Utara Malaysia.

Thi, N. C. T. (2017). the Impact of Female Board of Directors on Firm Performance and Dividend Payout Policies: Evidence From Vietnam. *International Research Journal of Finance and Economics*, (164), 56–67.

Uwalomwa, U., Olamide, O., & Francis, I. (2015). The Effects of Corporate Governance Mechanisms on Firms Dividend Payout Policy in Nigeria. *Journal of Accounting and Auditing: Research & Practice*, *2015*, 1–12. doi:10.5171/2015.313679

Wellalage, N. H., & Locke, S. (2013). Women on board, firm financial performance and agency costs. *Asian Journal of Business Ethics*, *2*(2), 113–127. doi:10.100713520-012-0020-x

Yahya, F., & Ghazali, Z. B. (2017). The effectiveness of board governance and dividend policy as alignment mechanisms to firm performance and CEO compensation. *Cogent Business & Management*, *4*(1), 1–20. doi:10.1080/23311975.2017.1398124

Zulkafli, A.H. bin, Samad, M.F. bt. A. & Ismail, M.I. (2003). *Corporate Governance in Malaysia*. Academic Press.

Compilation of References

Abadi, A. M. (2022). Kleptocracy and Foreign Loan Decision-Making Process: Insights from Malaysia's Deals and Renegotiations with China. *Journal of Current Southeast Asian Affairs*, *41*(1), 135–158. doi:10.1177/18681034211058470

Abd Aziz, H., & Abd Ghadas, Z. A. (2019). the Propose Governance Framework for Shariah Corporation. *International Journal of Law, Government and Communication*, 84–90. doi:10.35631/ijlgc.415009

Abd-ElZaher, M. A. E. (2014). Different types of inks having certain medicolegal importance: Deciphering the faded and physically erased handwriting. *Egyptian Journal of Forensic Sciences*, *4*(2), 39–44. doi:10.1016/j.ejfs.2013.09.002

Abels, P. B., & Martelli, J. T. (2013, April 5). CEO Duality: How Many Hats Are Too Many? *Corporate Governance*, *13*(2), 135–147. doi:10.1108/14720701311316625

Abu-Hussin, M. F., Idris, A., Yaakop, M. R. M., & Salleh, M. A. (2021). Essential Factors Influencing Malaysia's Relations with the United Arab Emirates. *Contemporary Review of the Middle East*, *8*(4), 477–495. doi:10.1177/23477989211031785

Adam, S. B., Al-Aidaros, A. M. H., & Ishak, S. B. (2018). The moderating effect of Islamic work ethics on the relationship between corporate governance and performance of Islamic financial institutions in Nigeria: A proposed framework. *Journal of Social Sciences Research, 2018*(Special Issue 6), 1041–1048. doi:10.32861/jssr.spi6.1041.1048

Adams, C. A. (2017). Conceptualising the contemporary corporate value creation process. *Accounting, Auditing & Accountability Journal*, *30*(4), 906–931. doi:10.1108/AAAJ-04-2016-2529

Ahmad, A., & Ishak, M. S. I. (2021). Shari'ah Governance of Islamic Non-Banking Financial Institutions in Malaysia: A Conceptual Review. *The Journal of Management Theory and Practice*, *2*(1), 70–77. doi:10.37231/jmtp.2021.2.1.91

Ahmed, S. I. (2020, February 4). *Luckin Coffee share price may nearly double to $60 on U.S. exchanges: Hedge fund Citron Capital.* Retrieved June 19, 2023, from Reuters: https://www.reuters.com/article/us-luckin-coffee-stock-citron-idUSKBN1ZY2EK

Ahmed, S. U., & Rahman, M. (2014). Incorporating ESG Risk in Bank-Lending in Bangladesh. *International Research Journal of Finance and Economics*, (120), 23–34.

Akben-Selcuk, E. (2019). Corporate social responsibility and financial performance: The moderating role of ownership concentration in Turkey. *Sustainability*, *11*(13), 36–43. doi:10.3390u11133643

Al Shaher, S., & Zreik, M. (2022). Reflections on the China-Malaysia Economic Partnership. *The Journal of Asian Finance, Economics and Business*, *9*(3), 229–234.

Alam Choudhury, M., & Nurul Alam, M. (2013). Corporate governance in Islamic perspective. *International Journal of Islamic and Middle Eastern Finance and Management*, *6*(3), 180–199. doi:10.1108/IMEFM-10-2012-0101

Alam, M. K. (2022). A proposed centralized Shariah governance framework for Islamic banks in Bangladesh. *Journal of Islamic Accounting and Business Research*, *13*(2), 364–389. doi:10.1108/JIABR-03-2021-0106

Alam, M. K., Ab Rahman, S., Mustafa, H., Shah, S. M., & Hossain, M. S. (2019). Shariah governance framework of islamic banks in bangladesh: Practices, problems and recommendations. *Asian Economic and Financial Review*, *9*(1), 118–132. doi:10.18488/journal.aefr.2019.91.118.132

Alam, M. K., Rahman, M. M., Islam, F. T., Adedeji, B. S., Mannan, M. A., & Sahabuddin, M. (2021). The practices of Shariah governance systems of Islamic banks in Bangladesh. *Pacific Accounting Review*, *33*(4), 505–524. doi:10.1108/PAR-10-2020-0195

Alam, M., & Thakur, O. A. (2022). Why does Bangladesh require a centralized shariah governance framework for Islamic banks? *Journal of Nusantara Studies*, *7*(1), 24–42. doi:10.24200/jonus.vol7iss1pp24-42

Albitar, K., Hussainey, K., Kolade, N., & Gerged, A. (2020). ESG disclosure and firm performance before and after IR: The moderating role of governance mechanisms. *International Journal of Accounting & Information Management*, *28*(3), 429–444. doi:10.1108/IJAIM-09-2019-0108

Al-Dhamari, R. A., & Ismail, K. N. I. K. (2013). Governance structure, ownership structure and earnings predictability: Malaysian evidence. *Asian Academy of Management Journal of Accounting and Finance*, *9*(1), 1–23.

Algabry, L., Alhabshi, S. M., Soualhi, Y., & Alaeddin, O. (2020). Conceptual framework of internal Sharīʿah audit effectiveness factors in Islamic banks. *ISRA International Journal of Islamic Finance*, *12*(2), 171–193. doi:10.1108/IJIF-09-2018-0097

Ali, S., Naseem, M. A., Jian, J., Rehman, R. U., Malik, F., & Ahmad, M. I. (2022, August 9). "How" and "When" CEO Duality Matter? Case of a Developing Economy. *Sage Journals*, 1–15.

Ali, A. M. (2016). 1MDB: The Audit Firms" Questions. *Journal of Public Administration and Governance*, *6*(1), 73–86. doi:10.5296/jpag.v6i1.9057

Almutairi, A. R., & Quttainah, M. A. (2020). Foreign directors and corporate governance in Islamic banks. *Journal of Islamic Accounting and Business Research*, *11*(3), 765–791. doi:10.1108/JIABR-07-2017-0104

Al-Rahahleh, A. S. (2017). Corporate Governance Quality, Board Gender Diversity and Corporate Dividend Policy: Evidence from Jordan. *Australasian Accounting, Business and Finance Journal*, *11*(2), 86–104.

Alzeaideen, K. A., & Al-Rawash, S. Z. (2014). The Effect of Ownership Structure on Share Price Volatility of Listed Companies in Amman Stock Exchange. *Research Journal of Finance and Accounting*, *5*(6), 192–201.

Amis, J. M., Mair, J., & Munir, K. A. (2020). The organizational reproduction of inequality. *The Academy of Management Annals*, *14*(1), 195–230. doi:10.5465/annals.2017.0033

Amrani, O., & Najab, A. (2023). The Impact of Multi-Layer Corporate Governance on Banks' Performance under the GFC and the COVID-19: A Cross-Country Panel Analysis Approach. *Journal of Risk and Financial Management*, *16*(1), 15. Advance online publication. doi:10.3390/jrfm16010015

Anderson, M. (1998). The electronic check architecture. Financial Services Technology Consortium, 123.

Anissa, N. D. (2018). Toward A Comprehensive Sharia Governance Framework for Islamic Finance: A Contribution to the Debate. *International Journal of Management Sciences and Business Research*, *7*(11), 14–26. http://www.ijmsbr.com

Anker, R. (1977). The effect of group-level variables on fertility in a rural Indian sample. *The Journal of Development Studies*, *14*(1), 63–76. doi:10.1080/00220387708421662

Arena, C., Bozzolan, S., & Michelon, G. (2015). Environmental reporting: Transparency to stakeholders or stakeholder manipulation? An analysis of disclosure tone and the role of the board of directors. *Corporate Social Responsibility and Environmental Management*, *22*(6), 346–361. doi:10.1002/csr.1350

Aribi, Z. A., & Gao, S. (2010). Corporate social responsibility disclosure: A comparison between Islamic and conventional financial institutions. *Journal of Financial Reporting and Accounting*, *8*(2), 72–91. doi:10.1108/19852511011088352

Arjalies, D. L. (2010). A social movement perspective on finance: How socially responsible investment mattered. *Journal of Business Ethics*, *92*(S1), 57–78. doi:10.100710551-010-0634-7

Ayaz Assistant Professor, M., Shakeel Shah Assistant Professor, H., & Bin Yusuf, J. (2018). Islamic Banking and Finance Review Legal and Corporate Governance Framework for Islamic Banks in Pakistan. *Islamic Banking and Finance Review*, *5*(01), 24–37. doi:10.32350/ibfr.2018.05.02

Ayondo Ltd. (2016). *FinTech and Social Trading Pioneer ayondo aims for Singapore listing* [Press release]. Retrieved from https://links.sgx.com/FileOpen/Ayondo_PressRelease_20160413_Final.ashx?App=ArchiveAnnouncement&FileID=398927&AnncID=03JWW0J6EA8WSLHO

Ayondo Ltd. (2018a). *Annual Report 2018*. Retrieved from https://links.sgx.com/FileOpen/ayondo_Annual%20Report%20FY2018.ashx?App=Announcement&FileID=563273

Ayondo Ltd. (2018b). *Audited Financial Statements for the Financial Year Ended 31 December 2017*. Retrieved from https://links.sgx.com/FileOpen/ayondo_FY2017%20results%20_090518.ashx?App=Announcement&FileID=504781

Ayondo Ltd. (2018c). *Offer document dated 15 March 2018* [Press release]. Retrieved from https://boersengefluester.de/wp-content/uploads/assets/annuals/2016/A2JG3A.pdf

Ayondo Ltd. (2018d). *Unaudited Financial Statements for the First Quarter ended 31 March 2018*. Retrieved from https://links.sgx.com/FileOpen/ayondo_1Q2018%20results_090518.ashx?App=Announcement&FileID=504782

Ayondo Ltd. (2019a). *Application to the Singapore Exchange Securities Trading Limited for further extensions of time to (I) Release the company's unaudited financial statements for the financial year ended 31 December 2019 ("FY2018"), (II) Hold Annual General Meeting ("AGM") for FY2018, and (III) Release the company's unaudited financial statements for financial period ended 31 March 2019 ("1Q2019")* [Press release]. Retrieved from https://links.sgx.com/FileOpen/ayondo%20-%20Further%20Extension%20of%20Time%20for%20FS%20and%20AGM_Final_290319.ashx?App=Announcement&FileID=549439

Ayondo Ltd. (2019b). *Receipt of Letter of Demand* [Press release]. Retrieved from https://links.sgx.com/FileOpen/ayondo_Receipt%20of%20Letter%20of%20Demand_Final_170419.ashx?App=Announcement&FileID=553766

Ayondo Ltd. (2019c). *Results of application to the Accounting and Corporate Regulatory Authority ("ACRA") for extension of time to hold Annual General Meeting ("AGM") for the financial year ended 31 December 2018 ("FY2018")* [Press release]. Retrieved from https://links.sgx.com/FileOpen/ayondo-%20Results%20of%20ACRA%20Application%20for%20EOT_Final_030419.ashx?App=Announcement&FileID=550163

Ayondo Ltd. (2019d). *Sale And Purchase Agreement In Relation To The Disposal Of The Entire Issued Shares Of Ayondo Markets Limited* [Press release]. Retrieved from https://links.sgx.com/FileOpen/ayondo_Announcement%20on%20the%20BUX%20SPA_Final_080519.ashx?App=Announcement&FileID=558337

Ayondo Ltd. (2019e). *Update pursuant to rule 703(1) of Section B: Rules of Catalist of the Listing Manual of the SGX-ST: A. Update on Ayondo Markets Limited B. Heads of Terms with BUX Holding B.V.* [Press release]. Retrieved from https://links.sgx.com/FileOpen/ayondo%20-%20Update%20Announcement_Final_140219.ashx?App=Announcement&FileID=543645

Baksh-Soodeen, R., Etchart, L., Onubogu, E., & Johnson, T. (Eds.). (2005). *Gender mainstreaming in conflict transformation: Building sustainable peace*. Commonwealth Secretariat.

Baltagi, B. H. (2008). Forecasting with panel data. *Journal of Forecasting*, *27*(2), 153–173. doi:10.1002/for.1047

Banaji, J. (2004). *Institutional investors and nominee directors. In Corporate Governance, Economic Reforms and Development: The Indian Experience*. Oxford University Press.

Banking Staff Writer, N. S. (2019). Ayondo explores sale of UK subsidiary to Dutch fintech BUX. *NS Banking*. Retrieved from https://www.nsbanking.com/news/ayondo-markets-sale-bux/

Barker, R., & Eccles, R. G. (2019). *Should FASB and IASB be responsible for setting standards for nonfinancial information?* Saïd Business School, University of Oxford.

Basel Committee on Banking Supervision. (2023). *The Basel Framework*. Bank for International Settlements.

Batool, Z., & Javid, A. Y. (2014). *Dividend Policy and Role of Corporate Governance in Manufacturing Sector of Pakistan*. Academic Press.

Bernardi, C., & Stark, A. W. (2018). Environmental, social and governance disclosure, integrated reporting, and the accuracy of analyst forecasts. *The British Accounting Review*, *50*(1), 16–31. doi:10.1016/j.bar.2016.10.001

Bhabra, H. S., Hossain, A. T., & Karmakar, V. R. (2020). An overview of C-SOX and directions for future research. *Managerial Finance*, *46*(2), 254–266. doi:10.1108/MF-10-2018-0530

Bhabra, H., & Hossain, A. T. (2018). SOX vs C-SOX: Which one works better? *Managerial Finance*, *44*(8), 1031–1046. doi:10.1108/MF-03-2018-0097

Bhatia, M., & Gulati, R. (2020). Does board effectiveness matter for bank performance? Evidence from India. *International Journal of Comparative Management*, *3*(1-2), 9–52. doi:10.1504/IJCM.2020.107335

Bhatti, M., & Bhatti, I. (2009). Development in legal Issues of Corporate Governance in Islamic Finance. *Journal of Economic and Administrative Sciences*, *25*(1), 67–91. doi:10.1108/10264116200900004

Bhuyian, M., & Hussain, M. (2020, June 06). Bangladesh moves 17 notches up on Environmental Performance Index. *The Business Standard*.

Booth, J. R., & Deli, D. N. (1999). On executives of financial institutions as outside directors. *Journal of Corporate Finance*, *5*(3), 227–250. doi:10.1016/S0929-1199(99)00004-8

Broughton, A., & Miller, L. (2009). Women in senior management: Is the glass ceiling still intact? *ISGUC The Journal of Industrial Relations and Human Resources*, *11*(5), 7–24. doi:10.4026/1303-2860.2009.0122.x

Brown, G., & Peterson, R. S. (2022). *Disaster in the Boardroom*. Springer Books. doi:10.1007/978-3-030-91658-9

Brun, J. P., Sotiropoulou, A., Gray, L., & Scott, C. (2021). *Asset recovery handbook: a guide for practitioners*. World Bank Publications.

Bubna, A., & Gopalan, R. (2012). Bank Involvement in Firm Management, Panacea or a Pain? *Panacea or a Pain, 1-35.* https://papers.ssrn.com/sol3/papers.cfm?abstract_id=2024801

Bukhari, K. S., Awan, H. M., & Ahmed, F. (2013). An evaluation of corporate governance practices of Islamic banks versus Islamic bank windows of conventional banks: A case of Pakistan. *Management Research Review*, *36*(4), 400–416. doi:10.1108/01409171311315003

Bu, Q. (2021, September 03). The anatomy of Holding Foreign Companies Accountable Act (HFCAA): A panacea or a double-edge sword? *Capital Markets Law Journal*, *16*(4), 503–527. doi:10.1093/cmlj/kmab022

Bussin, M., Wöcke, A., & Deysel, B. (2023). The impact of remuneration governance on chief executive officer overpayment. *Suid-Afrikaanse Tydskrif vir Ekonomiese en Bestuurswetenskappe*, *26*(1). Advance online publication. doi:10.4102ajems.v26i1.4860

Byoun, S., Chang, K. & Kim, Y.S. (2016). Does Corporate Board Diversity Affect Corporate Payout Policy? *Journal of Financial Studies*, *45*(1), 48–101.

Camilleri, M.A. (2022). Walking the talk about corporate social responsibility communication: an elaboration likelihood model perspective. *Business Ethics, the Environment & Responsibility*, *31*(3), 649-661.

Campbell, K., & Mínguez-Vera, A. (2008). Gender diversity in the boardroom and firm financial performance. *Journal of Business Ethics*, *83*(3), 435–451. doi:10.100710551-007-9630-y

Case, W. (2017). Stress testing leadership in Malaysia: The 1MDB scandal and Najib Tun Razak. *The Pacific Review*, *30*(5), 633–654. doi:10.1080/09512748.2017.1282538

Cha, P.C. (2015). *The Effect of Corporate Governance on Dividend Policy: Trading/Services Sector in Malaysia*. Universiti Tunku Abdul Rahman.

Chang, C. C., Chang, S. C., & Lee, J. S. (2009). An on-line electronic check system with mutual authentication. *Computers & Electrical Engineering*, *35*(5), 757–763. doi:10.1016/j.compeleceng.2009.02.007

Chen, J., Leung, W. S., & Goergen, M. (2017). The impact of board gender composition on dividend payouts. *Journal of Corporate Finance*, *43*, 86–105. doi:10.1016/j.jcorpfin.2017.01.001

Chen, V. (2022). Corporate Law and Political Economy in a Kleptocracy. *The American Journal of Comparative Law*, *70*(3), 480–509. doi:10.1093/ajcl/avac041

Chua, T. (2013). GRP appoints Peter Moe as director. *Singapore Business Review*. Retrieved from https://sbr.com.sg/manufacturing/people/grp-appoints-peter-moe-director

Chung, Y. L., Tan, H. C. P., How, C. X., & Tan, C. E. (2022). *The impact of corruption on innovation activities: The case of Malaysia* [Doctoral dissertation]. UTAR.

Cicchiello, A. F., Fellegara, A. M., Kazemikhasragh, A., & Monferrà, S. (2021). Gender diversity on corporate boards: How Asian and African women contribute to sustainability reporting activity. *Gender in Management*, *36*(7), 801–820. doi:10.1108/GM-05-2020-0147

Coley, B. (2020, December 17). *Luckin Coffee Agrees to Pay $180 Million Fine for Fraud Scandal*. Retrieved July 23, 2023, from QSR: https://www.qsrmagazine.com/finance/luckin-coffee-agrees-pay-180-million-fine-fraud-scandal

Colon, D. (2005). The Foreign Bank Exemption to the Sarbanes-Oxley Prohibition on Loans to Directors and Officers. *Journal of International Business and Law*, *4*(1), 123–151.

Dalton, D. R., Daily, C. M., Johnson, J. L., & Ellstrand, A. E. (1999). Number of directors and financial performance: A meta-analysis. *Academy of Management Journal*, *42*(6), 674–686. doi:10.2307/256988

Dam, L., & Scholtens, B. (2013). Ownership concentration and CSR policy of European multinational enterprises. *Journal of Business Ethics*, *118*(1), 117–126. doi:10.100710551-012-1574-1

Deegan, C. (2002). Introduction: The legitimising effect of social and environmental disclosures–a theoretical foundation. *Accounting, Auditing & Accountability Journal*, *15*(3), 282–311. doi:10.1108/09513570210435852

Department of Public Enterprises. (2019). *Public Enterprises Survey, 2018-2019*. https://dpe.gov.in/public-enterprises-survey-2018-19

Dettman, S. (2020). Authoritarian innovations and democratic reform in the "New Malaysia". *Democratization*, *27*(6), 1037–1052. doi:10.1080/13510347.2019.1705791

Dettman, S., & Gomez, E. T. (2020). Political financing reform: Politics, policies and patronage in Malaysia. *Journal of Contemporary Asia*, *50*(1), 36–55. doi:10.1080/00472336.2019.1571218

Dimovski, B., Lombardi, L., Ratcliffe, C., & Cooper, B. J. (2016). Australian Real Estate Management and Development companies and women directors. *Property Management*, *34*(1), 18–28. doi:10.1108/PM-12-2014-0052

Dimson, E., Karakas, O., & Li, X. (2015). Active ownership. *Review of Financial Studies*, *28*(12), 3225–3268. doi:10.1093/rfs/hhv044

Dissanayake, D., Tilt, C., & Xydias-Lobo, M. (2016). Sustainability reporting by publicly listed companies in Sri Lanka. *Journal of Cleaner Production*, *129*, 169–182. doi:10.1016/j.jclepro.2016.04.086

Dittmann, I., Maug, E., & Schneider, C. (2010). Bankers on the boards of German firms: What they do, what they are worth, and why they are (still) there. *Review of Finance*, *14*(1), 35–71. doi:10.1093/rof/rfp007

Dwivedi, N. (2007). Determinants of Board Effectiveness: Evidence from Large Indian Firms. *Indore Management Journal*, *2*(1), 1–15.

Elmagrhi, M. H. (2017). Corporate governance and dividend payout policy in the UK listed SMEs: The effects of corporate board characteristics. *International Journal of Accounting and Information Management*, *25*(4), 459–483. doi:10.1108/IJAIM-02-2017-0020

Enguix, L. P. (2021). The new EU remuneration policy as good but not desired corporate governance mechanism and the role of CSR disclosing. *Sustainability (Switzerland)*, *13*(10). Advance online publication. doi:10.3390u13105476

Ferdous, C. S. (2018). Corporate governance in Bangladesh: Evidence of compliance. *International Business Research*, *11*(3), 88–109. doi:10.5539/ibr.v11n3p88

Ferrell, O. C., & Fraedrich, J. (2021). *Business ethics: Ethical decision making and cases*. Cengage Learning.

Fisher, R., van Staden, C., & Richards, G. (2019). Watch that tone: An investigation of the use and stylistic consequences of tone in corporate accountability disclosures. *Accounting, Auditing & Accountability Journal*, *33*(1), 77–105. doi:10.1108/AAAJ-10-2016-2745

Friede, G., Busch, T., & Bassen, A. (2015). ESG and financial performance: Aggregated evidence from more than 2,000 empirical studies. *Journal of Sustainable Finance & Investment*, *5*(4), 210–233. doi:10.1080/20430795.2015.1118917

Galbreath, J. (2013). ESG in focus: The Australian evidence. *Journal of Business Ethics*, *118*(3), 529–541. doi:10.100710551-012-1607-9

Garcia-Sanchez, I. M., Cuadrado-Ballesteros, B., & Sepulveda, C. (2014). Does media pressure moderate CSR disclosures by external directors? *Management Decision, London*, *52*(6), 1014–1045. doi:10.1108/MD-09-2013-0446

George, C., & Venkiteswaran, G. (2019). *Media and power in Southeast Asia*. Cambridge University Press. doi:10.1017/9781108665643

Gerged, A. M., Albitar, K., & Alhaddad, L. (2021). Corporate environmental disclosure and earnings management—The moderating role of corporate governance structures. *International Journal of Finance & Economics*, *28*(3), 2789–2810. doi:10.1002/ijfe.2564

Ghandali, S., & Moghaddam, M. E. (2009). Off-Line Persian Signature Identification and Verification Based on Image Registration and Fusion. *Journal of Multimedia*, *4*(3). Advance online publication. doi:10.4304/jmm.4.3.137-144

Ghayad, R. (2008). Corporate governance and the global performance of Islamic banks. *Humanomics*, *24*(3), 207–216. doi:10.1108/08288660810899368

Ghosh, S. (2018). Banker directors and firm performance: Are family firms different? *Future Business Journal*, *4*(1), 1–15. doi:10.1016/j.fbj.2017.11.002

Gin, O. K. (2017). *Historical dictionary of Malaysia*. Rowman & Littlefield.

Gnanarajah, R. (2020). Introduction to Financial Services: Accounting and Auditing Regulatory Structure, U.S. and International. Congressional Research Service. Congressional Research Service.

Goel, A. (2021). Board Composition and Performance of Indian Companies: The Moderating Effect of CEO Duality. *SCMS Journal of Indian Management, 18*(4).

Gomez, E. T., Cheong, K. C., & Wong, C. Y. (2021). Regime changes, state-business ties and remaining in the middle-income trap: The case of Malaysia. *Journal of Contemporary Asia, 51*(5), 782–802. doi:10.1080/00472336.2021.1933138

Gomez, E. T., Padmanabhan, T., Kamaruddin, N., Bhalla, S., & Fisal, F. (2017). *Minister of Finance Incorporated: Ownership and control of corporate Malaysia*. Springer.

Graus, S., Rehman, S. U., & García, J. S. (2020). Corporate Social Responsibility and Environmental Performance: The Mediating Role of Environmental Strategy and Green Innovation. *Technological Forecasting and Social Change, 16*, 120262.

Gray, W. (2013). *Why Exclude Financial Firms from Quantitative Studies*. Alpha Architect.

Guerrero-Villegas, J., Pérez-Calero, L., Hurtado-González, J. M., & Giráldez-Puig, P. (2018). Board Attributes and Corporate Social Responsibility Disclosure: A Meta-Analysis. *Sustainability, 10*(12), 4808. doi:10.3390u10124808

Gupta, N., Mahakud, J., Tripathi, P. M., Agarwal, T., & Bakhshi, P. (2021). Do nominee directors influence bank performance. *Corporate Ownership & Control, 19*(1), 121–145. doi:10.22495/cocv19i1art10

Habiba, U., Ali, R., & Ashfaq, A. (2016). From patriarchy to neopatriarchy: Experiences of women from Pakistan. *International Journal of Humanities and Social Science, 6*(3), 212–221.

Hailu, S. M., & Tekdoğan, Ö. F. (2023). Ensuring The Compliance of Islamic Finance Applications with Shariah Principles in Ethiopia: The Way Forward. *Hitit İlahiyat Dergisi*. doi:10.14395/hid.1247875

Hamdan, H., Razak, D. A., Huridi, H., & Uddin, N. (2021). Factors contributing to financial literacy among MSMEs in Klang Valley. *Turkish Online Journal of Qualitative Inquiry, 12*(6), 9223–9232. https://www.researchgate.net/publication/353646187

Hamilton-Hart, N. (2018). *Asian states, Asian bankers: central banking in Southeast Asia*. Cornell University Press. doi:10.7591/9781501721731

Hans, D. B. (2018). SGX to see first fintech listing on Catalist board with Ayondo. *Reuters*. Retrieved from https://news.finchcapital.com/post/102ernp/sgx-to-see-first-fintech-listing-on-catalist-board-with-ayondo

Harun, M. S., Hussainey, K., Mohd Kharuddin, K. A., & Al Farooque, O. (2020). CSR Disclosure, Corporate Governance and Firm Value: A study on GCC Islamic Banks. *International Journal of Accounting and Information Management, 28*(4), 607–638. doi:10.1108/IJAIM-08-2019-0103

Hashim, H. A., Salleh, Z., Shuhaimi, I., & Ismail, N. A. N. (2020). The risk of financial fraud: A management perspective. *Journal of Financial Crime*, *27*(4), 1143–1159. doi:10.1108/JFC-04-2020-0062

Hassan, M. K., Farhat, J., & Al-zu'bi, B. (2003). Dividend signalling hypothesis and short term. *Islamic Economic Studies*, *11*(1), 1–30.

Heminway, J. M. (2019). Me, Too and# MeToo: Women in Congress and the Boardroom. *Geo. Wash. L. Rev.*, *87*, 1079.

Heo, K. (2018). *Effects of corporate governance on the performance of state-owned enterprises*. The World Bank. doi:10.1596/1813-9450-8555

Hermalin, B., & Weisbach, M. (2003). Board of directors as an endogenously determined institution: A survey of the economic literature. *Economic Policy Review*, (April), 7–26.

Hess, D. (2021). The management and oversight of human rights due diligence. *American Business Law Journal*, *58*(4), 751–798. doi:10.1111/ablj.12197

Hope, B., & Wright, T. (2018). Billion dollar whale: The man who fooled Wall Street, Hollywood, and the world. Hachette UK.

Horta, H., & Tang, L. (2023). Male and female academics' gendered perceptions of academic work and career progression in China. *Higher Education Quarterly*, *77*(3), 515–536. doi:10.1111/hequ.12419

Hossain, D. M. (2017). *Exploring the Main Discourses and Power Relations in The Disclosure on Social Inequality Issues in Corporate Narratives* [Unpublished Doctoral Thesis]. IIUM, Malaysia.

Howitt, D., & Cramer, D. (2011). *Introduction to Research Methods in Psychology (3rdedn.)*. Pearson.

Htay, S. N. N. (2012). Towards Islamic worldview based corporate governance framework. *Corporate Governances Practices in Malaysia*, 17–36. http://irep.iium.edu.my/29629/

Ikunda, C., Muiru, M., & Kamau, S. M. (2016). The Impact of Corporate Governance on Dividend Payout of Manufacturing Firms Listed at the Nairobi Securities Exchange. *Journal of Finance and Accounting*, *4*(5), 254–261. doi:10.11648/j.jfa.20160405.12

Im, J., & Chung, Y. (2017). The effects of insider ownership and board composition on firm performance in the restaurant industry. *The Journal of Hospitality Financial Management*, *25*(1), 4–16. doi:10.1080/10913211.2017.1313604

Iqbal, S. (2013). The impact of corporate governance on the dividend decision of firms : Evidence from Pakistan. *African Journal of Business Management*, *7*(11), 811–817.

Jahanzeb, A. (2016). Impact of Corporate Governance and Firm-Level Control Variables on Dividend Policy of Service Trade Sector of Malaysia. *Journal of Economic and Social Development*, *3*(2), 102–111.

Jain, N., & Mukherji, S. (2010). The Perception of 'Glass Ceiling' in Indian Organizations: An Exploratory Study. *South Asian Journal of Management*, *17*(1).

Jallai. (2020). Ethical standards for tax planning by corporations. In *Ethics and Taxation*. Springer.

Jallali, S., & Zoghlami, F. (2022). Does risk governance mediate the impact of governance and risk management on banks' performance? Evidence from a selected sample of Islamic banks. *Journal of Financial Regulation and Compliance*, *30*(4), 439–464. doi:10.1108/JFRC-04-2021-0037

Jamil, A., Mohd Ghazali, N. A., & Puat Nelson, S. (2021). The influence of corporate governance structure on sustainability reporting in Malaysia. *Social Responsibility Journal*, *17*(8), 1251–1278. doi:10.1108/SRJ-08-2020-0310

Jan, A. A., Lai, F. W., Draz, M. U., Tahir, M., Ali, S. E. A., Zahid, M., & Shad, M. K. (2021). Integrating sustainability practices into islamic corporate governance for sustainable firm performance: From the lens of agency and stakeholder theories. *Quality & Quantity*. Advance online publication. doi:10.100711135-021-01261-0

Jan, A. A., Lai, F. W., & Tahir, M. (2021). Developing an Islamic Corporate Governance framework to examine sustainability performance in Islamic Banks and Financial Institutions. *Journal of Cleaner Production*, *315*, 128099. Advance online publication. doi:10.1016/j.jclepro.2021.128099

Jan, A., Rahman, H. U., Zahid, M., Salameh, A. A., Khan, P. A., Al-Faryan, M. A. S., Che Aziz, R. B., & Ali, H. E. (2023). Islamic corporate sustainability practices index aligned with SDGs towards better financial performance: Evidence from the Malaysian and Indonesian Islamic banking industry. *Journal of Cleaner Production*, *405*, 136860. Advance online publication. doi:10.1016/j.jclepro.2023.136860

Jans, M., & Eulerich, M. (2022). Process mining for financial auditing. In *Process Mining Handbook* (pp. 445–467). Springer International Publishing. doi:10.1007/978-3-031-08848-3_15

Jauhar, J., & Lau, V. (2018). The 'Glass Ceiling' and Women's Career Advancement to Top Management: The Moderating Effect of Social Support. *Global Business and Management Research*, *10*(1).

Jayadev, M. (2016). *Debt, Defaults, and, Corporate Governance*. IIM Banglore.

Jensen, M., & Meckling, W. (1976). Theory of the firm: Managerial behavior, agency costs and ownership structure. *Journal of Financial Economics*, *3*(4), 305–360. doi:10.1016/0304-405X(76)90026-X

Jiao, L. (2020, July 14). *Pinduoduo and Luckin Coffee Show China's Corporate Governance Dilemmas*. Retrieved July 24, 2023, from Nikkei Asia: https://asia.nikkei.com/Opinion/Pinduoduo-and-Luckin-Coffee-show-China-s-corporate-governance-dilemmas

Johns, M. L. (2013). Breaking the glass ceiling: Structural, cultural, and organizational barriers preventing women from achieving senior and executive positions. *Perspectives in Health Information Management*, (Winter).

Jones, D. S. (2020). 1MDB corruption scandal in Malaysia: A study of failings in control and accountability. *Public Administration and Policy*, *23*(1), 59–72. doi:10.1108/PAP-11-2019-0032

Jones, D. S. (2022). Challenges in combating corruption in Malaysia: Issues of leadership, culture and money politics. *Public Administration and Policy*, *25*(2), 136–149. doi:10.1108/PAP-01-2022-0002

Jusoh, S., Abd Razak, M. F., & Mazlan, M. A. (2017). Malaysia and Investor-State Dispute Settlement: Learning from Experience. *The Journal of World Investment & Trade*, *18*(5-6), 890–917. doi:10.1163/22119000-12340065

Jye, N. R. (2019). Ayondo interim CEO to quit after less than 6 months on the job. *The Straits Times*. Retrieved from https://www.straitstimes.com/business/companies-markets/ayondo-interim-ceo-to-quit-after-less-than-6-months-on-the-job

Kabra, N., Bhattacharya, P., Tanwar, S., & Tyagi, S. (2020). MudraChain: Blockchain-based framework for automated cheque clearance in financial institutions. *Future Generation Computer Systems*, *102*, 574–587. doi:10.1016/j.future.2019.08.035

Kang, S. K., & Kaplan, S. (2019). Working toward gender diversity and inclusion in medicine: Myths and solutions. *Lancet*, *393*(10171), 579–586. doi:10.1016/S0140-6736(18)33138-6 PMID:30739693

Kao, M. F., Hodgkinson, L., & Jaafar, A. (2019). Ownership structure, Board of directors and firm performance: Evidence from Taiwan. *Corporate Governance: The International Journal of Business in Society*, *19*(1), 189–216. doi:10.1108/CG-04-2018-0144

Kaplan, S. N., & Minton, B. A. (1994). Appointments of outsiders to Japanese boards: Determinants and implications for managers. *Journal of Financial Economics*, *36*(2), 225–258. doi:10.1016/0304-405X(94)90025-6

Kaul, A., & Agarwal, R. (2022). Neither here nor there: reconciling nominee directors' dual loyalties under the Indian Companies Act 2013. *Oxford University Commonwealth Law Journal, 22*(2), 205-228. https://www.tandfonline.com/doi/abs/10.1080/14729342.2022.2151793

Kausar Alam, M., Ab Rahman, S., Ahad Thakur, O., Abdul Bashir, M., Hosen, S., Alam, M. K., Ab Rahman, S., Thakur, O., Bashir, M. A., & Hosen, S. (2020). The Reasons Behind the Absence of a Comprehensive Shariah Governance Framework of Islamic Banks in Bangladesh. International Journal of Economics and Business Administration, 8(1).

Kezar, A. J. (Ed.). (2020). Rethinking leadership in a complex, multicultural, and global environment: New concepts and models for higher education. Stylus Publishing, LLC.

Kezar, A. J. (Ed.). (2023). *Rethinking leadership in a complex, multicultural, and global environment: New concepts and models for higher education*. Taylor & Francis. doi:10.4324/9781003446842

Khan, H., Azizul Islam, M., Kayeser Fatima, J., & Ahmed, K. (2011). Corporate sustainability reporting of major commercial banks in line with GRI: Bangladesh evidence. *Social Responsibility Journal*, *7*(3), 347–362. doi:10.1108/17471111111154509

Kim, K. H. (2007). Exploring the interactions between Asian culture (Confucianism) and creativity. *The Journal of Creative Behavior*, *41*(1), 28–53. doi:10.1002/j.2162-6057.2007.tb01280.x

Kiranmai, J., & Mishra, R. K. (2019). Corporate Governance Practices in Listed State-owned Enterprises in India: An Empirical Research. *Indian Journal of Corporate Governance*, *12*(1), 94–121. doi:10.1177/0974686219849760

Klettner, A., Clarke, T., & Boersma, M. (2016). Strategic and regulatory approaches to increasing women in leadership: Multilevel targets and mandatory quotas as levers for cultural change. *Journal of Business Ethics*, *133*(3), 395–419. doi:10.100710551-014-2069-z

Kok, S. K., & Shahgholian, A. (2023). The impact of proximity within elite corporate networks on the Shariah governance-firm performance nexus: Evidence from the global Shariah elite. *Emerging Markets Review*, *54*, 100998. Advance online publication. doi:10.1016/j.ememar.2023.100998

KPMG. (2022). https://kpmg.com/xx/en/home/insights/2022/09/survey-of sustainability-reporting-2022/esg.html

Krook, M. L., Lovenduski, J., & Squires, J. (2009). Gender quotas and models of political citizenship. *British Journal of Political Science*, *39*(4), 781–803. doi:10.1017/S0007123409990123

Kroszner, R. S., & Strahan, P. E. (2001). Bankers on boards: Monitoring, conflicts of interest, and lender liability. *Journal of Financial Economics*, *62*(3), 415–452. doi:10.1016/S0304-405X(01)00082-4

Kurawa, J. M., & Ishaku, A. (2014). The Effect Of Corporate Governance On Dividend Policy Of Listed Banks In Nigeria : A Panel Data Analysis. *The Journal of Finance*, *2*(8), 1–12.

Lachance-Grzela, M., & Bouchard, G. (2010). Why do women do the lion's share of housework? A decade of research. *Sex Roles*, *63*(11-12), 767–780. doi:10.100711199-010-9797-z

Lagasio, V., & Cucari, N. (2019). Corporate governance and environmental social governance disclosure: A meta analytical review. *Corporate Social Responsibility and Environmental Management*, *26*(4), 701–711. doi:10.1002/csr.1716

Lam, F. (2019). Ayondo gets statutory demand of payment for S$165,800; gets nod to delay FY2018 results, AGM. *The Business Times*. Retrieved from https://www.businesstimes.com.sg/companies-markets/ayondo-gets-statutory-demand-payment-s165800-gets-nod-delay-fy2018-results-agm

Lamanda, G., & Tamásné Vőneki, Z. (2023). Is ESG disclosure associated with bank performance? Evidence from the Visegrad Four countries. *Management of Environmental Quality*. Advance online publication. doi:10.1108/MEQ-02-2023-0064

Langevoort, D. C. (2017). Cultures of compliance. *The American Criminal Law Review*, *54*, 933.

Larcker, D. F., Richardson, S. A., & Tuna, I. (2005, May 16). *How Important is Corporate Governance?* Philadelphia: The Wharton School University of Pennsylvania.

Lee, J. (2017). Starland's S$158m RTO with fintech firm Ayondo lapses. *The Business Times*. Retrieved from https://www.businesstimes.com.sg/companies-markets/starlands-s158m-rto-fintech-firm-ayondo-lapses

Lee, P. C. (2016). Fintech Ayondo to list on SGX through $158 mil reverse takeover of Starland. *The Edge Malaysia*. Retrieved from https://theedgemalaysia.com/article/fintech-ayondo-list-sgx-through-s158-mil-reverse-takeover-starland

Lee, S. Y., & Yu, S. (2020, September 22). *China fines Luckin Coffee and linked firms a total of $9 million* (M. Anantharaman, & R. Gopalakrishnan, Eds.). Retrieved July 22, 2023, from Reuters: https://www.reuters.com/article/luckin-coffee-investigation-fine-idINKCN26D07O

Lee, C. M. (2016). *Fault lines in a rising Asia*. Brookings Institution Press.

Leow, A. (2018a). Ayondo's IPO sees public applications come in at four-and-half times the number of offer shares. *The Business Times*. Retrieved from https://www.businesstimes.com.sg/companies-markets/ayondos-ipo-sees-public-applications-come-four-and-half-times-number-offer-shares

Leow, A. (2018b). Fintech Ayondo registers offer documents for Catalist listing. *The Business Times*. Retrieved from https://www.businesstimes.com.sg/companies-markets/fintech-ayondo-registers-offer-documents-catalist-listing

Leow, A. (2018c). Starland decides not to convert S$1.03 million loan into Ayondo shares; will be repaid in cash after IPO. *The Business Times*. Retrieved from https://www.businesstimes.com.sg/companies-markets/starland-decides-not-convert-s103-million-loan-ayondo-shares-will-be-repaid-cash

Levi, M. (2020). Evaluating the control of money laundering and its underlying offences: The search for meaningful data. *Asian Journal of Criminology*, *15*(4), 301–320. doi:10.100711417-020-09319-y PMID:32837603

Levi, M. (2022). Lawyers as money laundering enablers? An evolving and contentious relationship. *Global Crime*, *23*(2), 126–147. doi:10.1080/17440572.2022.2089122

Levine, R. (2004). *The corporate governance of banks: A concise discussion of concepts and evidence*. The World Bank. doi:10.1596/1813-9450-3404

Liang, N., & Useem, M. (2009). Profiles of Corporate Governance in Leading Countries: China. In A. Burmajster & A. Jolly (Eds.), *The Handbook of International Corporate Governance: A Definitive Guide* (2nd ed., pp. 167–175). Kogan Page Ltd.

Liao, G., Hou, P., Shen, X., & Albitar, K. (2021). The impact of economic policy uncertainty on stock returns: The role of corporate environmental responsibility engagement. *International Journal of Finance & Economics*, *26*(3), 4386–4392. doi:10.1002/ijfe.2020

Lim, G., Li, C., & Ji, X. (2022). Chinese financial statecraft in Southeast Asia: An analysis of China's infrastructure provision in Malaysia. *The Pacific Review*, *35*(4), 647–675. doi:10.1080/09512748.2020.1868556

Lin, T. W. (2004). Corporate Governance in China: Recent Developments, Key Problems, and Solutions. *Journal of Accounting and Corporate Governance*, *1*(1), 1–23.

Li, Y., Gong, M., Zhang, X., & Koh, L. (2018). The Impact of Environmental, Social, and Governance Disclosure on Firm Value: The Role of CEO Power. *The British Accounting Review*, *50*(1), 60–75. doi:10.1016/j.bar.2017.09.007

Li, Z., Liao, G., & Albitar, K. (2020). Does corporate environmental responsibility engagement affect firm value? The mediating role of corporate innovation. *Business Strategy and the Environment*, *29*(3), 1045–1055. doi:10.1002/bse.2416

Loewenberg, S. (2008, February 26). *SOX's outside reach a model for foreign markets*. Retrieved June 19, 2023, from Politico: https://www.politico.com/story/2008/02/soxs-outside-reach-a-model-for-foreign-markets-008678

Low, D. C., Roberts, H., & Whiting, R. H. (2015). Board gender diversity and firm performance: Empirical evidence from Hong Kong, South Korea, Malaysia and Singapore. *Pacific-Basin Finance Journal*, *35*, 381–401. doi:10.1016/j.pacfin.2015.02.008

Lucas, A. (2020, April 2). *Shares of China's Luckin Coffee plummet 80% after investigation finds COO fabricated sales*. Retrieved June 18, 2023, from CNBC: https://www.cnbc.com/2020/04/02/luckin-coffee-stock-plummets-after-investigation-finds-coo-fabricated-sales.html

Lückerath-Rovers, M. (2013). Women on boards and firm performance. *The Journal of Management and Governance*, *17*(2), 491–509. doi:10.100710997-011-9186-1

Luminor Financial Holdings Limited. (2023). *About Us*. Retrieved from https://www.luminorfinancialholdings.com/aboutus

Macarie, F., & Moldovan, O. (2012). Gender discrimination in management: Theoretical and empirical perspectives. *Transylvanian Review of Administrative Sciences*, (35E), 153–172.

Madaan, D. A., Mehta, K., & Sharma, R. (2022). A Revisit to Research on Corporate Governance Using Systematic Literature Review. *ECS Transactions*, *107*(1), 4035–4049. doi:10.1149/10701.4035ecst

Mahoney, J. P. (2020, April 17). *Inspection of PCAOB-Registered Chinese Auditor*. Retrieved July 21, 2023, from Harvard Law School Forum on Corporate Governance: https://corpgov.law.harvard.edu/2020/04/17/inspection-of-pcaob-registered-chinese-auditor/

Mak, Y. T. (2013). *GRP should clarify board appointment*. Retrieved from https://governanceforstakeholders.com/2013/09/29/grp-should-clarify-board-appointment/#:~:text=SGX%20should%20query%20GRP%20further,by%20the%20board%20and%20NC

Mak, Y. T. (2019). *No sign of governance*. Retrieved from https://governanceforstakeholders.com/2019/03/03/no-sign-of-governance/

Mamatzakis, E., Alexakis, C., Al Yahyaee, K., Pappas, V., Mobarek, A., & Mollah, S. (2023). Does corporate governance affect the performance and stability of Islamic banks? *Corporate Governance (Bingley)*, *23*(4), 888–919. doi:10.1108/CG-05-2022-0217

Mansourinia, E. (2013). The Effect of Board Size, Board Independence and CEO Duality on Dividend Policy of Companies: Evidence from Tehran Stock Exchange. *International Journal of Economy. Management and Social Sciences*, *2*(6), 237–241.

Martinez, I. (2020, June 16). *Luckin Coffee Delays Publishing 2019 Annual Report Over Fraud Probe*. Retrieved July 23, 2023, from S&P Global Market Intelligence: https://www.spglobal.com/marketintelligence/en/news-insights/latest-news-headlines/luckin-coffee-delays-publishing-2019-annual-report-over-fraud-probe-59058938

Marzuki, M. M., Majid, W. Z. N. A., Azis, N. K., Rosman, R., & Abdulatiff, N. K. H. (2020). Fraud risk management model: A content analysis approach. *The Journal of Asian Finance, Economics and Business*, *7*(10), 717–728.

Maskell-Pretz, M., & Hopkins, W. E. (1997). Women in engineering: Toward a barrier-free work environment. *Journal of Management Engineering*, *13*(1), 32–37. doi:10.1061/(ASCE)0742-597X(1997)13:1(32)

Mazlan, P. N. B. M., Hersh, N. F., Masron, T. A., & Malim, N. A. K. (2023). Islamic finance and governance indicators: Empirical evidence from Islamic finance-permitting countries. *International Journal of Disclosure and Governance*. Advance online publication. doi:10.105741310-023-00177-5

Mbo, M., & Adjasi, C. (2017). Drivers of organisational performance in state owned enterprises. *International Journal of Productivity and Performance Management*, *66*(3), 405–423. Advance online publication. doi:10.1108/IJPPM-11-2015-0177

Md Nasir, N. A., & Hashim, H. A. (2021). Corporate governance performance and financial statement fraud: Evidence from Malaysia. *Journal of Financial Crime*, *28*(3), 797–809. doi:10.1108/JFC-09-2020-0182

Mehdi, M., Sahut, J.-M., & Teulon, F. (2017). Do corporate governance and ownership structure impact dividend policy in emerging market during the financial crisis? *Journal of Applied Accounting Research*, *18*(3), 274–297. doi:10.1108/JAAR-07-2014-0079

Mehta, K., & Sharma, R. (2016). SMEs and corporate social responsibility: Indian perception. *SCMS Journal of Indian Management*, *13*(3), 58–67.

Menon, J. (2017). Government-linked Companies: Impact on the Malaysian Economy. *Policy Ideas*, *45*, 1–26.

Mergaliyev, A., Asutay, M., Avdukic, A., & Karbhari, Y. (2021). Higher Ethical Objective (Maqasid al-Shari'ah) Augmented Framework for Islamic Banks: Assessing Ethical Performance and Exploring Its Determinants. *Journal of Business Ethics*, *170*(4), 797–834. doi:10.100710551-019-04331-4

Merkl-Davies, D., & Koller, V. (2012). 'Metaphoring' people out of this world: A critical discourse analysis of a chairman's statement of a UK defence firm. *Accounting Forum*, *36*(3), 178–193. doi:10.1016/j.accfor.2012.02.005

Mills, G., Obasanjo, O., van der Merwe, E., & Desalegn, H. (2020). *The Asian Aspiration: Why and How Africa Should Emulate Asia—and What It Should Avoid*. Oxford University Press.

Mishra, S. (2020). Do Independent Directors Improve Firm Performance? Evidence from India. *Global Business Review*, 1–19. doi:10.1177/0972150920917310

Mnif, Y., & Tahari, M. (2021). The effect of Islamic banks' specific corporate governance mechanisms on compliance with AAOIFI governance standards. *Journal of Islamic Accounting and Business Research*, *12*(1), 21–43. doi:10.1108/JIABR-11-2018-0188

Mohamad, R., & Saad, N. M. (2016). Power distance culture and the construction of the followership identity. *Asia Pacific Journal of Advanced Business and Social Studies*, *2*(1), 149–160.

Mollah, S., & Zaman, M. (2015). Shari'ah supervision, corporate governance and performance: Conventional vs. Islamic banks. *Journal of Banking & Finance*, *58*, 418–435. doi:10.1016/j.jbankfin.2015.04.030

Morck, R., & Nakamura, M. (1999). Banks and corporate control in Japan. *The Journal of Finance*, *54*(1), 319–339. doi:10.1111/0022-1082.00106

Morrison, A. M., & Von Glinow, M. A. (1990). Women and minorities in management. American Psychological Association.

Muddy Waters Research. (2020, January 31). *MuddyWatersResearch @muddywatersre*. Retrieved June 19, 2023, from Twitter: https://twitter.com/muddywatersre/status/1223274746017722371

Muhtar. (2014). Effect Of The Audit Committee, Capital Structure, Managerial Ownership Structure, Management Of Profit And Dividend Policy Value Company Group Public In Indonesia Stock Exchange. *Journal of Research in Business and Management*, *2*(11), 40–49.

Mui, R. (2018). Ayondo, Singapore's 1st listed fintech firm, opens trading debut at 24 cents. *The Straits Times*. Retrieved from https://www.straitstimes.com/business/companies-markets/ayondo-opens-on-trading-debut-at-s024#:~:text=Home-,Ayondo%2C%20Singapore%27s%201st%20listed%20fintech%20firm%2C%20opens,trading%20debut%20at%2024%20cents&text=SINGAPORE%20%2D%20Global%20fintech%20group%20Ayondo,listed%20on%20the%20Singapore%20bourse

Muneeza, A., & Hassan, R. (2014). Shari'ah corporate governance: The need for a special governance code. *Corporate Governance (Bingley)*, *14*(1), 120–129. doi:10.1108/CG-02-2011-0015

Murphy, M. J., & Smolarski, J. M. (2020). Religion and CSR: An Islamic "Political" Model of Corporate Governance. *Business & Society*, *59*(5), 823–854. doi:10.1177/0007650317749222

Mutamimah, M., & Saputri, P. L. (2023). Corporate governance and financing risk in Islamic banks in Indonesia. *Journal of Islamic Accounting and Business Research*, *14*(3), 436–450. doi:10.1108/JIABR-09-2021-0268

Muzaffar, C. (2022). *Protector: An Analysis of the Concept and Practice of Loyalty in Leader-Led Relationships Within Malay Society*. Strategic Information and Research Development Centre.

Nachane, D. M., Ghosh, S., & Ray, P. (2005). Bank nominee directors and corporate performance: Micro-evidence for India. *Economic and Political Weekly*, 1216–1223. https://www.jstor.org/stable/4416370

Nasdaq. (2019). *ESG reporting guide 2.0, A support resource for companies.* Nasdaq.

National Committee On Corporate Governance. (n.d.). *The 8 Corporate Governance Principles*. Retrieved 2023 July, from National Committee On Corporate Governance: https://nccg.mu/8-corporate-governance-principles

Naysary, B., Salleh, M. C. M., & Abdullah, N. I. (2020). A comprehensive appraisal of Sharīʿah governance practices in Malaysian Islamic banks. *ISRA International Journal of Islamic Finance*, *12*(3), 381–400. doi:10.1108/IJIF-09-2018-0104

Neo, R. (2021). The failed construction of fake news as a security threat in Malaysia. *Contemporary Politics*, *27*(3), 316–335. doi:10.1080/13569775.2021.1884397

Newman, C., Chama, P. K., Mugisha, M., Matsiko, C. W., & Oketcho, V. (2017). Reasons behind current gender imbalances in senior global health roles and the practice and policy changes that can catalyze organizational change. *Global Health, Epidemiology and Genomics, 2*, e19.

Nicolo, G., Zampone, G., Sannino, G., & Tiron-Tudor, A. (2023). Worldwide evidence of corporate governance influence on ESG disclosure in the utilities sector. *Utilities Policy*, *82*, 101549. doi:10.1016/j.jup.2023.101549

Noordin, N. H., & Kassim, S. (2019). Does Shariah committee composition influence Shariah governance disclosure?: Evidence from Malaysian Islamic banks. *Journal of Islamic Accounting and Business Research*, *10*(2), 158–184. doi:10.1108/JIABR-04-2016-0047

Nor, N. H. M., Firdaus, A., & Kaur, S. (2020). Rise of the 5th estate: How online public discourse on Najib Razak's 1MDB scandal foreshadowed Pakatan Harapan's win in the 14th general election. *Jurnal Komunikasi: Malaysian Journal of Communication*, *36*(2), 179–195.

Nosratabadi, S., Mosavi, A., Shamshirband, S., Kazimieras Zavadskas, E., Rakotonirainy, A., & Chau, K. W. (2019). Sustainable Business Models: A Review. *Sustainability*, *11*(6), 1663. doi:10.3390u11061663

Nwogugu, M. I. (2019). *Complex Systems*. Multi-Sided Incentives and Risk Perception in Companies.

Olorede, T., Abogun, S., & Olowookere, J. (2022). Executive Compensation, Corporate Governance and Financial Reporting Quality: Evidence from listed firms in Nigeria. *Istanbul Management Journal*, *0*(93), 1–19. doi:10.26650/imj.2022.93.001

Pahlevi, R. W. (2023). Mapping of Islamic corporate governance research: a bibliometric analysis. In Journal of Islamic Accounting and Business Research (Vol. 14, Issue 4, pp. 538–553). Emerald Publishing. doi:10.1108/JIABR-12-2021-0314

PaisaBazaar. (2023). *What is a Cheque – Types, Features, Chequebook, Advantages*. Retrieved from https://www.paisabazaar.com/banking/what-is-cheque/

Pajo, K., McGregor, J., & Cleland, J. (1997). Profiling the pioneers: Women directors on New Zealand's corporate boards. *Women in Management Review*, *12*(5), 174–181. doi:10.1108/09649429710182341

Payne, D. C. (2005). *The Glass Ceiling Ten Years Later: A Study of the Professional Woman's Perception of Success in Corporate America* [Doctoral dissertation]. Capella University.

Penga, Z., & Yang, Y. (2020, November 13). A Ripple in the Muddy Waters: The Luckin Coffee Scandal and Short Selling Attacks. *SSRN*.

Peng, M. W., Bruton, G. D., Stan, C. V., & Huang, Y. (2016). Theories of the (state-owned) firm. *Asia Pacific Journal of Management*, *33*(2), 293–317. doi:10.100710490-016-9462-3

Peng, Z., Yang, Y., & Wu, R. (2022, June). The Luckin Coffee scandal and short selling attacks. *Journal of Behavioral and Experimental Finance*, *34*, 34. doi:10.1016/j.jbef.2022.100629

Peregrine, M. W. (2021, December 20). *The Lasting, Positive Impact of Sarbanes-Oxley*. Retrieved June 18, 2023, from Harvard Law School Forum on Corporate Governance: https://corpgov.law.harvard.edu/2021/12/20/the-lasting-positive-impact-of-sarbanes-oxley/

Phillips, S. D., & Imhoff, A. R. (1997). Women and career development: A decade of research. *Annual Review of Psychology*, *48*(1), 31–59. doi:10.1146/annurev.psych.48.1.31 PMID:9046555

Pillai, S. (2019a). Ayondo CFO quits in under a year over 'differences with management'. *The Business Times*. Retrieved from https://www.businesstimes.com.sg/companies-markets/ayondo-cfo-quits-under-year-over-differences-management

Pillai, S. (2019b). Ayondo shareholders vote to dispose UK unit. *The Business Times*. Retrieved from https://www.businesstimes.com.sg/companies-markets/ayondo-shareholders-vote-dispose-uk-unit

Pitre, R., & Claiborne, C. (2021). Corporate ethical training: An answer to white-collar crimes. *The Journal of Values Based Leadership*, *14*(2), 11. doi:10.22543/0733.142.1362

Plastun, A., Makarenko, I., Khomutenko, L., Osetrova, O., & Shcherbakov, P. (2020). SDGs and ESG disclosure regulation: Is there an impact? Evidence from Top-50 world economies. *Problems and Perspectives in Management*, *18*(2), 231–245. doi:10.21511/ppm.18(2).2020.20

Ponnu, C. H. (2008). Corporate Governance Structures and the Performance of Malaysian Public Listed Companies. *International Review of Business Research Papers*, *4*(2), 217–230.

Pucheta-Martinez, M. C., & Bel-oms, I. (2016). The Board of Directors and Dividend Policy: The Effect of Gender Diversity. *Industrial and Corporate Change*, *25*(3), 523–547. doi:10.1093/icc/dtv040

Qudah, H., Malahim, S., Airout, R., Alomari, M., Hamour, A. A., & Alqudah, M. (2023). Islamic Finance in the Era of Financial Technology: A Bibliometric Review of Future Trends. *International Journal of Financial Studies*, *11*(2), 76. doi:10.3390/ijfs11020076

Rajan, R. G. (1992). 'Insiders and outsiders: The choice between informed and arm' s-length debt'. *The Journal of Finance*, *47*(4), 1367–1400. doi:10.1111/j.1540-6261.1992.tb04662.x

Rajender, M., & Pal, R. (2014, January). Detection of manipulated cheque images in cheque truncation system using mismatch in pixels. In *2014 2nd International Conference on Business and Information Management (ICBIM)* (pp. 30-35). IEEE. 10.1109/ICBIM.2014.6970928

Rantanen, J., Muchiri, F., & Lehtinen, S. (2020). Decent work, ILO's response to the globalization of working life: Basic concepts and global implementation with special reference to occupational health. *International Journal of Environmental Research and Public Health*, *17*(10), 3351. doi:10.3390/ijerph17103351 PMID:32408597

Rashid, A., Akmal, M., & Shah, S. M. A. R. (2023). Corporate governance and risk management in Islamic and convectional financial institutions: Explaining the role of institutional quality. *Journal of Islamic Accounting and Business Research*. Advance online publication. doi:10.1108/JIABR-12-2021-0317

Razak, D. A., Hamdan, H., & Uddin, M. N. (2020). The Effect of The Demographic Factors of Micro-Entrepreneur on Financial Literacy: Case of Amanah Ikthiar Malaysia (AIM). *International Journal of Business, Economics and Law, 21*(3), 47–56. https://www.researchgate.net/publication/343404101

Reinsurance Group of American. (2014). *RGA Global Reinsurance Company, Ltd., Labuan Branch Malaysian Life Reinsurance Group Berhad (MLRe)*. RGA.

Rose, C. (2007). Does female board representation influence firm performance? The Danish evidence. *Corporate Governance*, *15*(2), 404–413. doi:10.1111/j.1467-8683.2007.00570.x

Rosli Abdul Aziz, A. A.-R. (2019). Best Practices for Internal Shariah Governance Framework: Lessons from Malaysian Islamic Banks. *Asian Journal of Accounting and Governance*, *12*(1), 1–14. doi:10.17576/AJAG-2019-12-15

RSQ Technology Ventures GmbH. (2023). *About Us*. Retrieved from https://ayondo.com/en/about-us

Sadek, D. M., Rahim, K. A., & Abas, Z. (2018). Islamic Corporate Governance In Islamic Financial Institutions. *International Journal of Academic Research in Business and Social Sciences*, *8*(4). Advance online publication. doi:10.6007/IJARBSS/v8-i4/3993

Salleh, K., Husaini, M. F., Bidin, A., Harun, N., & Hamid, A. (2021). The Duties and Conflicts of Nominee Directors: The Legal Position in Malaysia. *Psychology and Education*, *58*(2), 1577–1583. doi:10.17762/pae.v58i2.2311

Sani, A. A., & Musa, A. M. (2017). Corporate Board Attributes and Dividend Payout Policy of Listed Deposit Money Banks in Nigeria. *International Journal of Research in IT, Management and Engineering*, *7*(1), 7–13.

Saravanamuttu, J., & Mohamad, M. (2020). The monetisation of consent and its limits: Explaining political dominance and decline in Malaysia. *Journal of Contemporary Asia*, *50*(1), 56–73. doi:10.1080/00472336.2019.1569710

Saurbh, S. (2019). *Economic Value Added for competitive advantage a case of Indian enterprises*. Cambridge Scholar Publishing.

Schwartz, D., Youngs, N., & Britto, A. (2014). The ripple protocol consensus algorithm. *Ripple Labs Inc White Paper, 5*(8), 151.

Schwartz, F. N. (1989). Management women and the new facts of life. *Women in Management Review*, *4*(5). Advance online publication. doi:10.1108/EUM0000000001789

Securities and Exchange Commission vs Luckin Coffee, Inc., 1:20-cv-10631 (United States District Court Southern District of New York December 16, 2020).

Securities Commission Malaysia. (2017). *Malaysian Code on Corporate Governance, Securities Commission Malaysia, 2011. Malaysian Corporate Governance Blueprint 2011*. Author.

Sencal, H., & Asutay, M. (2021). Ethical disclosure in the Shari'ah annual reports of Islamic banks: Discourse on Shari'ah governance, quantitative empirics and qualitative analysis. *Corporate Governance (Bingley)*, *21*(1), 175–211. doi:10.1108/CG-01-2020-0037

Shahid, M.S., Rizwan, M., & Bucha, M.H. (2016). Ownership Structure, Board Size, Board Composition and Dividend Policy : New Evidence From Two Emerging Markets. *Journal of Business Studies*, *12*(2), 25–36.

Shamsudheen, S. V., Rosly, S. A., & Muneeza, A. (2023). Assessing ethical praxis of ethical (Islamic) financial institutions: a survey of empirical discoveries. *International Journal of Law and Management*. doi:10.1108/IJLMA-11-2022-0256

Shamsudheen, S. V., & Rosly, S. A. (2021). Measuring ethical judgement on ethical choice in an ethical system: A confirmatory study on Islamic banks in UAE. *International Journal of Islamic and Middle Eastern Finance and Management*, *14*(2), 301–316. doi:10.1108/IMEFM-03-2018-0112

Shan, Y. G., & Round, D. K. (2012). China's Corporate Governance: Emerging Issues and Problems. *Modern Asian Studies*, *46*(5), 1316–1344. doi:10.1017/S0026749X1200008X

Sharma, R., Mehta, K., & Goel, A. (2022). Non-linear relationship between board size and performance of Indian companies. *The Journal of Management and Governance*, 1–25. doi:10.100710997-022-09651-8

Shawtari, F. A., Mohamad, M. H. S., Rashid, H. M. A., & Moh'd Ayedh, A. (2017). Board characteristics and real performance in Malaysian state-owned enterprises (SOEs). *International Journal of Productivity and Performance Management*, *66*(8), 1064–1086. doi:10.1108/IJPPM-12-2015-0188

Shicong, D. (2020, April 27). *China Sends Team to Luckin Coffee to Probe Accounting Fraud.* (P. Thomas, Editor) Retrieved July 24, 2023, from Yicai Global: https://www.yicaiglobal.com/news/china-sends-team-to-luckin-coffee-to-probe-accounting-fraud

Shicong, D. (2020, July 16). *Auditor EY Denies Liability for Luckin Coffee's Financial Scandal.* Retrieved July 22, 2023, from Yicai Global: https://www.yicaiglobal.com/news/auditor-ey-denies-liability-for-luckin-coffee-financial-scandal

Shukla, M. (2017). Losing the tag of 'independent director'-role played by nominee directors in determining firm performance. In *6th International Conference on Trade, Business, Economics and Law* (p. 22). Academic Press.

Siddiquee, N. A., & Zafarullah, H. (2022). Absolute power, absolute venality: The politics of corruption and anti-corruption in Malaysia. *Public Integrity*, *24*(1), 1–17. doi:10.1080/10999922.2020.1830541

Simpson, R. (1997). Have times changed? Career barriers and the token woman manager. *British Journal of Management*, *8*(s1), 121–130. doi:10.1111/1467-8551.8.s1.10

Singapore Exchange Limited. (2019a). *Ayondo Ltd - Change - Announcement of Cessation: Resignation of Executive Director and Chief Executive Officer*. Author.

Singapore Exchange Limited. (2019b). *Ayondo Ltd - Change - Announcement of Cessation: Retirement of Independent Director* [Press release]. Retrieved from https://links.sgx.com/1.0.0/corporate-announcements/QKOCQXS97KFR3FIN/a13d4038e33c996cad1268f40a24d7be11716a4e399bcb39b4e5264f9c337a60

Singapore Exchange Regulation Pte Ltd. (2019). *Ayondo Ltd - Notice of Compliance* [Press release]. Retrieved from https://links.sgx.com/FileOpen/Notice%20of%20Compliance-ayondo-16April2019.ashx?App=Announcement&FileID=553554

Singh, K., Singh, N., & Kushwaha, D. S. (2018, September). An interoperable and secure e-wallet architecture based on digital ledger technology using blockchain. In *2018 international conference on computing, power and communication technologies (GUCON)* (pp. 165-169). IEEE.

Singh, N., Kumar, T., & Vardhan, M. (2021). Blockchain-based e-cheque clearing framework with trust based consensus mechanism. *Cluster Computing*, *24*(2), 851–865. doi:10.100710586-020-03163-6

Sloan, L., Joyner, M., Stakeman, C., & Schmitz, C. (2018). Critical multiculturalism and intersectionality in a complex world. Oxford University Press.

Smith, D. (2022). *Fraud and Corruption: Cases and Materials*. Springer Nature. doi:10.1007/978-3-031-10063-5

Sprigg, H. R. (n.d.). *The Importance of Corporate Governance*. Retrieved may 27, 2023, from SpriggHR: https://sprigghr.com/blog/board-management/the-importance-of-corporate-governance/

Srivastava, G., & Kathuria, V. (2020). Impact of corporate governance norms on the performance of Indian utilities. *Energy Policy*, *140*, 111414. doi:10.1016/j.enpol.2020.111414

Stevenson, A., & Wong, E. (2020, April 30). *Chinese Coffee Chain's Scandal Renews U.S. Calls for Oversight*. Retrieved June 17, 2023, from The New York Times: https://www.nytimes.com/2020/04/30/business/luckin-coffee-china-fraud-wall-street.html

Stocksbnb. (2018). *Ayondo Ltd: The alternative asset management platform*. Retrieved from https://www.stocksbnb.com/reports/ayondo-ltd-the-alternative-asset%20-management-platform/

Subramaniam, R., & Devi, S. S. (2011). Corporate Governance and Dividend Policy in Malaysia. *2010 International Conference on Business and Economics*, 200–207.

Sultana, S., Zainal, D., & Zulkifli, N. (2017). The influence of environmental, social and governance (ESG) on investment decisions: The Bangladesh perspective. *Pertanika Journal of Social Science & Humanities*, *25*, 155–173.

Sultana, S., Zulkifli, N., & Zainal, D. (2018). Environmental, social and governance (ESG) and investment decision in Bangladesh. *Sustainability*, *10*(6), 1831. doi:10.3390u10061831

Support innovative projects with star. (2019). *Starbase*. Retrieved from https://starbase.co/contracts

Suzuki, K. (n.d.). *Japan exercises US-style control*. Retrieved June 20, 2023, from Mori Hamada & Matsumoto Japan: https://www.mhmjapan.com/content/files/00014813/20071019suzuki.pdf

Swandaru, R., & Muneeza, A. (2022). Can fraud in Islamic financial institutions be prevented using high standards of shariah governance? *International Journal of Law and Management*, *64*(6), 469–485. doi:10.1108/IJLMA-07-2022-0162

Tahir, S. H. (2016). Effect of Corporate Governance Index on Dividend Policy: An Investigation of Textile Industry of Pakistan. *Journal of Economic and Social Development*, *3*(1), 139–146.

Tahir, S. H., Aslam, M. A., & Akhtar, M. A. (2014). the Impact of Board Characteristics and Ownership Structure on Corporate Dividend Policy in Canada. *The International Journal's Research Journal of Economics and Business Studies*, *3*(6), 18–24.

Tan, W. C. (2015). *Corporate Governance Structure and Performance of Malaysian Listed Companies*. Universiti Utara Malaysia.

Tay, H. M. (2019). Fintech firm Ayondo stares at a spate of resignations from its top brass. *Deal Street Asia*. Retrieved from https://www.dealstreetasia.com/stories/ayondo-resignations-142505/

Tay, V. (2019). Ayondo inks deal to sell UK unit for £5.7m. *The Business Times*. Retrieved from https://www.businesstimes.com.sg/companies-markets/ayondo-inks-deal-sell-uk-unit-ps57m

Teichmann, F. M. J., & Falker, M. C. (2021). The 1MDB case and the Swiss banking sector. *Journal of Money Laundering Control*, *24*(2), 278–290. doi:10.1108/JMLC-04-2020-0037

Thi, N. C. T. (2017). the Impact of Female Board of Directors on Firm Performance and Dividend Payout Policies: Evidence From Vietnam. *International Research Journal of Finance and Economics*, (164), 56–67.

Thompson, R. M., Alleyne, P., & Charles-Soverall, W. (2019). Exploring governance issues among boards of directors within state-owned enterprises in Barbados. *International Journal of Public Sector Management*, *32*(3), 264–281. Advance online publication. doi:10.1108/IJPSM-04-2018-0099

Tschorsch, F., & Scheuermann, B. (2016). Bitcoin and beyond: A technical survey on decentralized digital currencies. *IEEE Communications Surveys and Tutorials*, *18*(3), 2084–2123. doi:10.1109/COMST.2016.2535718

Uddin, M. N., Hamdan, H., Che Embi, N. A., Kassim, S., & Saad, N. B. M. (2020). Governance Structure of Microfinance Institutions: A Comparison of Models and Its Implication on Social Impact and Poverty Reduction. *Journal of Ibn Haldun Studies*, *5*(1), 95–118. doi:10.36657/ihcd.2020.68

Uddin, Md. N., Hamdan, H., Saad, N. B., Haque, A., Kassim, S., Embi, N. A. C., & Agarwal, K. (2022). The Governance Structure of Microfinance Institutions: A Comparison of Models of Sustainability and their Implication on Outreach. *Asian Journal of Economics. Business and Accounting*, *22*(19), 104–123. doi:10.9734/ajeba/2022/v22i1930662

Ullah, M. H., & Rahman, M. A. (2015). Corporate social responsibility reporting practices in banking companies in Bangladesh: Impact of regulatory change. *Journal of Financial Reporting and Accounting*, *13*(2), 200–225. doi:10.1108/JFRA-05-2013-0038

Umezaki, S. (2019). The Malaysian economy after the global financial crisis: International capital flows, exchange rates, and policy responses. *Public Policy Review*, *15*(1), 69–98.

Umma, H., Khan, M., Sultana, R., & Acharjee, K. (2023). Impact of corporate governance on ESG and Financial performance: A comparison between Commercial and Islamic Banks. *The Journal of Business*, *8*(1), 1–14.

University of Lincoln. (2022, June 16). *What are the Core Principles of Corporate Governance?* Retrieved July 21, 2023, from University of Lincoln: https://online.lincoln.ac.uk/what-are-the-core-principles-of-corporate-governance/

Uwalomwa, U., Olamide, O., & Francis, I. (2015). The Effects of Corporate Governance Mechanisms on Firms Dividend Payout Policy in Nigeria. *Journal of Accounting and Auditing: Research & Practice*, *2015*, 1–12. doi:10.5171/2015.313679

van Dijk, T. A. (1990). The future of the field: Discourse analysis in the 1990s. *Text*, *10*, 133–156.

Velayutham, S., & Hasan, R. (2021). Sovereign wealth funds and corporate social responsibility: A comparison of Norway's Government Pension Fund Global and Abu Dhabi Fund for Development. *Public Administration and Policy*, *24*(2), 139–151. doi:10.1108/PAP-08-2020-0037

Wang, J. (2020, May 13). *Fall From Grace: Luckin Coffee's Former Billionaire CEO Fired Amid Fraud Scandal*. Retrieved July 12, 2023, from Forbes: https://www.forbes.com/sites/jenniferwang/2020/05/13/fall-from-grace-luckin-coffees-former-billionaire-ceo-fired-amid-fraud-scandal/

Waring, A. (2016). *Corporate risk and governance: an end to mismanagement, tunnel vision and quackery*. Routledge. doi:10.4324/9781315574318

Wellalage, N. H., & Locke, S. (2013). Women on board, firm financial performance and agency costs. *Asian Journal of Business Ethics*, *2*(2), 113–127. doi:10.100713520-012-0020-x

Welsh, B. (2022). *The End of Umno? Essays on Malaysia's Former Dominant Party*. Strategic Information and Research Development Centre.

West, M. A., Hwang, S., Maier, R. V., Ahuja, N., Angelos, P., Bass, B. L., Brasel, K. J., Chen, H., Davis, K. A., Eberlein, T. J., Fong, Y., Greenberg, C. C., Lillemoe, K. D., McCarthy, M. C., Michelassi, F., Numann, P. J., Parangi, S., Reyes, J. D., Sanfey, H. A., ... Wren, S. M. (2018). Ensuring equity, diversity, and inclusion in academic surgery: An American Surgical Association white paper. *Annals of Surgery*, *268*(3), 403–407. doi:10.1097/SLA.0000000000002937 PMID:30004923

Widdowson, H. G. (2007). *Discourse Analysis*. Oxford University Press.

Wood, J. (2020). *Why this moment could be decisive for tackling climate change: Report*. https://www.weforum.org/agenda/2020/07/how-covid-19-could-spark-climate-change-recovery-sustainability/WorldEconomicForum

Xi, C., & Huang, Y. (2021, July 8). *Are US-Listed Chinese Firms a Minefield? A Board Perspective*. Retrieved July 19, 2023, from Oxford Business Law Blog: https://blogs.law.ox.ac.uk/business-law-blog/blog/2021/07/are-us-listed-chinese-firms-minefield-board-perspective

Yahya, F., & Ghazali, Z. B. (2017). The effectiveness of board governance and dividend policy as alignment mechanisms to firm performance and CEO compensation. *Cogent Business & Management*, *4*(1), 1–20. doi:10.1080/23311975.2017.1398124

Yang, J. (2020, July 16). *Ernst & Young Says It Isn't Responsible for Luckin Coffee's Accounting Misconduct*. Retrieved July 22, 2023, from Wall Street Journal: https://www.wsj.com/articles/ernst-young-says-it-isnt-responsible-for-luckin-coffees-accounting-misconduct-11594909084

Yiannakis, C. (2010). *The moderating role of self-directedness in a Job Demands-Job Resources Model for working women*. University of Johannesburg.

Ying, M., Tikuye, G. A., & Shan, H. (2021). Impacts of Firm Performance on Corporate Social Responsibility Practices: The Mediation Role of Corporate Governance in Ethiopia Corporate Business. *Sustainability*, *13*(17), 9717. doi:10.3390u13179717

Yu, E.-y., Van Luu, B., & Chen, C. H. (2020). Greenwashing in environmental, social and governance disclosures. *Research in International Business and Finance*, *52*, 101192. doi:10.1016/j.ribaf.2020.101192

Zahid, S. N., & Khan, I. (2019). Islamic Corporate Governance: The Significance and Functioning of Shari'ah Supervisory Board in Islamic Banking. *Turkish Journal of Islamic Economics*, *6*(1), 87–108. doi:10.26414/A048

Ziems-Mueller, W. J. (2011). *A Qualitative Inquiry of Barriers Facing Female Faculty Desiring Career Progression into Higher Education Administration* [Doctoral dissertation]. University of Phoenix.

Zreik, M. (2023). Governance in Post-COVID-19 China: Challenges, Responses, and Opportunities. In Multidisciplinary Approaches to Organizational Governance During Health Crises (pp. 214-235). IGI Global.

Zreik, M., Iqbal, B. A., & Rahman, M. N. (2022). Outward FDI: determinants and flows in emerging economies: evidence from China. *China and WTO Review*, *8*(2), 385–402. doi:10.14330/cwr.2022.8.2.07

Zreik, M., Marzuki, S. Z., & Iqbal, B. A. (2023). Deepening Financial Inclusion through Digitization: A Case Study of Microfinance in China. *ASEAN Entrepreneurship Journal*, *9*(2), 9–21.

Zulkafli, A.H. bin, Samad, M.F. bt. A. & Ismail, M.I. (2003). *Corporate Governance in Malaysia*. Academic Press.

About the Contributors

Rashedul Hasan boasts a decade of experience in teaching accounting and finance-related modules, underpinned by a strong academic foundation. His qualifications include a Bachelor's degree in Accounting and Finance, a Master's degree in Finance, and a PhD in Accounting. In addition to his academic accomplishments, Dr. Hasan holds prestigious certifications, including membership in the Chartered Institute of Management Accountants (CIMA) and fellowship status with the Higher Education Academy (FHEA). As a certified CIMA accountant, he possesses the unique ability to enhance students' proficiency in cost and management accounting. His teaching prowess is further acknowledged by the Chartered Association of Business Schools (CABS), which has conferred upon him the Certified Management and Business Educator (CMBE) certificate. Dr. Hasan's scholarly contributions are notable, with a substantial body of work encompassing over 40 publications in esteemed journals such as Business Strategy and Environment, Finance Research Letters, Global Finance Journal, Thunderbird International Business Review, and Borsa Istanbul Review. His commitment to academic excellence extends to serving as an Associate Editor for the Quarterly Journal of Accounting and Finance, International Journal of Islamic and Middle Eastern Finance and Management, and the Journal of Economic Cooperation and Development. A dedicated participant in the academic community, Dr Hasan actively engages in conferences both within the United Kingdom and on the international stage. His scholarly impact is further amplified by the publication of his book, "Central Bank Digital Currency and the Global Financial System – Theory and Practice," by De Gruyter. Dr. Hasan's research interests are wide-ranging, encompassing pivotal areas such as corporate governance, fintech, sustainability reporting, and Islamic finance.

* * *

Muhammad Ashfaq is a professor of business administration with a focus on Finance and Accounting at IU International University of Applied Sciences in Germany. He is widely recognized as an outstanding and experienced business and finance expert with more than 16 years of international experience. In addition to his professorship at IU, he is the Academic Director International and Program Director of Digital Business. He is also a regular visiting faculty member at Wittenborg University of Applied Sciences in the Netherlands, LSi Business School in Cambodia, and the international MBA program at Coburg University, Germany. Prof. Ashfaq earned his doctor of philosophy on the topic: "Knowledge, Attitude and Practices toward Islamic Banking and Finance: An Empirical Analysis of Retail Consumers in Germany" from the University of Tübingen Germany. He was also awarded the prestigious LGFW (Baden Württenberg State Government) scholarship for his Ph.D. Prof. Ashfaq holds an MBA in Financial Management from Coburg University in Germany. Prof. Ashfaq has worked for several years in the industry in various countries and has obtained valuable experience in various management, consultancy and leadership roles in international companies such as Pfizer, Amanah IIFE, IAC Accountants and IT Electronic Service. He has played a key role in the conceptualization, development and accreditation of study programs in various countries such as the Netherlands, Pakistan, Germany, the UK, Cambodia and most recently developed an extensive and innovative study program Digital Business for undergraduate students, and M.Sc. Finance, Accounting & Taxation at IU International University of Applied Sciences, Germany. He also played a pivotal role in the curriculum development of study programs such as BSc (Hons) Banking & Finance and MSc Banking & Finance for the London Institute of Banking and Finance. Prof. Ashfaq is a member of various research groups, and he is a well-accomplished interdisciplinary researcher. He has published four books as lead author, dozens of scientific journal articles and book chapters. Prof. Ashfaq is the author of the book "Islamic Banking and Finance in Europe: the Case of Germany and the United Kingdom". He is also the lead co-author of the book "Central Bank Digital Currencies and the Global Financial System: Theory and Practice" published by the De Gruyter, Germany. He has contributed to the development of the Islamic financial industry through his cutting-edge research, industry specific trainings and global initiatives for human capital development and organizational capacity building. Prof. Ashfaq has also conducted a number of lectures and facilitated training programs for many financial, academic and multinational institutions on the topic of Islamic banking and finance, digital transformation of financial services industry such as Central Bank of Somaliland and Bank Alfalah. Prof. Ashfaq is passionate about the personal and professional development of young learners and C-suite management at various levels across different industries. He was awarded the Young Scholars Research Award by Bilkent University, Turkey in 2015 for his cutting-edge research contribution to the area of Islamic finance. He also conducted a TV lecture series on Islamic finance for Paghiam TV Network. Prof. Ashfaq is a certified coach and consultant from HDW Network (NRW) Germany and a certified Train the Trainer from the Australian Centre for Education and Training (ACET) Melbourne. He has earned certification in Innovation Management and Entrepreneurship from International Summer University Carinthia, Austria. Prof. Ashfaq has spoken on the topic of Islamic banking and finance, FinTech, business ethics, sustainable development goals at conferences in more than 35 countries worldwide, and has served as a peer-review referee for a number of international conferences and journals. Recently, prof. Ashfaq has been awarded the Amity Global Academic Excellence Award by Amity University India for his impeccable credentials in the world of education.

Archana Goel is an assistant professor at Chitkara Business School. She has done M. Com, B.Ed., and Ph.D. and has 12 years of corporate and academic experience. Her Ph.D. is in corporate governance. Her research areas include corporate governance, mergers and acquisitions, financial reporting, ESG, etc. She specialises in teaching accounts, statistics, research methodology and finance courses. She has around 20 papers published in national and international journals of repute and has attended many national and international conferences. Several patents have been granted to her. Currently, she is guiding one Ph.D. scholar as well.

Ahsanul Haque is a professor in Marketing, Department of Business Administration, International Islamic University Malaysia. He showed research interest in the areas of international marketing, digital marketing, consumer behaviour, Internet marketing, Islamic marketing, and other marketing and management areas.

Siddharth Kanojia is an Assistant Professor of Law at Jindal School of Banking & Finance, O.P. Jindal Global University, India. Presently, he is also a visiting professor at Indian Institute of Management Sirmaur. He holds a Ph.D in Corporate Law & Governance, LL.M in International Business and Commercial Law, LL.B and BBS in Finance. Before coming to academics, he has worked at Jersey Island based Intellectual Property Management Company as Legal Consultant and Manchester based Start-up Company as Legal Advisor. Till date, he has 16 publications including the SCOPUS and WoS indexed journals. He is also an active member in Human Development and Capability Association, USA and Development Studies Association, U.K.

Lubza Nihar Khaliq is an Associate Professor, Accounting and Finance, GITAM School of Business at the GITAM Deemed to be University, Visakhapatnam Campus. She is an avid researcher and has written several research papers and case studies published in reputed outlets. She is a peer reviewer in various research journals.

Vijaya Kittu Manda has nearly 12+ years of experience in capital markets, financial planning, and investing. He is an Advocate, a technocrat, an academician, a book writer, and a stock market enthusiast. He has 10 University Postgraduate Degrees, is NISM Certified in multiple subjects and just submitted his Ph.D. thesis on Mutual Funds. Associated with Smart Investment publications for several years, he contributed over 650 articles to the outlet. He is the author of various books and the Chief Editor for a Management Book Series named Perspectives on Business Management and Economics (PBME), writers research papers and case studies, and is a speaker and resource person for colleges and universities. He conducts Kittu's Wealth Journey Seminars & Webinars in India and abroad on various stock market trading and investing topics.

Kiran Mehta is a seasoned educator, consultant, trainer, and researcher with nearly two decades of experience. With an impressive background spanning more than twenty years in teaching and research, she has cultivated a robust research portfolio featuring over 135+ publications in renowned journals and conferences. Her scholarly work has graced numerous international publications such as Emerald, Taylor & Francis, and Sage. Dr. Mehta is also the author of "Financial Services," a widely recognized textbook published by CENGAGE. She has also authored many edited books by Wiley, DeGruyter and IGI Global. She has contributed valuable study materials for various Indian educational institutions. Her research interests encompass climate finance, sustainable business practices, portfolio management, stock market efficiency, technology in education, and entrepreneurship.

Niaz Mohammad is working as an Assistant Professor, Faculty of business administration, American International University-Bangladesh (AIUB). He has completed his MBA and BBA specializing in Accounting & Information Systems (AIS), Faculty of Business Studies, University of Dhaka. Besides teaching at AIUB, he is also completed his CMA from ICMAB (Institute of Cost and Management Accountants of Bangladesh) and Associate Member of Cost and Management Accountants of Bangladesh. He has some experience in the corporate sector and worked as an Executive Officer in the Internal Control and Compliance department of IDLC Finance Limited, a leading non-banking financial institution in Bangladesh. In addition, he also published research papers in local and international journals. So far, he has published a good number of journal articles mostly in internationally referred journals, and attended different conferences locally and internationally. His research areas are integrated reporting, sustainability reporting, corporate social responsibility and intellectual capital. Currently, he is pursuing his Doctor of Philosophy (Phd) in Accounting at University of Dhaka.

Iberedem Obot is an erudite scholar and professional with a robust background in law. His academic journey commenced in Nigeria, where he secured a Law degree (LL.B) in 2012, before advancing to the Nigerian Law School where he obtained the license to practice law in the country in 2014. Subsequently, he attended the University of Westminster, London, UK, and obtained a Master of Laws (LL.M) in Corporate Finance Law in 2016. His thirst for academia propelled him to pursue and successfully obtain a Doctor of Philosophy (PhD) in Law from Coventry University, UK, in 2023. Dr. Obot's career embodies a blend of academic and professional engagements, showcasing a convergence of theoretical and practical applications of law. He tenured as a Researcher at the Centre for Counter Fraud Awareness (CCFA) in Nigeria, between 2019 and 2020. During this period, he helped in providing information on Politically Exposed Persons (PEPs), produced educational materials on compliance-related issues, and drafted policy documents, thereby underscoring his commitment to knowledge dissemination and practical legal solutions. In 2021, Dr. Obot transitioned to a role as an Analyst at AML/CFT Resources Nigeria Ltd, where he is involved in developing training materials on anti-money laundering safety procedures and contributing to strategy meetings for developing compliance frameworks. His foray into academia has encompassed tutoring and socio-legal research, with a particular interest in investigating the value of soft law instruments as compliance mechanisms for international law provisions. Dr. Obot has also showcased a remarkable ability to share his knowledge and insights through publications. He has attained proficiency in legal drafting and an understanding of corporate finance law that has been invaluable in the projects he has undertaken. His journey reflects a harmonious blend of academic rigor, and professional diligence, making him a distinguished individual in the legal and academic arenas.

Abdullah Sarwar is currently a Senior Lecturer of Marketing and the Deputy Dean (Student Experience & Alumni) at the Faculty of Management, Multimedia University (MMU), Cyberjaya, Malaysia. He was educated at the University Tun Abdul Razzak, Malaysia and graduated with a master's degree in business administration after serving 5 years in Bangladesh Army as a commissioned officer. He then worked as a corporate manager for another 3 years before attending International Islamic University Malaysia for his PhD degree in Business Administration. He then embarked on an academic career, which has both embraced teaching undergraduate and postgraduate students and research. He is currently a member of the American Psychological Association (APA). He has published more than 80 academic articles in various international journals and conferences in the field of marketing and management. He has been awarded the "Emerald Literati Network Awards for Excellence" in the category of highly commended paper 2016. He has also distinguished himself as a trainer and has played a pivotal role in consultancy and research. He is currently an active trainer/consultant for Unifi, Telekom Malaysia for "Digital Marketing with E-Learning" while indulging in academic research by mentoring PhD and master's students. His research interest covers consumer behaviour, digital marketing, Islamic marketing, service marketing, marketing strategy and tourism marketing. He can be contacted at sunabdullah@gmail.com.

Renuka Sharma boasts over two decades of rich teaching and research experience, establishing a substantial research portfolio with 130+ publications in esteemed journals and conferences. Her research interests encompass a wide array of topics, assessing the interplay of toxic air pollution, health spending, and economic growth to prioritizing critical success factors in e-learning systems. Sustainability remains a focal point, exploring metrics like energy efficiency and liquidity risk in addition to responsible investing. She also investigates behavioural aspects, including customer switching behaviour and cryptocurrency investor psychology. Dr. Sharma's prolific research has graced prestigious journals like the International Review of Economics & Finance and the International Journal of Business Excellence. An accomplished author, editor, trainer, educator, and consultant, she authored "Financial Services" and edited multiple books, with more in progress. Her educational contributions extend to developing course materials, online resources, and case studies. Beyond academia, she imparts expert lectures and collaborates on consultancy projects with the Department of Science and Technology, Government of India. Dr. Sharma's comprehensive contributions underscore her profound influence on the field of finance.

Aysa Siddika is a Research Fellow at the Faculty of Management, Cyberjaya Campus, Multimedia University. With over eight years of experience in the commercial banking sector, she specializes in credit risk management and operational management. In 2018, she successfully obtained her PhD in Business Administration from the International Islamic University of Malaysia. Prior to that, she earned her MBA in Finance and Bachelor's degree in Business Administration from Jahangirnagar University, Dhaka, Bangladesh. She has authored a number of articles in the area of bank capital and bank risk management, Islamic finance, fintech, ERP, social media marketing, mental wellbeing, etc.

Paul N. C. Tiong holds a PhD in accounting, is a professionally qualified accountant, and a member of Advance HE. He has more than 10 years of work experience in the corporate sector. In academia, Paul has taught accounting and finance courses of a number of universities, at undergraduate and postgraduate levels. Paul's research interest is in corporate governance, business ethics and sustainability reporting. He has written peer-reviewed and professional journal articles and conference papers on these topics.

Md Nazim Uddin specializes in banking and finance, with a focus on financial technology, inclusion, and digital finance. His expertise extends to ESG, corporate governance, transparency, and sustainable development goals. He also contributes to research areas like managerial ability, microfinance, and Islamic microfinance.

Yiqian Zhang embarked on her academic journey at London South Bank University, securing a BA and an MSc in International Accounting and Finance. Her educational voyage culminated at Coventry University where she earned a Ph.D. in Accounting. Now serving as an Assistant Lecturer at Coventry University, Dr. Zhang imparts knowledge across diverse financial and accounting modules, such as Financial Accounting Foundations and Corporate Governance and Ethics. Her pedagogical approach extends beyond traditional teaching to include academic progress coaching, providing holistic mentorship to students. In her tenure as a Research Assistant at Coventry University, Dr. Zhang made notable contributions to projects focused on Accounting Regulation, Corporate Governance, and Technology Affordances. Dr. Zhang is a recognized Fellow of Higher Education (FHEA) and a member of the British Accounting and Finance Association. Her research interests encompass financial reporting accountability, accounting quality measurements, and corporate governance. Through her scholarly and research pursuits, Dr. Zhang continues to explore complex financial paradigms, significantly enriching the academic discourse in accounting and finance.

Mohamad Zreik is a recognized scholar in International Relations. His extensive knowledge spans Middle Eastern Studies, China-Arab relations, East Asian and Asian Affairs, Eurasian geopolitics, and Political Economy, providing him a unique viewpoint in his field. Dr. Zreik is a proud recipient of a PhD from Central China Normal University (Wuhan). He's written numerous acclaimed papers, many focusing on China's Belt and Road Initiative and its Arab-region impact. His groundbreaking research has established him as a leading expert in his field. His significant contributions make him a crucial figure in understanding contemporary international relations.

Index

G

I

L

M

N

O

P

Q

R

S

T

W

www.ingramcontent.com/pod-product-compliance
Lightning Source LLC
LaVergne TN
LVHW061537290926
849162LV00004B/820